ILLUMINATING LETTERS

Studies in Print Culture and the History of the Book

Editorial Advisory Board

Illuminating Letters

Typography and Literary Interpretation

EDITED BY

Paul C. Gutjahr AND **Megan L. Benton**

University of Massachusetts Press
AMHERST

Copyright © 2001 by University of Massachusetts Press
All rights reserved
Printed in the United States of America
LC 00-055178
ISBN 1-55849-288-7
Set in Adobe Garamond and Gill Sans by Graphic Composition, Inc.
Designed by Jack Harrison
Printed and bound by Sheridan Books

Library of Congress Cataloging-in-Publication Data

Illuminating letters : typography and literary interpretation / edited by Paul C. Gutjahr
and Megan L. Benton.
    p. cm. — (Studies in print culture and the history of the book)
Includes bibliographical references (p.) and index.
ISBN 1-55849-288-7 (alk. paper)
1. Graphic design (Typography)—History.
2. Book design—History.
I. Gutjahr, Paul C. II. Benton, Megan. III. Series.

Z246 .I44 2000
686.2′2′09—dc21
                    00-055178

British Library Cataloguing in Publication data are available.

This book is published with the support and cooperation of the University of Massachusetts Boston.

For our parents

Harold and Ilene Gutjahr
Peter and Lydia Beckman

Contents

Acknowledgments

All books are collaborative efforts. A glance back over the three years spent putting this collection together vividly reminds us how many people help bring a book to completion. A simple "thank you" hardly suffices to express our gratitude, but we wish everyone connected with this project to know that without their expertise, humor, encouragement, and knowledge this collection would have remained little more than the dream of a group of scholars who have long marveled at the beauty and importance of typography.

We would like to express particular gratitude to Paul Wright and the University of Massachusetts Press for unwavering support of this project. Paul has been a wonderful friend to scholars interested in print culture studies. This volume is just one of many he has sponsored that significantly enrich a wide range of scholarship devoted to the power and pleasures that surround the printed word.

We also thank the Yale Program in Religion and American History endowed by the Pew Foundation, directed by Jon Butler and Harry Stout, for a grant that gave Paul Gutjahr the space to begin mapping this collection. Ray (Palatino) Smith has also been a great encouragement, ceaselessly cheering on this seemingly "crazy font project." In addition, we gratefully acknowledge the support of the Center for the Study of Religion at Princeton University, directed by Robert Wuthnow and Marie Griffith; the Christian Scholars Foundation, directed by Bernard Draper; the English Department at Indiana University; and Pacific Lutheran University's Regency Fellowship program.

As always, our greatest debt of gratitude goes to family. We particularly thank our parents, and we dedicate this volume to them in appreciation for their unfailing love and support. As his young sons embark on the great journey of learning to write, Paul is constantly reminded of the importance, the mutability, and the joys of letterforms. Finally, we thank our partners, Cathy Gutjahr and Paul Benton, whose journeys of learning constantly inspire our own.

P. C. G.   M. L. B.

ILLUMINATING LETTERS

Introduction

Reading the Invisible

PAUL C. GUTJAHR and MEGAN L. BENTON

Virtually from the beginning of his career in 1915, the eminent American publisher Alfred A. Knopf placed a colophon on the last page of each book bearing his imprint. This statement informed readers about key elements of the book's making: where it was printed, the paper used, the designer, and particularly the name, origin, and brief characteristics of the type used to print its text. To this day, readers of Knopf books encounter this perhaps mysterious message; most probably pay it little attention or are puzzled by its presence. To many it seems superfluous and self-indulgent. Why then is it there?

"Why, indeed?" wondered William A. Dwiggins, Knopf's leading book designer in those early decades. In 1939 he gently scoffed at his friend's colophonic habit. "It's all shop talk," Dwiggins remarked. "He [Knopf] likes 'em. He thinks it gives the books tone, I daresay. I think it doesn't matter a damn one way or the other. All that shop detail is zero. They don't care to know and they don't *need* to know. Just make your book so it will read handily and let it go at that."[1] Readers, Dwiggins insisted, neither cared about nor benefited from any behind-the-scenes technical details about type, paper, and the like. If handled properly, he implied, typography—the selection and arrangement of type and other visual elements on a page—and especially type itself should be invisible, deferential servants to the text they convey. When type does its job well, all the reader should "see" is the text's message.

The ethic of typographic invisibility has prevailed throughout much of modern Western bookmaking and publishing. The notion was immortalized in a stirring speech by Beatrice Warde in 1932 when she likened good book typography to a crystal goblet. True connoisseurs of wine would prefer crystal to the finest gilded chalice, she declared, because "everything about it is calculated to *reveal* rather than to hide the beautiful thing which it was meant to *contain*." So too are

---

1. William A. Dwiggins, "Twenty Years After" (1939), in *Books and Printing: A Treasury for Typophiles,* ed. Paul A. Bennett, rev. ed. (Cleveland: World, 1951), 147.

text and reader best served by typography that strives to be unseen, she explained. "The mental eye focusses *through* type and not *upon* it. . . . The type which, through any arbitrary warping of design or excess of 'color,' gets in the way of the mental picture to be conveyed, is a bad type."[2] Type should be self-effacing and supremely humble; type that intrudes upon a reader's awareness, she warned, was bad: distracting, impudent, *visible*.

Much has changed since 1932. Although some may still prefer that those who serve others' needs retire into deferential transparency, we know that such "servants" are not invisible. We also know, although we may not have given it much thought, that types are not invisible either. They too have names, faces, personalities, jobs they are good at and others they are not, benefactors and detractors, ancestors and offspring. And thanks to computers, most of us now have at least rudimentary skills in manipulating type to suit our purposes: what sophomore writer has not discovered that an eight-page labor can be stretched to ten with a quick switch to fourteen-point type? With modern word processing and desktop publishing software we make a myriad of typographic decisions each time we produce a text, or we tacitly approve the decisions we allow the software to make for us. But both as writers and as readers, we often fail to notice, much less fully consider, the role of type and typography in making a text not only visible but meaningful.

In fact, too often our own experience at the keyboard leads us to conflate writing and typography, so that the latter seems to disappear as a discrete and independent function. It is an easy and natural confusion, since when we create personal documents—a term paper, a letter, instructions to the babysitter, and so on—writing and typography are virtually synonymous: the form given the text by its writer is the form that the reader receives. In the larger world of professionally published texts, however, the distinction is profound. There a book's content and its form are not created simultaneously by a single person. As a familiar truism in the publishing world reminds us, writers don't write books—they write texts. A book is created when a text is transformed by print, when it is literally shaped into a material object whose visual and tactile features render it perceptible and accessible to others.

For most readers this formal, intermediate presence of print is so familiar and conventional that it is indeed virtually transparent and so unseen and unpondered; we see only text on the page. But it is impossible to read the words on a page without also reading, albeit usually on a subconscious level, the visual text of the page itself. "Typography is to literature as musical performance is to composition," writes the poet-typographer Robert Bringhurst. Just as we can hear music only by listening to a particular performance of it, we can read a text only by reading a typographic presentation of it. Typography, then, is what Bringhurst

2. Beatrice Warde, "Printing Should Be Invisible" (1932), in ibid., 109, 113.

calls "an essential act of interpretation, full of endless opportunities for insight or obtuseness."[3]

This is a bold assertion. It interjects typography into an already crowded and contested arena: the complex thing that we call the "text." It also leads straight into the thorny question of who or what produces meaning in a text: The author's unique visions and expressions? Transcendent, universal truths? Language itself? Or a typographer's mediating perceptions of some combination of these elements, as Bringhurst asserts? Perhaps even the typography itself, an independent kind of visual language in its own right, employed but not finally controlled by a designer's intentions? The essays in this volume contend that type and typography are indeed an intrinsic part of the text that a reader encounters when he or she reads a book.

Scholars have long recognized that a book is much more than simply text. In recent decades a great deal of fruitful thinking and research has revolved around closer scrutiny of "the book" as a constellation of social, cultural, economic, technological, aesthetic, and commercial as well as literary and linguistic forces. Beginning with the 1958 landmark work by Lucien Febvre and Henri-Jean Martin, *L'Apparition du livre* (translated into English as *The Coming of the Book*), scholars in a wide range of fields have amply illustrated that there is a great deal to be learned from studying books. Delineating the relatively new interdisciplinary field broadly known as "history of the book" or history of "print culture," these scholars have demonstrated that the study of publishing, printing, authorship, bookselling, and reading constitutes an important dimension of social, intellectual, and cultural history.[4]

Illuminating Letters focuses on one particular aspect of book history, the relationship between a text's typography and its literary interpretation. It is thus grounded in the assertion that both the material form of a text and any interpretation of it are inflected by the historical contexts in which they are made. This general notion that the "materiality" of any cultural object necessarily affects its

3. Robert Bringhurst, *The Elements of Typographic Style,* 2d ed. (Point Roberts, Wash.: Hartley & Marks, 1996), 19.

4. Lucien Febvre and Henri-Jean Martin, *The Coming of the Book: The Impact of Printing, 1450–1800,* trans. David Gerard, ed. Geoffrey Nowell-Smith and David Wootton (1958; London: Verso, 1984). Subsequent seminal work establishing this field includes Elizabeth Eisenstein, *The Printing Press as an Agent of Change* (New York: Cambridge University Press, 1979); and several multivolume national history projects, notably the *Cambridge History of the Book in Britain,* 7 vols., ed. D. F. McKenzie, David McKittrick, and Ian Willison, and *The History of the Book in America,* 5 vols., ed. David Hall (both Cambridge: Cambridge University Press, 2000 and forthcoming). For helpful assertions about the nature and direction of this emerging interdisciplinary field, see Robert Darnton's groundbreaking 1982 essay "What Is the History of Books?" reprinted in Cathy N. Davidson, ed., *Reading in America: Literature and Social History* (Baltimore: Johns Hopkins University Press, 1989), 27–52; John B. Hench, "Toward a History of the Book in America," *Publishing Research Quarterly* 10 (Fall 1994): 9–21; and Thomas R. Adams and Nicholas Barker, "A New Model for the Study of the Book," in *A Potencie of Life: Books in Society,* ed. Nicholas Barker (London: The British Library, 1993), 5–43.

meaning has been thoroughly articulated in relation to books by D. F. McKenzie in *Bibliography and the Sociology of Texts* (1986), and others have explored and extended its ramifications. The literary critic Jerome McGann, for example, contends that the material and typographic forms of a text, what he calls its "bibliographical codes," together with the commercial layers of its identity—prices, advertisements, distribution channels, and so forth—necessarily and essentially contribute to the meanings of the text, *"whether we are aware of such matters when we make our meanings or whether we are not."* George Bornstein and Theresa Tinkle have edited *The Iconic Page in Manuscript, Print, and Digital Culture* (1998), an important volume whose essays illustrate the influence of material form on a text's reception and meanings. As Michele Moylan and Lane Stiles, editors of a volume of studies that showcase this theoretical approach to American literature, argue, there is "no such thing as a text unmediated by its materiality." Accordingly, "the material text [serves] as a nexus in the intersection of literature, culture, and history."[5]

As these scholars have shown, however, the relationship between how and why a book is produced and how and why it is read is often complex, even at times perverse. The meanings made from the text of a printed book derive not only from the many facets that shape how the author, designer, and publisher construct that book but also from the conditions—personal, political, social, and so on—in which the reader encounters it. Highly useful here is the distinction that Michel de Certeau draws between *strategies* of cultural production and *tactics* of cultural consumption.[6] Strategies describe the practices of those who create cultural products like texts or books—how they envision, compose, revise, edit, design, package, price, and distribute them. Tactics, on the other hand, describe how those who receive or "consume" these cultural goods in fact use them, understand them, derive meaning and value from them. Strategies of production usually attempt to influence tactics of consumption, and sometimes they succeed, but they certainly do not control them. Users' tactics often sidestep creators' intentions, and sometimes they subvert them. Readers may perceive meanings that neither author nor publisher intended, or they may fail or refuse to conform to expected understandings. This subversive slipperiness is of course partly rooted in the nature of language, but it is also inherent in aspects of a text's materiality, including its typography.

5. D. F. McKenzie, *Bibliography and the Sociology of Texts* (London: The British Library, 1986); Jerome McGann, *The Textual Condition* (Princeton: Princeton University Press, 1991), 12–13; George Bornstein and Theresa Tinkle, eds., *The Iconic Page in Manuscript, Print, and Digital Culture* (Ann Arbor: University of Michigan Press, 1998); Michele Moylan and Lane Stiles, eds., *Reading Books: Essays on the Material Text and Literature in America* (Amherst: University of Massachusetts Press, 1996), 12. Another important theoretical work germane to these assertions is Gérard Genette's *Paratexts: Thresholds of Interpretation,* trans. Jane E. Lewin (1987; Cambridge: Cambridge University Press, 1997).
6. Michel de Certeau, *The Practices of Everyday Life,* trans. Steven Rendall (Berkeley: University of California Press, 1984), xix–xxii. See especially the chapter titled "Reading as Poaching," 165–76.

An impressive array of important scholarship has begun to explore this complex network of agency and influence in the creation of textual meaning. The French cultural historian Roger Chartier has shown that the material aspects of inexpensive editions known as the Bibliotèque bleue—well-known texts peddled for more than two centuries throughout pre-Revolution France—yield important clues suggesting how and why they were both produced and read. By analyzing the typography as well as the content of texts in the margins of early modern English books, Evelyn Tribble "shows that the page can be seen as a territory of contestation upon which issues of political, religious, social, and literary authority are fought."[7] And Claire Badaracco has chronicled the extraordinary care given by the R. R. Donnelley Company's Lakeside Press to the design, illustration, and printing of its heralded "Four American Books." In this project, which culminated in 1930, fine limited editions of Melville's *Moby Dick,* Thoreau's *Walden,* Dana's *Two Years Before the Mast,* and the *Tales of Edgar Allan Poe* were produced in bibliophilic forms both to exalt American literature and to promote the printing firm's bookmaking prowess.[8]

In her study *The Visible Word* (1994), the critic Johanna Drucker distinguishes between two fundamental kinds of typography, resulting in what she calls the marked and the unmarked text. A marked text bears highly noticeable typographic features that explicitly, even aggressively, manipulate how it is read. Varieties of type styles and sizes, selected uses of boldface and color, and so on function prominently to direct the reader's eye and mind, shepherding their understandings of the text. Such typography is typically commercial and bureaucratic; it overtly aims to "sell" a particular message and to provoke a particular behavior from the reader.

Drucker's study focuses on the highly marked typography of early twentieth-century experimental artists who sought to foreground typography itself. This volume, however, primarily looks at the typography of unmarked texts, so-called because it purports to efface its interpretive enterprise. Drucker describes "the even, gray page of prose and poetic convention" as an unmarked, "literary" text because, she contends, it bears no (obvious) marks of typographic manipulation by author, printer, or publisher. With its typography seemingly invisible, its text seems neutral and natural to the reader—and therefore true. The unmarked text ostensibly exudes an "authority which transcends the mere material presence of

7. Roger Chartier, "The *Bibliothèque bleue* and Popular Reading," in *The Cultural Uses of Print in Early Modern France,* trans. Lydia G. Cochrane (Princeton: Princeton University Press, 1987); Evelyn Tribble, *Margins and Marginality: The Printed Page in Early Modern England* (Charlottesville: University Press of Virginia, 1993), 2. For studies focusing on more modern texts and authors, see, for example, Jerome McGann's *Black Riders: The Visible Language of Modernism* (Princeton: Princeton University Press, 1993).

8. Claire Badaracco, *American Culture and the Marketplace: R. R. Donnelley's Four American Books Campaign, 1926–1930* (Washington, D.C.: Library of Congress, 1992). See also Badaracco's larger study, *Trading Words: Poetry, Typography, and Illustrated Books in the Modern Literary Economy* (Baltimore: Johns Hopkins University Press, 1995), which examines the strategic roles of typography in serving modern commercial purposes.

words on a page." Through its discreet typography the unmarked text is simply "there, and the unmarked author [is] indeed the Author of the Text as pure Word."[9]

We assert, however, that literary texts are no less "marked" by their typography than more commercial or functional texts. Once given visual form, any text is implicitly coded by that form in ways that signal, however subtly, its nature and purpose and how its creators wish it to be approached and valued. A stage production of *Hamlet* in modern dress may seem more "marked" than another that adheres scrupulously to conventions of Shakespearean costume, staging, and so on, but it is not. Each feature of both productions represents an interpretive choice made by a director, actor, or stage manager, and is filtered through the physical and verbal skills and qualities of the actors. The words may be Hamlet's, but the uniquely inflected body and voice are Branagh's or Olivier's. The body and the voice make a difference. Type and typography make a difference.

To better understand the role of type in literary interpretation one must examine both the apparent *strategies* behind its selection and arrangement and the *tactics* it may provoke or enable in readers' responses. Typography is an interpretive act, but one that must in turn be evaluated: Is it insightful, or obtuse? Consonant or dissonant with the linguistic text? "Transparent" or obtrusive? To answer that question, the wise reader must look at that which purports to not be there. To perceive typography's interpretive powers we must learn to see and read the invisible.

Can an ordinary reader, untrained in its forms and methods, develop an "eye" for typography as the music lover cultivates an "ear" for detecting a particular musician's performance of a score? Alfred Knopf certainly believed so. We also vigorously contend that yes, ordinary readers can readily learn to see what strives to be transparent. No matter how clear its glass, a window is perfectly visible when one simply alters one's gaze.

This collection is devoted to exploring both the typographic strategies of those who produce books and the interpretive tactics of readers who make sense of a text's presentation. It is important to clarify, however, that none of the included essays focuses on typographic theory or analysis per se. Like Chartier, Tribble, and Badaracco (and many other scholars working in this rich new vein of textual

9. Johanna Drucker, *The Visible Word: Experimental Typography and Modern Art, 1909–1923* (Chicago: University of Chicago Press, 1994), 46, 95. For a broader sense of modern theoretical approaches to Western book typography, see, for example, Jan Tschichold, *The New Typography,* trans. Ruari McLean (1928; Berkeley: University of California Press, 1995); Jan Tschichold, *The Form of the Book,* ed. Robert Bringhurst (Point Roberts, Wash.: Hartley & Marks, 1991); Eric Gill, *An Essay on Typography* (1936; Boston: Godine, 1993); Harry Duncan, *Doors of Perception* (Austin, Tex.: W. Thomas Taylor, 1987); Herbert Spencer, *Pioneers of Modern Typography,* rev. ed. (Cambridge: MIT Press, 1982); and various theoretical discussions in the quarterly journal *Visible Language* and the irregularly published serials *Serif* and *Matrix.*

studies), these authors are neither professional book designers nor typographic critics. Rather, they are primarily concerned with literary and cultural meanings. Each author began as we hope our readers may begin, with a curiosity about the particular visual and physical printed forms of a specific text or genre. In each case that curiosity led to a closer inspection of aspects, implications, and consequences of those forms. In other words, each author has made the "invisible" not only visible but illuminating. We hope that these case studies will encourage readers to look in fresh ways at how texts are presented in print, and at how those presentations shape understandings of the texts' meanings and value. We believe these essays provide helpful models of that process of discovery and insight.

Because these essays are intended to introduce literary scholars, both experienced and beginning, to the interpretive layers of typography, they neither assume nor require that readers be well versed in typographic terminology, procedures, or theory. Only a very brief and simple introduction to the nature, structure, and evolution of type itself is needed here. Figure 1 illustrates the basic vocabulary for understanding the nonprofessional discussions of type in these essays. References to *serifs*, for example, indicate the small strokes at the beginning or end of the main strokes of a letter. Type without serifs, which first began to appear in the nineteenth century, is described as *sans serif* or *sanserif*. Another important feature of type anatomy is the *x-height*, or distance between the baseline on which the letters rest and the top of such lowercase letters as a, c, e, m, r, and x. The extensions of other lowercase letters (g, j, p, q, y) below the baseline are called *descenders*, while the parts of letters (b, d, f, h, k, l, t) that extend above the x-height are called *ascenders*. The distance from the baseline of one line of type to the baseline of the next is called the *leading*, because when composing metal type the typesetter adjusts vertical space by inserting thin strips of lead between the lines. Type is measured in *points*; there are approximately 72 points to the inch.

Although the full variety of typefaces has grown exponentially with the advent of digital design and desktop publishing, type used for reading matter—and particularly texts of books—remains a fairly small subset of that larger, dizzying spectrum of style. While there are many systems of classifying and characterizing type, a particularly intelligent and thorough one that focuses on type for text composition is offered by Robert Bringhurst in his highly regarded handbook, *The Elements of Typographic Style* (1992). Bringhurst relates shifts in fundamental elements of letterforms' shapes—the axis of letters with rounded strokes, or *bowls*; the presence or shape of serifs; the contrast between thick and thin strokes; and so on—to broader periods of cultural style: renaissance, baroque, neoclassical, romantic, realist, modernist, and the like (see figure 2).[10] This scheme

10. See chapter 7, "Historical Interlude," and prefatory illustrations of these type categories in Bringhurst's *Elements of Typographic Style*, 119–42, 12–15. For further reading on type itself, see Sebastian Carter, *Twentieth-Century Type Designers* (New York: Taplinger, 1987); Frederic W. Goudy, *Typologia: Stud-*

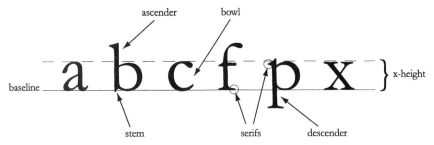

FIGURE 1. Basic anatomy of the roman letterform.

emphasizes the intimate relationship between type and the cultural climates in which it is created and used, a relationship that we too contend is fundamental to any informed understanding of typography.

Written language is of course a vast subject, spanning many cultures and millennia. The parameters of this volume are more manageable: the essays address only printed productions of texts in the English language. They therefore do not directly deal with manuscript traditions that preceded the advent of Western mechanical printing in the mid-fifteenth century, or with recent electronic editions (although the visual dimensions of each are highly significant and worthy of precisely the kind of study we advocate here).

Although these momentous shifts in the technology of textual production make easy boundaries, it is important to note that letterforms and page layout conventions typically blur those boundaries. The earliest types cast by Johann Gutenberg and his associates in Mainz, Germany, in the 1430s and 1440s scrupulously mimicked contemporary medieval letterforms, for example, just as the earliest printed pages were virtually indistinguishable from their handwritten counterparts. The visual qualities of type and typography have steadily evolved to accommodate the limitations of changing bookmaking technologies and to exploit their strengths, but the process has been far more complex than such a formulaic equation suggests. Technology is an essential factor in the history of type and typography, but—as in the history of any cultural product—it is not the only important influence.[11]

The variety of type styles that emerged soon after printing well illustrate this fact. While the technology of typecasting and printing was identical throughout Europe, significantly different types appeared, reflecting national or regional tra-

ies in Type Design and Type Making (Berkeley: University of California Press, 1940); Ruari McLean, ed., *Typographers on Type: An Illustrated Anthology from William Morris to the Present Day* (New York: Norton, 1995); and Charles Bigelow, Paul Hayden Duensing, and Linnea Gentry, eds., *Fine Print on Type: The Best of Fine Print Magazine on Type and Typography* (San Francisco: Bedford Arts, 1988).

11. For a comprehensive introduction to the technical processes of book production since Gutenberg, see Philip Gaskell, *A New Introduction to Bibliography* (New York: Oxford University Press, 1972). See also D. C. Greetham, *Textual Scholarship: An Introduction* (New York: Garland, 1994), 77–151.

ditions and varying intellectual and political interests. In Germany and northern Europe, type resembled dominant scribal letterforms there, those we know today as "gothic" or "blackletter." In Italy, however, types quickly followed the humanist letterforms we now call "roman," letterforms associated with the great scholarly and linguistic discoveries of the Renaissance. By 1500 an alternative letterform developed by Italian Renaissance calligraphy masters was captured in a type style we call "italic." Figures 3, 4, and 5 illustrate these three basic styles, which have remained foremost in Western book production for five hundred years. They quickly came to register broad cultural and ideological as well as nationalist connotations; blackletter, for example, became associated with religious and espe-

FIGURE 2. Evolving styles of text type, illustrating Robert Bringhurst's cultural classification system.

Garamond roman & italic
Renaissance (fifteenth and sixteenth centuries)

Caslon roman & italic
Baroque (seventeenth century)

Baskerville roman & Italic
Neoclassical (eighteenth century)

Bodoni roman & italic
Romantic (eighteenth and nineteenth centuries)

Helvetica roman & italic
Realist (nineteenth and early twentieth centuries)

Palatino roman & italic
Modernist (twentieth century)

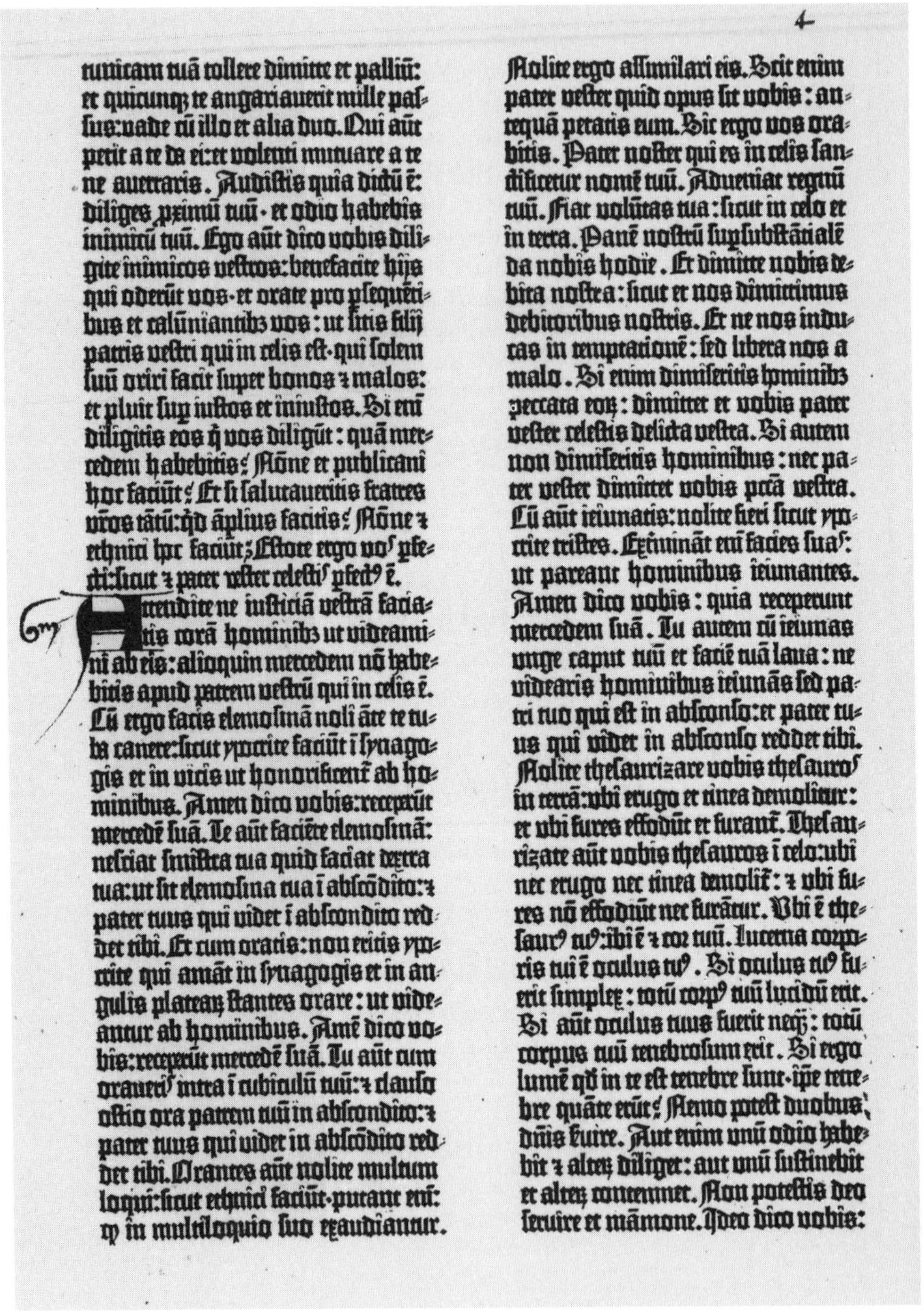

tunicam tuā tollere dimitte ei et palliū:
et quicunqȝ te angariaverit mille passus: vade cū illo et alia duo. Qui aūt
petit a te da ei: et volenti mutuare a te
ne avertaris. Audistis quia dictū ē:
diliges proximū tuū · et odio habebis
inimicū tuū. Ego aūt dico vobis dili-
gite inimicos vestros: benefacite hijs
qui oderūt vos · et orate pro psequēti-
bus et calūniantibȝ vos: ut sitis filij
patris vestri qui in celis est · qui solem
suū oriri facit super bonos ⁊ malos:
et pluit sup iustos et iniustos. Si enī
diligitis eos q vos diligūt: quā mercedem habebitis? Nōne et publicani
hoc faciūt? Et si salutaveritis fratres
vros tātū: qd āplius facitis? Nōne ⁊
ethnici hoc faciūt? Estote ergo vos pfe-
cti: sicut ⁊ pater vester celestis pfectus ē.
Attendite ne iusticiā vestrā facia-
tis corā hominibȝ ut videami-
ni ab eis: alioquin mercedem nō habebitis apud patrem vestrū qui in celis ē.
Cū ergo facis elemosinā noli āte te tu-
ba canere: sicut ypocrite faciūt ī synagogis et in vicis ut honorificent ab hominibus. Amen dico vobis: receperūt
mercedē suā. Te aūt faciēte elemosinā:
nesciat sinistra tua quid faciat dextra
tua: ut sit elemosina tua ī abscōdito: ⁊
pater tuus qui videt ī abscondito reddet tibi. Et cum oratis: non eritis ypocrite qui amāt in synagogis et in an-
gulis plateaȝ stantes orare: ut vide-
antur ab hominibus. Amē dico vobis: receperūt mercedē suā. Tu aūt cum
oraveris intra ī cubiculū tuū: ⁊ clauso
ostio ora patrem tuū in abscondito: ⁊
pater tuus qui videt in abscōdito reddet tibi. Orantes aūt nolite multum
loqui: sicut ethnici faciūt · putant enī
qȝ in multiloquio suo exaudiantur.

Nolite ergo assimilari eis. Scit enim
pater vester quid opus sit vobis: an-
tequā petatis eum. Sic ergo vos ora-
bitis. Pater noster qui es in celis san-
ctificetur nomē tuū. Adveniat regnū
tuū. Fiat voluntas tua: sicut in celo et
in terra. Panē nostrū supsubstātialē
da nobis hodie. Et dimitte nobis de-
bita nostra: sicut et nos dimittimus
debitoribus nostris. Et ne nos indu-
cas in temptationē: sed libera nos a
malo. Si enim dimiseritis hominibȝ
peccata eoȝ: dimittet et vobis pater
vester celestis delicta vestra. Si autem
non dimiseritis hominibus: nec pater vester dimittet vobis pctā vestra.
Cū aūt ieiunatis: nolite fieri sicut ypocrite tristes. Extermināt enī facies suas:
ut pareant hominibus ieiunantes.
Amen dico vobis: quia receperunt
mercedem suā. Tu autem cū ieiunas
unge caput tuū et faciē tuā lava: ne
videaris hominibus ieiunās sed pa-
tri tuo qui est in abscondito: et pater tuus qui videt in abscondito reddet tibi.
Nolite thesaurizare vobis thesauros
in terra: ubi erugo et tinea demolitur:
et ubi fures effodiūt et furantur. Thesau-
rizate aūt vobis thesauros ī celo: ubi
nec erugo nec tinea demolit: ⁊ ubi fures nō effodiūt nec furantur. Ubi ē the-
saurus tuus: ibi ē ⁊ cor tuū. Lucerna corpo-
ris tui ē oculus tuus. Si oculus tuus fuerit simplex: totū corpus tuū lucidū erit.
Si aūt oculus tuus fuerit nequā: totū
corpus tuū tenebrosum erit. Si ergo
lumē qd in te est tenebre sunt · ipe tenebre quāte erūt? Nemo potest duobus
dnis servire. Aut enim unū odio habe-
bit ⁊ alteȝ diliget: aut unū sustinebit
et alteȝ contemnet. Non potestis deo
servire et māmone. Ideo dico vobis:

FIGURE 3. An example of early blackletter type from Gutenberg's 1454 New Testament, Mainz, Germany. Courtesy of The Lilly Library, Indiana University Libraries, Bloomington.

cially Protestant texts, while roman and italic types prevailed for secular literary and scientific works.[12]

This collection is arranged to amplify two broad themes that resonate throughout the history of printed text production and that guide scholars' approaches to studying it. Although each writer initiated and pursued his or her investigation independently, their efforts coalesce neatly here to reflect a focal dichotomy: the respective roles played by printers and publishers, or by authors, in shaping the typographic presentation of a text. We attempt to explicate the points of coalescence and articulation in the pages that follow with brief interchapter bridge notes.

We begin, however, with an essay that spans the historical scope of the collection, suggesting both a range of ways in which type and typography affect literary interpretation and a larger sense of evolving typographic conventions and innovations. This essay also introduces our overarching contention that by its nature no typography can preserve a "pure" text, the unmediated word of its author. In "The Letter(s) of the Law: Four Centuries of Typography in the King James Bible," Paul Gutjahr argues that while some contend the word of God is immutable, the succession of types used in various editions of the King James Bible undermines that changelessness. Even though the core text of the King James translation has remained little altered since its first appearance in 1611, typographic changes over the centuries reflect the theological, social, and ideological battles that have raged over the Bible's production and reception. Those typographic changes, Gutjahr demonstrates, often played a profound role in biblical interpretation.

The next three chapters look in closer detail at the ways in which typographic decisions made by printers and publishers can manipulate, whether deliberately or inadvertently, the way a text is received and understood. Each essay examines how printers orchestrate textual meaning through type selection and how those choices reveal the ways in which type has been socially and culturally constructed, its features imbued with qualities that reinforce or subvert aspects of—in these three case studies—religious doctrine, gender, and race.

Sarah A. Kelen's "*Peirs Plohman* [*sic*] and 'the formidable array of black letter' in the Early Nineteenth Century" discusses the archaizing use of blackletter type in Thomas Dunham Whitaker's 1813 edition of the fourteenth-century allegory *Piers Plowman*. Whitaker's typographic decision distanced the medieval poem from its nineteenth-century readers iconically, just as his use of Middle English orthography rendered the text historically and linguistically remote. Kelen argues

12. Of the many excellent studies of the history of types and typography, among the best are Harry Carter, *A View of Early Typography* (Oxford: Oxford University Press, 1969); Robin Kinross, *Modern Typography: An Essay in Critical History* (London: Hyphen Press, 1992); Alexander Lawson, *Anatomy of a Typeface* (Boston: Godine, 1990); S. H. Steinberg, *Five Hundred Years of Printing*, 4th ed., rev. John Trevitt (1974; New Castle, Del.: Oak Knoll Books, 1996); and D. B. Updike, *Printing Types: Their History, Forms and Use*, 2d ed. (1922; Cambridge: Harvard University Press, 1937).

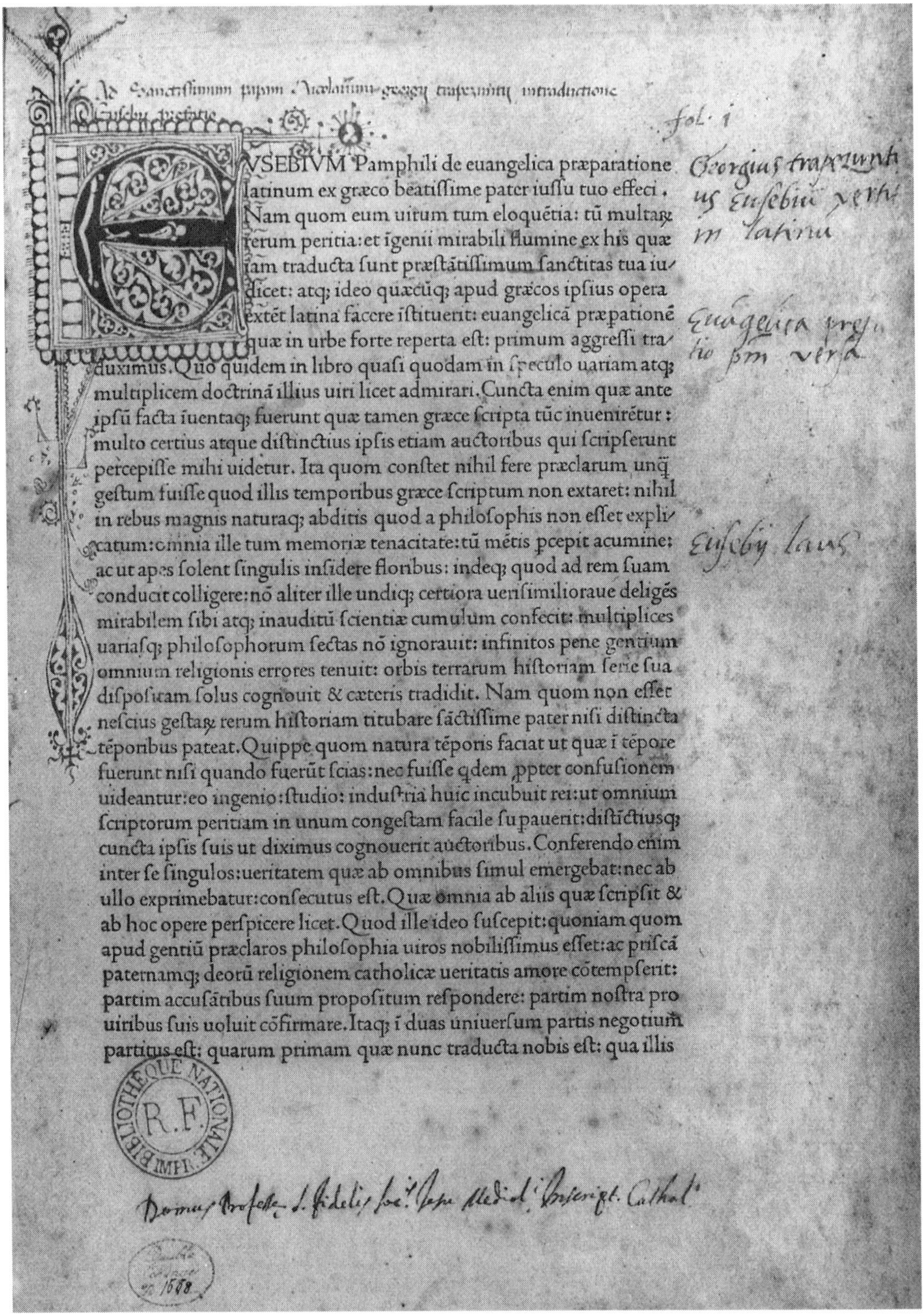

VSEBIVM Pamphili de euangelica præparatione latinum ex græco beatiſſime pater iuſſu tuo effeci. Nam quom eum uirum tum eloquétia: tu multaꝗ rerum peritia: et igenii mirabili flumine ex his quæ iam traducta ſunt præſtátiſſimum ſanctitas tua iudicet: atꝗ ideo quæcuq; apud græcos ipſius opera extet latina facere iſtituerit: euangelica præpationé quæ in urbe forte reperta eſt: primum aggreſſi tra/ duximus. Quo quidem in libro quaſi quodam in ſpeculo uariam atꝗ multiplicem doctrina illius uiri licet admirari. Cuncta enim quæ ante ipſu facta iuentaꝗ fuerunt quæ tamen græce ſcripta tuc inueniretur : multo certius atque diſtinctius ipſis etiam auctoribus qui ſcripſerunt percepiſſe mihi uidetur. Ita quom conſtet nihil fere præclarum unꝗ geſtum fuiſſe quod illis temporibus græce ſcriptum non extaret: nihil in rebus magnis naturaꝗ abditis quod a philoſophis non eſſet expli/ catum:omnia ille tum memoriæ tenacitate:tu métis pcepit acumine: ac ut apes ſolent ſingulis inſidere floribus: indeq; quod ad rem ſuam conducit colligere:no aliter ille undiq; certiora ueriſimilioraue deliges mirabilem ſibi atq; inauditu ſcientiæ cumulum confecit: multiplices uariaſq; philoſophorum ſectas no ignorauit: infinitos pene gentium omnium religionis errores tenuit: orbis terrarum hiſtoriam ſerie ſua diſpoſitam ſolus cognouit & cæteris tradidit. Nam quom non eſſet neſcius geſtaꝗ rerum hiſtoriam titubare ſáctiſſime pater niſi diſtincta téporibus pateat.Quippe quom natura téporis faciat ut quæ i tépore fuerunt niſi quando fuerut ſcias:neo fuiſſe qdem ꝓpter confuſionem uideantur:eo ingenio:ſtudio: induſtria huic incubuit rei:ut omnium ſcriptorum peritiam in unum congeſtam facile ſu pauerit:diſtictiusq; cuncta ipſis ſuis ut diximus cognouerit auctoribus.Conferendo enim inter ſe ſingulos:ueritatem quæ ab omnibus ſimul emergebat:nec ab ullo exprimebatur:confecutus eſt.Quæ omnia ab aliis quæ ſcripſit & ab hoc opere perſpicere licet.Quod ille ideo ſuſcepit:quoniam quom apud gentiu præclaros philoſophia uiros nobiliſſimus eſſet:ac priſca paternamq; deoru religionem catholicæ ueritatis amore cotempſerit: partim accuſátibus ſuum propoſitum reſpondere: partim noſtra pro uiribus ſuis uoluit cofirmare.Itaq; i duas uniuerſum partis negotium partius eſt: quarum primam quæ nunc traducta nobis eſt: qua illis

FIGURE 4. An example of early roman type. Eusebius, *De Evangelica Praeparatione,* printed by Nicolas Jenson, Venice, Italy, 1470. Courtesy of The Lilly Library, Indiana University Libraries, Bloomington.

30   I. SAMBVCI
                        Confilium.

N i l firmum fine lege ſtetit,ſtudijsꝗ, verendis
   C onſilio pacem,bellaꝗ, iuſta rege.
Q uod fine iudicio prudenti,& fuſcipis arte,
   F ædera fint,moueas feu quoque bella, perit.
M ilitiæ doctrina valet,ſanctusꝗ, Senatus,
   A tque domum tuta conditione tenet.
E n breuis à rixis concordia,diſſidiumꝗ,
   F it longum è ſocio pectore,ni caueas.
A ttica conceſſit belli ſua ſceptra Pericli,
   T yrtæo,& Sophocli fic quoque Sparta Duci.
P ax melior cunctis,te copia poſcit amœnam,
   T u reparas animos,te fine mœret ager.
E rgo feceſſus Cadmi,cultaꝗ, forores
   E t viuant quoſquos litera docta fouet.

                                        Cauſſæ

FIGURE 5. An example of early italic type. Sambaucus, *Emblemata,* printed by Robert
Granjon, Antwerp, Belgium, 1562. Courtesy of The Lilly Library, Indiana University
Libraries, Bloomington.

that Whitaker used the archaic blackletter type not out of a simple antiquarian fetishism of the old but to distance the medieval text's Catholicism from his modern, Protestant audience. Whitaker's edition thus manifests an anxiety about the status of Anglo-Catholicism that was prevalent between the Act of Union with Ireland in 1800 and the passage of Catholic Emancipation in 1829.

While Kelen explores the religious connotations of type in early nineteenth-century Britain, Megan Benton's essay, "Typography and Gender: Remasculating the Modern Book," challenges us to think about how letterforms gender the reading experience. She notes that the typographic revival of the late nineteenth century, spearheaded by the work of William Morris, Theodore Low De Vinne, and others, was in part a reaction against what they called the feminine look and feel of Victorian machine-made books. The ensuing reform called for a return to preindustrial models of typography, including more "robust" letterforms, and exalted design and publishing practices that, in De Vinne's word, "remasculated" the printed page. In repudiating as feminine, weak, and impoverished the light, thin letterforms favored by most nineteenth-century printers and their customers, reformers implicitly spurned as well the growing predominance of women writers and readers in modern book culture.

Beth McCoy then offers a new way to understand the early twentieth-century African American writer Nella Larsen's novel *Passing*. In "Perpetua(l) Notion: Typography, Economy, and Losing Nella Larsen," McCoy considers the effects of changing the text's type from the Caslon used in the original 1929 edition, published by Knopf, to the Perpetua type used for the novel's popular 1986 edition in the Rutgers University Press American Women Writers series. The latter edition's typography may make it more attractive and hence more inviting to scholars, McCoy contends, but the change also obscures the book's rich commentary on the literature and publishing practices of the Harlem Renaissance, which she finds embedded in the original edition's typography. Much of what Larsen wished her book to be about is lost, McCoy argues, when the original Caslon type is replaced in a later edition by another publisher.

By contrast, the final three chapters examine roles played by the other active agent in the creation of typographic meaning, the author. While authors have long been generally relegated to the sidelines by printers and typographers in most commercial publishing practices, savvy writers have often resisted such exclusion, eager to participate in if not control decisions about how their work is presented on paper. As modern technology increasingly empowers writers to create their own typography, it becomes more important than ever to understand how authorial involvement further reveals the dynamic power of type to inflect literary content.

In "The Autograph Manuscript in Print: Samuel Richardson's Type Font Manipulation in *Clarissa*," Steven Price argues that Richardson's knowledge of type and printing played a pivotal role in how he conceptualized and wrote *Clarissa*. A master printer as well as one of England's first novelists, Richardson used type to visually build the book's characterization and plot. Most notably, Price explains, Richardson deliberately chose type forms that would give his printed pages certain manuscript characteristics. By evoking those associations, Richardson hoped to lend credibility to his fictional text, which he feared would otherwise be too easily dismissed.

Leon Jackson's essay, " 'The Italics Are Mine': Edgar Allan Poe and the Semiotics of Print," explores Poe's frustrations with the printing errors that plagued his texts. Jackson contends that Poe understood acutely the ability of print both to enhance and to undermine a text's power and meanings. Although drawn to print by its cultural status and its ability to reach vast audiences, he increasingly felt stymied by a medium that he believed warped his work through typesetting imprecision and carelessness. Poe therefore proposed various ways to circumvent typographic mediation of the literary text; in particular, he sought to use printing methods that bypassed type altogether and so would not distort the meanings he intended for his texts.

Finally, Gene Kannenberg Jr. takes us into the realm of the American comic book in "Graphic Text, Graphic Context: Interpreting Custom Fonts and Hands in Contemporary Comics." While most readers believe that the visual elements of comics are confined to their graphic images, Kannenberg contends that the letterforms of the texts are also graphic images that similarly convey an author's intended meaning. Furthermore, he considers the influence of technology on interpretive practice by exploring how computerization has radically altered comic book production processes.

In many ways, letterforms are the most immediate and visible link between writer and reader. But letters are neither as immediate—without mediation— nor as intellectually visible as one might think. These essays remind us all that type exerts a powerful role in the interpretive process whether or not that influence is apparent to us. We hope that by helping to make that "invisible" typographic presence visible to the reader's eye, the book will also help readers understand how a printed text's typographic meaning and literary meaning are essentially intertwined. They may confirm or subvert, clarify or complicate each other, but they cannot finally be disentangled. No one can fully read a text's literary content without also reading its typographic form.

Chapter One

The Letter(s) of the Law: Four Centuries of Typography in the King James Bible

PAUL C. GUTJAHR

In the winter of 1604, James I set in motion the production of a book that would profoundly shape the cultural, religious, and linguistic life of the English-speaking world for the next four centuries. The book was a new translation of the Holy Bible, and while it came to be known as the authorized version in England, in the United States it would take the name of its sponsoring monarch: King James. The King James Bible has remained widely popular over the past four hundred years, a fact attested to not only in sales figures but in the amount of attention scholars have paid it. Within this scholarly interest, however, precious little work has focused on the production of various King James editions and how the book's materiality has often exercised an immense influence on its interpretation. Scholars have largely ignored the fact that this translation reached its readers in myriad editions over the centuries, editions whose shifting distribution practices, bindings, illustrations, and typographical presentation have all helped shape the meaning of the biblical text.

This essay examines just one of the numerous intersections between the King James's materiality and its content. In the thousands of editions of the King James that have come off the presses since 1611, the celestial words of scripture have been represented by terrestrial letterforms. By exploring the presence and changing nature of the various type designs used to present the King James's text, one comes to the stark realization that typography can exercise an all-too-often ignored influence on textual interpretation.

Because well over four thousand editions of the King James have been printed in the United States and England alone over the past four hundred years, an exhaustive scholarly treatment of the interpretive influence of biblical typography is impossible.[1] Instead, I examine the ability of type to influence the biblical text's

1. Other countries, such as the Netherlands, also produced the King James Bible in great quantities. The standard bibliographies of various Bible editions printed in the United States and Britain are T. H. Darlow and H. F. Moule, *Historical Catalogue of the Printed Editions of Holy Scripture* (New York: Kraus

meaning by looking at four specific editions of the King James produced between 1611 and 1931. These four volumes have been chosen because they serve as striking, but not uncommon, examples of how letterforms can signify a multitude of meanings. To help the reader appreciate the range of possible signification found in various Bible letterforms, I have superimposed the following analytical rubrics on these four Bible editions: tradition, social status, religious sensibility, and theological interpretation. The use of these broad categories should not blind one to the fact that typefaces rarely, if ever, signify meaning on just one level. For example, while gothic type might invoke associations with monastic manuscript reproduction and religious texts, it might simultaneously signal social distinctions such as a specific level of education.

Although the four analytical rubrics often blur into one another, they do provide initial reference points that help one explore the ability of letterforms to hold multivalent meanings which deeply influence a reader's experience of a specific biblical text. Through these categories, one can begin to appreciate that biblical typefaces are yet one more factor that needs to be weighed in considering how certain biblical editions and certain biblical texts have been interpreted. Typefaces have the ability to hold their own meanings, accent in unique ways the words they are relaying, and even contradict the messages they are supposed to represent.

Tradition

When James I ascended to the English throne in 1603, there were three English versions of the Scripture prominent in England: the Great Bible (1539), the Geneva Bible (1560), and the Bishops' Bible (1568). Of these, the Geneva Bible enjoyed the greatest popularity, having been translated in an accessible idiom and favored by English Puritans. The Puritans, however, were not entirely happy with the Geneva Bible and appealed to James I for a "newe translation of the Bible, because those which were allowed in the raignes of Henri the eight, and Edward the sixt, were corrupt and not aunswerable to the truth of the Originall."[2] James readily agreed. For some time, he had been bothered by what he considered seditious commentary in the Geneva version, and so he gave his blessing to the work of a new translation—a translation he made sure would include only cross references and philological commentary in its margins. Forty-seven scholars worked for three years on the new translation, and in 1611 the first King James Bibles came off the presses. Once released, the version steadily gained in popularity; fifty years after its introduction, it had clearly replaced the Geneva as the most popular version of the Bible in English.

Reprint Corporation, 1963), and Margaret T. Hills, *The English Bible in America* (New York: American Bible Society, 1962).

2. As quoted in S. L. Greenslade, ed., *The Cambridge History of the Bible: The West from the Reformation to the Present Day* (London: Cambridge University Press, 1963), 3:164.

Robert Barker was the first printer to produce an edition of the King James. Barker had inherited the office of King's Printer from his father, Christopher. This office gave him "sole monopoly of printing the Bible, either as a whole or in parts, the Book of Common Prayer, and all official documents, and this was extended by King James to include all Statutes, hitherto the monopoly of other printers."[3] As the king's printer, Barker bore the entire cost of the printing the new King James Bible, a huge expense, but also an expense that promised vast profits. For unknown reasons, however, the first folios of the King James Bible were to be among the last great books produced by Barker. Even though his name would continue to appear on royal imprints as late as the 1640s, the office of King's Printer began to slip away from him in the 1610s. Many of the imprints published in the 1610s were only nominally under his control. He died in 1645, having spent the last decade of his life in debtor's prison.[4]

The decline of Barker's career in no way detracts from the beauty of his 1611 folio edition of King James Bible. From this edition's binding to its paper, the book bore all the marks of the period's finest printing. What concerns us here are the levels of discourse nestled within Barker's typographic choices. Barker used four basic forms of type throughout the volume: gothic, roman, roman italic, and illuminated letters (figure 6). Such typographic diversity signals how letterforms can serve as interpretive devices for the words they signify.

The Bible's core text is presented in a gothic type, a letterform characterized by a dense and dark feel.[5] Barker's choice of gothic was highly traditional in that it resonated with the letterforms scribes had used for centuries to reproduce various documents, including the Bible. Gutenberg had manufactured such a type font to echo the script used by the ecclesiastical scribes in Germany, and early sellers of machine-made books often lied to their customers telling them that their wares had been produced by scribes.[6] Thus, gothic script invoked the ecclesiastical tradition of book production. In accordance with Western culture's reluctance to change anything associated with religious tradition, gothic letter faces were used in religious books long after roman type was adopted in the majority of Western printing.[7] In a sense, the eternal, changeless nature of God's words was reflected in the changeless nature of the type used to convey those words.

Barker also used gothic type to delineate what was sacred writ, as opposed to

3. Henry R. Plomer, "The King's Printing House under the Stuarts," *The Library* 2, no. 2 (1901): 354.

4. For the most complete account of Barker's role as royal printer, see ibid., 353–75. See also William K. Sessions, *The King's Printer: At Newcastle upon Tyne in 1639, at Bristol in 1643–1645, at Exeter in 1645–1646* (York, Eng.: Ebor Press, 1982).

5. J. L. Frazier, *Type Lore: Popular Fonts of Today, Their Origin and Use* (Chicago: Published by the Author, 1925), 23, 31.

6. Ibid., 25. Frederic W. Goudy, *Typologia: Studies in Type Design & Type Making* (Berkeley: University of California Press, 1940), 40. A. F. Johnson, *Type Designs: Their History and Development,* 2d ed. (New York: London House & Maxwell, 1959), 3–4.

7. James Deetz, *In Small Things Forgotten: The Archaeology of Early American Life* (New York: Anchor Books, 1977), 50–51, 88. See also Lewis Binford, "Archaeology as Anthropology," *American Antiquity* 28 (October 1962): 217–25. Alexander Lawson, *Anatomy of a Typeface* (Boston: Godine, 1990), 24.

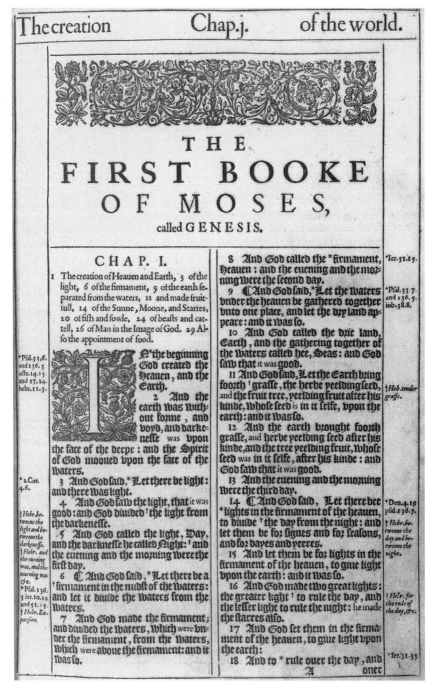

FIGURE 6. The first page of Genesis in Robert Barker's 1611 folio edition of the King James Bible, showing different lettering styles. Courtesy of The Lilly Library, Indiana University Libraries, Bloomington.

what was human invention. He did this by using roman type for the chapter summaries (which often included some theological commentary), marginal notes, and words in the text itself that stood as interpolated meanings interpreted from the original texts. Throughout his 1611 folio edition, Barker carefully manipulated his typographical choices to make clear to his readers what was written by the hand of God and what was not.

As well as these typographic manipulations, Barker used illuminated letters to begin books and chapters. Illuminated letters again hark back to the scribal tradition of book production. Manuscript books were produced by a number of scribes who all had special talents and functions. *Antiquarii* dedicated themselves to restoring books and revising faulty texts, *librarii* copied the texts, and "rubricators" illustrated pages with various decorative letters, borders, and other designs.[8] Gutenberg left room on his Bible's pages so that rubricators could accent his machine-made book with decorative borders and letters, making the book look more like a handwritten production (figure 7). Eventually wood blocks and then other illustrating techniques would take the place of hand-painted decoration, but these decorative engravings often echoed what had preceded them in book production.[9] Illuminated letters thus became the descendants of these hand-drawn typographic ornaments and again reveal a marked persistence in the typographic conventions surrounding religious books.

What is particularly interesting here is Barker's choice of illuminated letters. The 1611 folio edition's illuminated letters fall into three general categories: floriated (sometimes with figures included), biblical historiated, and mythical. While floriated letters are the most prevalent, there is also a large number of historiated letters, and though one might well expect biblical figures in these historiated letters (figure 8), classical figures outnumber biblical figures three to one. Intriguing issues are raised by the pronounced presence of such non-biblical iconography. So many letters dedicated to classical mythology forces one to consider the intertextual implications of their presence on the text they are supposedly meant to represent.

Numerous scholars have noted that once illustrations are wedded to a written text a "third text" is created out of the verbal/visual textual fusion, which can exercise various influences on the reading experience and interpretive enterprise.[10] One is forced to ask why such illustrated letters would be used in a Bible edition when classical mythology was clearly a pagan, polytheistic belief system. What is even more puzzling is the way in which these letters are employed. These classical

---

8. Goudy, *Typologia,* 5.

9. Geoffrey Ashall Glaister, *Encyclopedia of the Book,* 2d ed. (New Castle, Del.: Oak Knoll Press, 1996), 313.

10. Examples include: J. Hillis Miller, *Illustration* (Cambridge: Harvard University Press, 1992), 67–70; Natalie Zemon Davis, "Printing and the People," in *Rethinking Popular Culture: Contemporary Perspectives in Cultural Studies,* ed. Chandra Mukerji and Michael Schudson (Berkeley: University of California Press, 1991), 83–84; and Stephen Behrendt, "Readers and Illustrated Texts," paper presented at the Modern Language Association Annual Meeting, San Diego, December 1994.

Figure 7. Representative page composed in gothic blackletter with hand-drawn decorative letters from Gutenberg's 1454 New Testament. Courtesy of The Lilly Library, Indiana University Libraries, Bloomington.

letters are not placed near biblical texts with which they might have even the most tangential connection.

The reason for their use may be impossible to determine with much certainty, but one plausible answer centers on the fact that classical mythology also pointed to classical training, a mark of education and gentility. Letters depicting Neptune astride a seahorse (figure 9) or laurel trees growing out of Daphne's hands (figure 10) may not "illuminate" the texts they accompany, but they do evoke in the reader a sense of self-esteem if one has had the benefits of a classical education and can therefore recognize the symbols being used.[11] In fact, clerics and those well educated enough to read and purchase Bibles had often been steeped in the classics, and these symbols simply reminded them of their privileged educational status.[12] Although the reasons behind the presence of such classical letters remain obscure, one thing is clear. The presence of these letters did not upset Barker's buyers because they continue to appear in later editions. Nodding to classical, if pagan, history did not diminish the edition's appeal.

Social Status

If classical overtones can be found in the illuminated letters of the 1611 Barker edition, similar devices to demarcate levels of social achievement and refinement appear in the first illustrated Bible printed in the United States. Isaiah Thomas, printer, publisher extraordinaire, and philanthropist, gave the United States its first indigenous illustrated English Bible when he released his magnificent King James folio edition in 1791. Thomas, an archetype of the American self-made man, championed a strain of Enlightenment thinking that espoused social, moral, and intellectual improvement as not only the right, but within the grasp, of all people.[13] He believed that enlightened rationality not only enabled one to better his or her position in the world, but benefited society in general by making it more courteous, refined, and charitable.[14]

The most visible manifestation of this belief in human potential and the bene-

11. For discussions of literacy as a means of class distinction in the period, see Keith Thomas, "The Meaning of Literacy in Early Modern England," in *The Written Word: Literacy in Transition,* ed. Gerd Baumann (Oxford: Clarendon Press, 1986), 97–131; David Cressy, *Literacy and the Social Order: Reading and Writing in Tudor and Stuart England* (New York: Cambridge University Press, 1980); and Jonathan Goldberg, *Writing Matter: From the Hands of the English Renaissance* (Stanford: Stanford University Press, 1990), 41–54.

12. For insight into the educational practices of this period, see: David Cressy, *Education in Tudor and Stuart England* (New York: St. Martin's, 1975), and Donald Clark, *John Milton at St. Paul's School* (New York: Columbia University Press), 65–184.

13. Biographical material on Isaiah Thomas (1749–1831) can be found in Clifton K. Shipton, *Isaiah Thomas: Printer, Patriot, and Philanthropist, 1749–1831* (Rochester, N.Y.: The Printing House of Leo Hart, 1948); Benjamin Franklin Thomas, *Memoir of Isaiah Thomas* (Boston: Published privately, 1874); Isaiah Thomas, *Three Autobiographical Fragments* (Worcester, Mass.: American Antiquarian Society, 1812); and Thomas, "The Diary of Isaiah Thomas 1805–1828," *Transactions and Collections of the American Antiquarian Society,* vols. 9–10 (Worcester, Mass.: American Antiquarian Society, 1909).

14. For discussions of the influence of various strains of Enlightenment thought on notions of refinement and cultural formation, see Richard Bushman, *The Refinement of America: Persons, Houses, Cities*

FIGURE 8. Historiated illuminated letter, depicting a Gospel writer at work, from the first page of John's Gospel in Robert Barker's 1611 folio edition of the King James Bible. Courtesy of The Lilly Library, Indiana University Libraries, Bloomington.

fits of refinement appears in his folio Bible of 1791, an edition Thomas touted as unrivaled in either craftsmanship or content. Setting out to prove correct the post-Revolution sentiment that American products were every bit as good as their British counterparts, Thomas embarked upon his Bible project with single-minded devotion. He constructed his own paper mill and bookbindery to aid the volume's production.[15] Driving his workers to the point of exhaustion, Thomas readied his luxurious folio edition (which he simultaneously produced with a more affordable quarto edition) in just over twelve months. Even the aged former printer Benjamin Franklin added his voice to the throngs that hailed Thomas's folio as the most beautiful book ever printed in America.[16]

Although scholars have pointed to Thomas's volume as a book of early, superior American craftsmanship, no attention has been given to how the book's typography echoed Thomas's desire to have the volume stand as a marker and a catalyst of enlightened humanity and gentility. Unlike Barker's first edition of the King James Bible, Thomas's edition was printed in a roman letterform (figure 11). On one level, Thomas was simply following the common typesetting trends of the day. By the mid-seventeenth century, roman letters had replaced gothic in Bible editions, and thus one level of typographic distinction disappeared from King James Bible editions.[17] No longer were the words of Scripture set apart by

(New York: Alfred A. Knopf, 1992), 3–206, and Richard Brown, *Knowledge Is Power: The Diffusion of Information in Early America, 1700–1865* (New York: Oxford University Press, 1989), 42–64.

15. Charles Lemuel Nichols, *Bibliography of Worcester from 1775–1848* (Worcester, Mass.: Printed privately, 1899), viii.

16. Ibid., ix.

17. Philip Gaskell, *A New Introduction to Bibliography* (New York: Oxford University Press, 1972), 20; A. F. Johnson, *Type Designs: Their History and Development,* 2d ed. (New York: London House & Maxwell, 1959), 10.

FIGURE 9. Illuminated letter depicting Neptune astride a seahorse in Robert Barker's 1611 folio edition of the King James Bible. Courtesy of The Lilly Library, Indiana University Libraries, Bloomington.

FIGURE 10. Illuminated letter depicting laurel trees growing out of Daphne's hands in Robert Barker's 1611 folio edition of the King James Bible. Courtesy of The Lilly Library, Indiana University Libraries, Bloomington.

THE
G O S P E L,
ACCORDING TO
SAINT MATTHEW.

CHAP. I.

1 The genealogy of Christ from Abraham to Joseph. 18 The miraculous conception of Mary; Joseph's doubts are satisfied by an angel: Jesus is born.

HE book of the generation of Jefus Chrift, the fon of David, the fon of Abraham.

2 Abraham begat Ifaac; and Ifaac begat Jacob; and Jacob begat Judas and his brethren;

3 And Judas begat Phares and Zara of Thamar; and Phares begat Efrom; and Efrom begat Aram;

4 And Aram begat Aminadab; and Aminadab begat Naaffon; and Naaffon begat Salmon;

5 And Salmon begat Booz of Rachab; and Booz begat Obed of Ruth; and Obed begat Jeffe;

6 And Jeffe begat David the king; and David the king begat Solomon of her *that had been the wife* of Urias;

7 And Solomon begat Roboam; and Roboam begat Abia; and Abia begat Afa;

8 And Afa begat Jofaphat; and Jofaphat begat Joram; and Joram begat Ozias;

9 And Ozias begat Joatham; and Joatham begat Achaz; and Achaz begat Ezekias;

10 And Ezekias begat Manaffes; and Manaffes begat Amon; and Amon begat Jofias;

11 And Jofias begat Jechonias and his brethren, about the time they were carried away to Babylon:

12 And after they were brought to Babylon, Jechonias begat Salathiel; and Salathiel begat Zorobabel;

13 And Zorobabel begat Abiud; and Abiud begat Eliakim; and Eliakim begat Azor;

14 And Azor begat Sadoc; and Sadoc begat Achim; and Achim begat Eliud;

15 And Eliud begat Eleazar; and Eleazar begat Matthan; and Matthan begat Jacob;

16 And Jacob begat Jofeph the hufband of Mary, of whom was born Jefus, who is called Chrift.

17 So all the generations from Abraham to David, *are* fourteen generations; and from David until the carrying away into Babylon, *are* fourteen generations; and from the carrying away into Babylon unto Chrift, *are* fourteen generations.

18 ¶ Now the birth of Jefus Chrift was on this wife: When as his mother Mary was efpoufed to Jofeph, before they came together, fhe was found with child of the Holy Ghoft.

19 Then Jofeph her hufband, being a juft *man*, and not willing to make her a publick example, was minded to put her away privily.

20 But while he thought on thefe things, behold, the angel of the Lord appeared unto him in a dream, faying, Jofeph, thou fon of David, fear not to take unto thee Mary thy wife: for that which is conceived in her is of the Holy Ghoft.

21 And fhe fhall bring forth a fon, and thou fhalt call his name JESUS: for he fhall fave his people from their fins.

22 Now all this was done, that it might be fulfilled which was fpoken of the Lord by the prophet, faying,

23 Behold, a virgin fhall be with child, and fhall bring forth a fon, and they fhall call his name Emmanuel, which being interpreted is, God with us.

24 Then Jofeph being raifed from fleep, did as the angel of the Lord had bidden him, and took unto him his wife:

25 And knew her not till fhe had brought forth her firftborn fon: and he called his name JESUS.

CHAP. II.

1 Wife men from the eaft come to Jerufalem to inquire after Chrift. 3 Herod is alarmed. 11 Jofeph fleeth into Egypt. 16 Herod's maffacre of the children. 19 On Herod's death, Chrift is brought to Nazareth.

NOW when Jefus was born in Bethlehem of Judea, in the days of Herod the king, behold, there came wife men from the eaft to Jerufalem,

2 Saying,

198 F

FIGURE 11. The roman type of Isaiah Thomas's 1791 folio Bible. Courtesy of The Lilly Library, Indiana University Libraries, Bloomington.

gothic type; Scripture and its accompanying commentary began to share the same type font. As well as this loss of typographic, and thus interpretive, distinction, it is also important to note that roman script first appeared in Italy and emerged out of an Italian humanist tradition during the Renaissance.[18] Consequently, although in keeping with the type trends of the day, Thomas's choice of roman type was also strikingly appropriate to the Enlightenment aesthetic that undergirded his entire folio Bible project.

Thomas's commitment to Enlightenment ideals is perhaps nowhere more evident than in his Bible's illustrations. For his Bible edition, Thomas commissioned fifty copperplate illustrations executed in the rococo style.[19] He probably chose the rococo style because of its close associations with enlightened rationality and "the very limit of upper-class refinement."[20] The rococo style was bent on portraying beauty, often in a sensuous way, as seen in the frequency with which it depicted eroticized representations of classical figures in the pleasure parks and villas of European aristocracy. Thomas attempted to recode the rococo for his Bible readers by fusing beauty with certain key virtues such as honesty, courage, and wisdom in the context of biblical scenes. For example, the folio's illustration titled "Susanna Surprised by the Elders in the Garden" is filled with the rococo conventions of S and C curves, cherubs and children, clamshells and nature motifs, and a pronounced emphasis on the feminine, while at the same time emphasizing Susanna's chastity and courage in resisting the lascivious advances of two elders (figure 12). By linking beauty and virtue, Thomas strove to refine his viewer's sensibilities and encourage them to think of virtuous action as a beautiful thing.[21] For Thomas, as well as many of his like-minded friends who held certain Enlightenment ideals, appreciations of beauty and virtue were key markers of the gentility found among the better classes.

The use of the rococo style did not stop with the Bible's illustrations, however; Thomas employed it extensively in his typographical choices. The title page is but the first hint that the enlightened aesthetic of the rococo will characterize the book's type; the words "Holy Bible" are illustrated with cherubic forms (figure

18. Johnson, *Type Designs,* 37.

19. The engravers included Joseph H. Seymour of Philadelphia, Amos Doolittle of New Haven, Samuel Hill, and H. Norman. Nichols, *Bibliography of Worcester,* 37.

20. For discussions of the influence of various strains of Enlightenment thought on notions of refinement and cultural formation, see Bushman, *The Refinement of America,* 3–206, and Brown, *Knowledge Is Power,* 42–64. For the rococo's connection to ideas of high culture and gentility, see William Park, *The Idea of Rococo* (Newark: University of Delaware Press, 1992), 42. See also Morrion H. Heckscher and Leslie Greene Bowman, *American Rococo, 1750–1775: Elegance in Ornament* (New York: Metropolitan Museum of Art, 1992), 4. Along with Park's and Heckshcher's works, good treatments of the rococo style in the eighteenth and nineteenth century include Jean Starobinski, Philippe Duboy, Akiko Fukai, Jun I. Kanai, Toshio Horii, Janet Arnold, and Martin Kamer, *Revolution in Fashion: European Clothing, 1715–1815* (New York: Abbeville, 1989); Eric M. Zafran, *The Rococo Age: French Masterpieces of the Eighteenth Century* (Atlanta: High Museum of Art, 1983); Michael Levey, *Rococo to Revolution: Major Trends in Eighteenth-Century Painting* (New York: Thames and Hudson, 1966).

21. For a good discussion of the role of feeling in the midst of eighteenth-century Enlightenment thought, see Simon Schama, *Citizens: A Chronicle of the French Revolution* (New York: Alfred A. Knopf, 1992), 145–62.

Engraved for THOMAS's N.º XXXI Edition of the Bible.

SUSANNA. I.19.

Jos.ᵗ H. Seymour sculp.

SUSANNA
surprised by the Elders in the Garden.

FIGURE 12. An illustration using rococo conventions in Isaiah Thomas's 1791 folio Bible. Courtesy of The Lilly Library, Indiana University Libraries, Bloomington.

28

13). Rococo period artists favored the use of cherubs and cherubic figures, conjuring a complex interplay between innocence and mischievousness, heavenly causes and earthly consequences. The rococo element continues in the illuminated letters found at the beginning of each book.

Instead of the mythic beasts and occasional biblical figure found in early Barker editions of the King James, Thomas used three illuminated letterforms in his volume: an intricately wrought engraved letter to begin each testament and either a floriated (figure 14) or a floriated factotum initial (figure 15) to begin each book. The use of the scrolled S and C lines in the former and the garden/nature invocations of the latter were type elements immensely popular in the French court of Louis XV, the place associated with the golden age of the rococo style.[22] Thus, Thomas's choice of type was calculated to bring far more than simple words to his readers: words encased in artistic aesthetics that helped define one's social status through various notions of refinement and gentility found in the late eighteenth century.

Religious Sensibility

Isaiah Thomas was but the first in a long line of American publishers interested in producing stunningly crafted Bible editions. In the early 1840s, the firm of Harper and Brothers released their mammoth (over thirteen pounds) *Illuminated Bible*. Many heralded it as "the most splendidly elegant edition of the Sacred Record ever issued."[23] It was a volume that would influence countless Bible editions that followed it, setting the standard for an ensuing vogue of large nineteenth-century family Bibles. The idea of producing such a Bible did not originate with any of the four Harper brothers. Even though their firm was fast becoming the largest publisher in the United States, the Harpers had not printed a Bible for almost twenty years when Joseph Alexander Adams, a New York printer and engraver, came to them with a proposal to produce the grandest Bible the United States had ever seen.[24]

What promised to make Adams's edition so special was its more than sixteen hundred illustrations. No previous American-made Bible had ever contained more than one hundred pictures. In addition to the spectacular number of engravings, Adams wanted his volume to be distinguished by the fact that the

22. Lewis F. Day, *Alphabets Old & New* (London: Senate, 1910) sample 152.

23. *Catalogue of Books Published by Harper & Brothers, 1845* (New York: Harper & Brothers, 1845), 13. See also Edward O'Callaghan, *A List of Editions of the Holy Scriptures and Parts Thereof* (Albany, N.Y.: Munsell & Rowland, 1861), 288–89; Frank Weitenkempf, "American Bible Illustration," *The Boston Public Library Quarterly* 3 (July 1958): 155; Joseph Henry Harper, *The House of Harper* (New York: Harper & Brothers, 1912), 80; *American Dictionary of Printing and Bookmaking* (New York: Howard Lockwood, 1984), 8; and David Bland, *A History of Book Illustration: The Illuminated Manuscript and the Printed Book*, 2d ed. rev. (Berkeley: University of California Press, 1969), 303.

24. Eugene Exman, *The House of Harper: One Hundred and Fifty Years of Publishing* (New York: Harper & Row, 1967), 24; Edward Spann, *The New Metropolis: New York City, 1840–1857* (New York: Columbia University Press, 1981), 409.

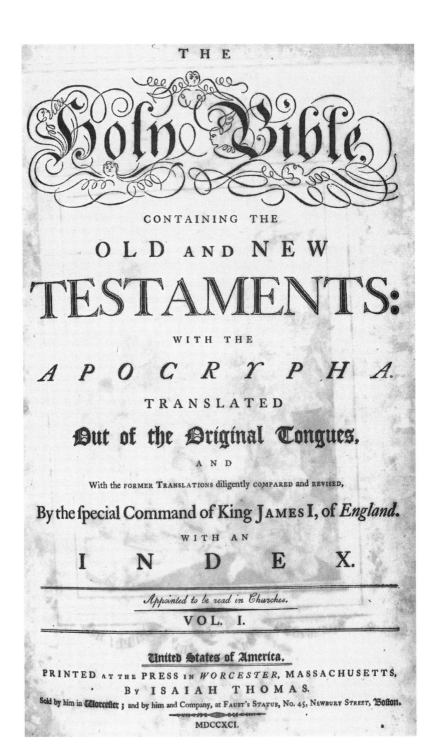

FIGURE 13. Rococo conventions complete with cherubic forms used to depict the words "Holy Bible." Courtesy of The Lilly Library, Indiana University Libraries, Bloomington.

FIGURE 14. Floriated illuminated letter in Isaiah Thomas's 1791 folio Bible. Courtesy of The Lilly Library, Indiana University Libraries, Bloomington.

FIGURE 15. Floriated factotum letter in Isaiah Thomas's 1791 folio Bible. Courtesy of The Lilly Library, Indiana University Libraries, Bloomington.

pictures would predominantly be on the same pages as the text, rather than following the far more common publishing practice of printing illustrations on separate sheets and then binding them with the text. Adams promised to accomplish this wonder through a new printing process called electrotyping, a procedure that involved coating stereotyped, wood block, or intaglio plates with a thin layer of copper, thereby strengthening them for use in high-speed, high-pressure presses. Electrotyping allowed for large print runs of extremely fine quality text and pictures, and the Harpers' *Illuminated Bible* was the first volume printed with the technology.[25]

Whether it was the Harper brothers's staunch Methodism, their keen sense of business acumen, or the allure of technological innovation that moved them to undertake such an expensive and potentially risky enterprise is impossible to say.[26] One thing, however, is clear: they believed in the project with an unrelenting fervor. They gave Adams a rare contract which allowed him both a large percentage of the edition's profits and complete charge of the edition's production.[27] They also aggressively advertised the volume by flooding newspapers, literary periodicals, and booksellers with publicity.[28] Rather than releasing the book all at once, Harper and Brothers decided to print the edition in fifty-four parts ranging from twenty-five to sixty-pages, at twenty-five cents per installment. They decided on an initial press run of 50,000 copies. Subscribers could purchase the installments as they appeared and then have them bound upon the edition's completion in 1846. To make these installments more enticing, the Harpers decided to print some pages in an expensive two-color format. In 1844 they ordered a new set of presses specially designed to facilitate the electrotyping printing process. The *Illuminated Bible* was an immediate success. The initial press run quickly sold out, and the Harpers printed 25,000 copies of the entire volume in 1846. Over the next two decades, sales remained strong enough for the firm to issue two more printings, in 1859 and 1866.[29]

What brief mention scholars have made of the *Illuminated Bible* has centered mostly on its heavily illustrated nature, bound to its use of electrotyping technology. Not surprisingly, the volume's typography is ignored. Typography here, however, is of particular importance, because it was the book's typography that initially threatened the popularity of the volume by keeping it from gaining the acceptance of various segments of the nation's clergy. Disapproval on a clerical level could have meant serious sales problems for the firm, and such disapproval was tied to certain religious and artistic sensibilities active among mid-nineteenth-century American Protestants.

As the title page of the Harper Bible reflects, the early nineteenth-century American publishing industry enjoyed an unprecedented diversity of type styles. New technology in the production of type, as well as the exploding print culture

25. Exman, *House of Harper*, 34–35. See also *American Dictionary of Printing*, 157–66, and Bamber Gascoigne, *How to Identify Prints* (London: Thames and Hudson, 1986), 33b, 72.

26. James C. Derby, *Fifty Years among Authors, Books, and Publishers* (New York: G. W. Carleton), 95; O'Callaghan, *A List of Editions*, 288–89.

27. Harper and Brothers Collection, Columbia University, *Contract Book* (New York: Chadwyck-Healy), Reel A1, 75–77.

28. Exman, *House of Harper*, 35. For an extended discussion of Harper and Brothers advertising strategies, see Ronald J. Zboray, *A Fictive People: Antebellum Economic Development and the American Reading Public* (New York: Oxford University Press, 1993), 56–68.

29. Harper and Brothers Collection, *Contract Book*, Reel A1, 330–331. See also Paris Marion Simms, *The Bible in America: Versions That Have Played their Part in the Making of the Republic* (New York: Wilson-Erickson, 1936), 266, and Harper, *House of Harper*, 80.

of the antebellum era, encouraged a wide-ranging use of new typefaces.[30] The *Illuminated Bible's* title page shows the eclectic nature of the type aesthetic of the day, in which placing as many different type styles together as possible was often the practice (figure 16).

The Harpers nonetheless took only limited advantage of the increasingly diverse nature of type fonts when they produced their *Illuminated Bible*. In most of its elements the *Illuminated Bible* followed the standard use of various sizes of roman and roman italic type. In setting the type for chapter summaries, marginal commentary, and the text itself, the Harpers maintained long-standing conventions of setting in roman italic type words that were not found in the primary text used for the scriptural translation. Font sizes also helped distinguish human and divine utterance. Smaller roman type was used in chapter summaries and in some marginal commentary to create a distinctive look for those words that could not be attributed to God. Italics were used in the text itself to set apart human interpretations of the text. In all of these typographical conventions, the Harpers simply followed the current biblical trends of their day. It was in their illuminated letters that they showed some potentially dangerous deviance.

One finds three styles of illuminated letters in the *Illuminated Bible*. First, there are letters full of the S and C curves and natural imagery reminiscent of Thomas's folio Bible and its rococo style. The high artistic aspirations of this style were still in force in early Victorian America.[31] Second, there is a style of letter full of sharp, robust perpendicular lines, which recalls the columns and artistic conventions of the neoclassical style that would later develop into a gothic architectural renaissance in the United States (figure 17).[32] The neoclassical style followed upon the heels of the rococo in both Europe and the United States and became a prevalent architectural and artistic style in the early American republic.

The neoclassical style is founded on the classic architecture of Greek and Roman, full of columns, domes, and broad, squat-based buildings. The style became popular in the United States largely because of its association with the best qualities of ancient Greek and Roman society, in which honesty, sacrificial service, and devotion to country were held out as the supreme virtues. A young American democracy admired these attributes and counted them as essential to the survival of a country that stood as the first great modern experiment in democracy.[33] It is no surprise that the illuminated letters of Harper's Bible played on such a popular style whose virtues so closely resonated with many biblical values. The volume's neoclassical letters were not the problem, however. The problem was the two letters found at the beginning of the Old and New Testaments.

The Harpers decided to present spectacularly elaborate illuminated letters at

30. Edmund G. Gress, *Fashions in American Typography, 1780–1930* (New York: Harper & Brothers, 1931), 31–78; Gaskell, *New Introduction to Bibliography*, 207–13.

31. John Maass, *The Victorian Home in America* (New York: Hawthorn Books, 1972), 8, 25.

32. James Early, *Romanticism and American Architecture* (New York: A. S. Barnes, 1965).

33. Colleen McDannell, *The Christian Home in Victorian America, 1840–1900* (Bloomington: Indiana University Press, 1986), 30.

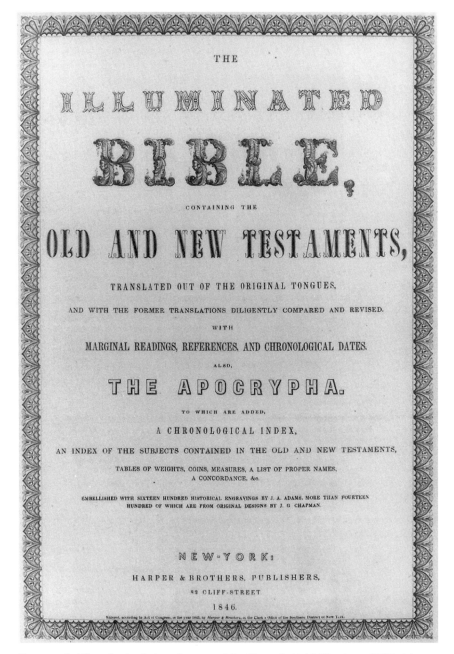

FIGURE 16. The eclectic choice of type used for Harper's 1846 *Illuminated Bible* title page. Courtesy of The Lilly Library, Indiana University Libraries, Bloomington.

FIGURE 17. Illuminated letters in neoclassical and rococo styles in Harper's 1846 *Illuminated Bible,* page 538. Courtesy of The Lilly Library, Indiana University Libraries, Bloomington.

the beginning of the two Testaments. The New Testament showed the evangelist Matthew hard at work writing his Gospel (figure 18). The Old Testament showed Adam and Eve in the midst of the Garden of Eden (figure 19). The problem with both these letters was that they depicted nudity. Matthew's Gospel was heralded by several naked angels, and the garden of Eden contained a nude Adam and Eve. This was a bold and provocative move on the part of the Harpers, and it met with significant resistance from a group of New Jersey clergymen who were outraged by the titillating nature of the pictures.[34]

Such resistance reveals something about American Protestantism of the time. Nudity, which for centuries had played an important role in European religious art, was under serious scrutiny in the United States, and this scrutiny came largely from more conservative American Protestants. European paintings and sculptures that involved nudity became points of clerical contention; debates raged over what was edifying art and what was simply titillating pornography. One of the most famous of the debates on this topic centered on an American sculpture named "The Greek Slave," which depicted a naked woman in chains and was viewed by more than 100,000 Americans in the 1840s.[35] American Protestants, divided even among themselves, mounted significant opposition to such displays of a naked human body.

Into this climate came the largest decorative letters of the *Illuminated Bible.* On one level, these letters were elegant pieces of typography, invoking the time-honored biblical tradition of illuminated letters. On another level, they were a dangerous affront to certain religious sensibilities. Those most committed to more conservative notions of religious display sought to have Harper's *Illuminated Bible* scorned.

Clearly, a letter is not simply a letter. Typography makes a difference when it

34. Eugene Exman, *The Brothers Harper* (New York: Harper and Row, 1965), 190.

35. Joy S. Kasson, "Narratives of the Female Body: *The Greek Slave,*" in *The Culture of Sentiment: Race, Gender, and Sentimentality in 19th Century America,* ed. Shirley Samuels (New York: Oxford University Press, 1992), 172–90.

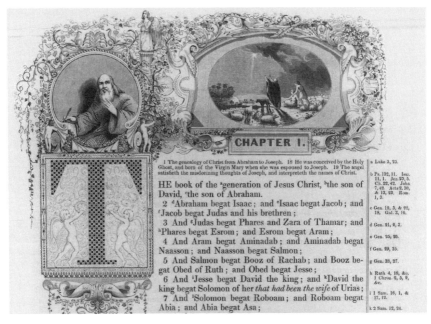

FIGURE 18. Elaborate illuminated letter depicting nudity at the beginning of Matthew's Gospel in Harper's 1846 *Illuminated Bible*. Courtesy of The Lilly Library, Indiana University Libraries, Bloomington.

FIGURE 19. Perhaps the most controversial illuminated letter in Harper's 1846 *Illuminated Bible* because of the nude figures of Adam and Eve, Old Testament, page 1. Courtesy of The Lilly Library, Indiana University Libraries, Bloomington.

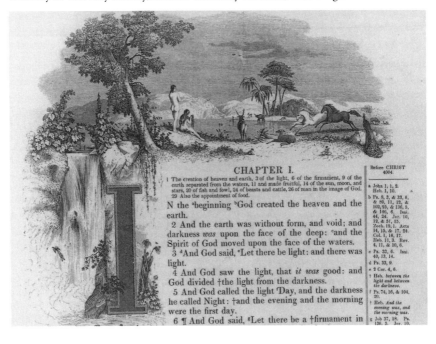

enters into wider cultural discussions on what one might consider appropriate and inappropriate representations in relation to sacred works. Although the Harpers' Bible would go on to become one of the most successful and influential Bible editions of the century, it is important to note that its typography was as serious an issue among many of its initial purchasers as its fine craftsmanship.

Theological Interpretation

By the twentieth century, illuminated letters were relegated almost exclusively to the most expensive Bible editions. Early in the century, small fine arts presses such as the Nonesuch Press and the Doves Press helped create a sort of renaissance of fine Bible production by printing magnificent editions of portions of the Scriptures.[36] Perhaps the most stunning biblical edition to appear in this period was the Golden Cockerel Press's edition of *The Four Gospels*. Robert Gibbings, who had taken over the Golden Cockerel Press in 1924, released this volume to universal acclaim in 1931.[37]

Gibbings called upon another artist and fine printer, Eric Gill, to help him produce *The Four Gospels*. Both Gibbings and Gill were the sons of Anglican clergymen, and hence combined an extensive knowledge of bookmaking with a deep familiarity with Scripture.[38] Gill had, in fact, been interested in illustrating the Gospels since 1913, so when Gibbings enlisted his aid in 1927, he had considered for well over a decade how he might want such an edition to look.[39] As with all Golden Cockerel imprints, the press run was small and specifically targeted for a collector's, rather than religious, market. The press run consisted of twelve copies on vellum and 488 copies on handmade paper.[40]

Gill and Gibbings abandoned many century-old traditions in printing their edition of the Gospels. Most noticeably, they did not use roman and roman italic typefaces to distinguish between divine and human words. Instead, with few— and therefore noticeable—exceptions, the entire text is set in the same font. They did, however, change the size, design, and positioning of their letters to make interpretive statements. For example, at the end of the Gospel of Mark, the edition employs a modified Greek font with a specifically Greek-like form of the letter "Y" to shout the words "Go Ye" (figure 20). Consequently, Mark's rendition of the Great Commission takes on the ancient overtones and authenticity of the original manuscripts and is emphasized by letters that command both the page and the reader.

Gibbings and Gill found other ways to format their type to echo the text's meaning. For example, in the genealogy found in Saint Luke's Gospel, the generations

36. Joel Silver, *The Bible in the Lilly Library* (Bloomington, Ind.: The Lilly Library, 1991), 36–37.

37. For various reviews of the edition, see John Dreyfus, *A Typographical Masterpiece* (San Francisco: The Book Club of California, 1990), 74–83.

38. Ibid., xi.

39. Ibid., 34.

40. Ibid., 71.

went & told them that had been with him, as they mourned and wept. And they, when they had heard that he was alive, and had been seen of her, believed not. ✴ After that he appeared in another form unto two of them, as they walked, and went into the country. And they went and told it unto the residue: neither believed they them. ✴ Afterward he appeared unto the eleven as they sat at meat, and upbraided them with their unbelief and hardness of heart, because they believed not them which had seen him after he was risen. And he said unto them,

GO YE

INTO ALL THE WORLD ◢ AND PREACH THE GOSPEL TO EVERY

CREATURE. HE THAT BELIEVETH AND IS BAPTIZED shall be saved; but he that believeth not shall be damned. And these signs shall follow them that believe; In my name shall they cast out devils; they shall speak with new tongues; They shall take up serpents; and if they drink any deadly thing, it shall not hurt them; they shall lay hands on the sick, and they shall recover. ✴ So then after the Lord had spoken unto them, he was received up into heaven, and sat on the right hand of God. And they went forth, and preached every where, the Lord working with them, and confirming the word with signs following. AMEN.

127

FIGURE 20. Modified Greek type in the Golden Cockerel Press's 1931 *The Four Gospels*, page 127. Courtesy of The Lilly Library, Indiana University Libraries, Bloomington.

are presented in a column format (figure 21). Such a typographical move gives a linear, extended feel to the text, echoing the extension of the various families back through the ages.

These typographical strategies of theological interpretation are extended to the illuminated letters that can be found throughout the volume. Unlike Bible editions that frequently used the same illuminated letters over and over again, the Golden Cockerel uses its illuminated words and letters only once, allowing for a tremendous amount of specification in their design. In all cases, the letters fit nicely into the passage they are set against. More than this, however, the illuminated letters often have a sense of collapsing various notions of timing. The illuminated "T" at the beginning of the Gospel of Matthew contains the baby Jesus in a womb signaling that Christ serves as the seed for all generations and yet he arrives at the end of the stated genealogy (figure 22). He is thus the alpha and the omega.

Another example of such temporal collapse is seen in the letter "A" that illuminates Christ's words as he distributes the elements for the last supper, pointing to the sacrament of communion by depicting the communion cup and wafer. Once again, beginnings and endings are connected as the genesis of this sacrament is linked to its later Anglican form (figure 23). This strategy is reinforced in the way the words found in the Anglican liturgy for communion are highlighted by capitals in the text.

Complementing their distinctive illuminated letters, Gibbings and Gill chose to employ illuminated words. This in itself is an interesting typographical choice with possible theological overtones. Instead of typography that simply stresses letters by placing them in an illuminated form, here the typography stresses entire words, harking back to the biblical emphasis on the Word itself.

This emphasis on the word and the theological implications of the illuminations are well demonstrated at the opening of the Gospel of John (figure 24). Here several interpretive connections are made in the decorative word. The beginning of the Gospel of John with its emphasis on the creative nature of God's word is stressed by placing Adam and Eve next to the figure of Jesus. God's creative activity is clearly linked in this illustration to God's redemptive action. The illustration explicitly portrays a linkage between John's text and the text of Genesis, a connection readers would appreciate only if they had a certain degree of biblical familiarity.

Another example of theological interpretation coming into play in an illuminated word is found in the twenty-sixth chapter of Matthew where the woman comes to anoint Jesus' feet with her hair (figure 25). Here the woman is anointing Jesus' feet in a way which the disciples do not understand. The illustration again collapses time by making the interpretive connection that this is the only anointing Jesus will receive for his burial, a point made through his outstretched hand pointing to the cross and tomb in the upper right-hand portion of the illuminated word.

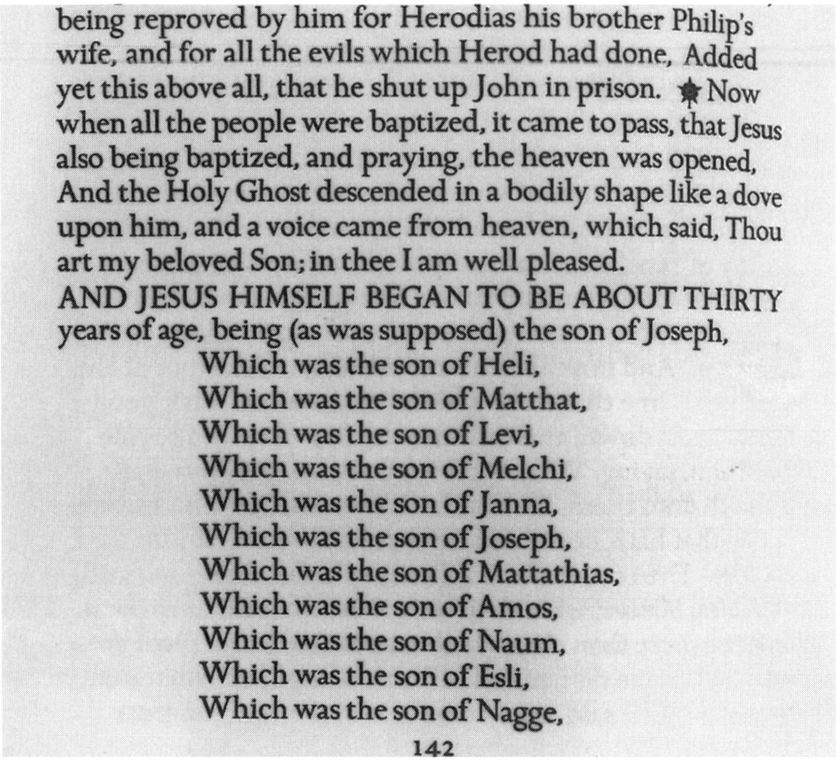

being reproved by him for Herodias his brother Philip's wife, and for all the evils which Herod had done, Added yet this above all, that he shut up John in prison. ✹ Now when all the people were baptized, it came to pass, that Jesus also being baptized, and praying, the heaven was opened, And the Holy Ghost descended in a bodily shape like a dove upon him, and a voice came from heaven, which said, Thou art my beloved Son; in thee I am well pleased.

AND JESUS HIMSELF BEGAN TO BE ABOUT THIRTY years of age, being (as was supposed) the son of Joseph,

> Which was the son of Heli,
> Which was the son of Matthat,
> Which was the son of Levi,
> Which was the son of Melchi,
> Which was the son of Janna,
> Which was the son of Joseph,
> Which was the son of Mattathias,
> Which was the son of Amos,
> Which was the son of Naum,
> Which was the son of Esli,
> Which was the son of Nagge,

142

FIGURE 21. Column format used to emphasize genealogical lineage in the Golden Cockerel Press's 1931 *The Four Gospels,* page 142. Courtesy of The Lilly Library, Indiana University Libraries, Bloomington.

FIGURE 22. Illuminated letter showing the baby Jesus in the Golden Cockerel Press's 1931 *The Four Gospels,* page 5. Courtesy of The Lilly Library, Indiana University Libraries, Bloomington.

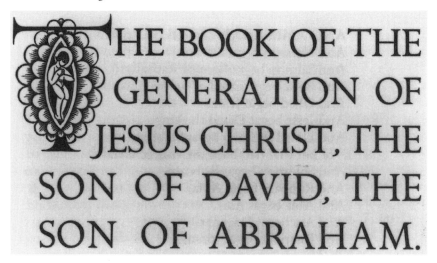

THE BOOK OF THE GENERATION OF JESUS CHRIST, THE SON OF DAVID, THE SON OF ABRAHAM.

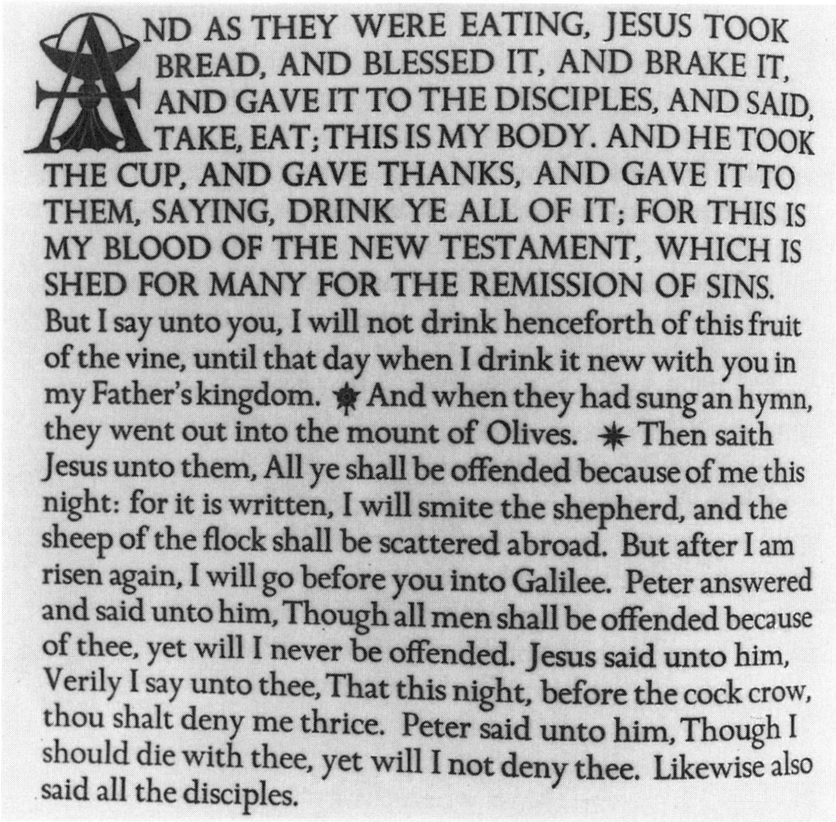

AND AS THEY WERE EATING, JESUS TOOK BREAD, AND BLESSED IT, AND BRAKE IT, AND GAVE IT TO THE DISCIPLES, AND SAID, TAKE, EAT; THIS IS MY BODY. AND HE TOOK THE CUP, AND GAVE THANKS, AND GAVE IT TO THEM, SAYING, DRINK YE ALL OF IT; FOR THIS IS MY BLOOD OF THE NEW TESTAMENT, WHICH IS SHED FOR MANY FOR THE REMISSION OF SINS. But I say unto you, I will not drink henceforth of this fruit of the vine, until that day when I drink it new with you in my Father's kingdom. ✱ And when they had sung an hymn, they went out into the mount of Olives. ✱ Then saith Jesus unto them, All ye shall be offended because of me this night: for it is written, I will smite the shepherd, and the sheep of the flock shall be scattered abroad. But after I am risen again, I will go before you into Galilee. Peter answered and said unto him, Though all men shall be offended because of thee, yet will I never be offended. Jesus said unto him, Verily I say unto thee, That this night, before the cock crow, thou shalt deny me thrice. Peter said unto him, Though I should die with thee, yet will I not deny thee. Likewise also said all the disciples.

FIGURE 23. Illuminated letter highlighting the communion wafer and cup in the Golden Cockerel Press's 1931 *The Four Gospels,* page 68. Courtesy of The Lilly Library, Indiana University Libraries, Bloomington.

Finally, while some traditional typographical conventions are eschewed in this edition, there exist certain traditional typographical elements that echo Bible production all the way back to the monastic scribes and Gutenberg. As the edition's depiction of John the Baptist's beheading shows (figure 26), the illuminated word is not confined within the justification of the book's margins. The executioner is literally allowed to step outside the normal bounds of the printed text, echoing the decorated letters of Gutenberg's Bible and the illuminations of countless monastic manuscripts. This strategy, which is used for every illuminated letter and word in the volume, gives the edition a more handcrafted feel. At the same time, the strategy also associates the text with a tradition of scriptural presentation dating back to the most ancient ecclesiastical manuscripts.

Although letters must obey certain rules of form to remain identifiable, it should not be forgotten that they can also be as distinctive and expressive as a person's

FIGURE 24. Illuminated word containing theological commentary in the Golden Cockerel Press's 1931 *The Four Gospels,* page 213. Courtesy of The Lilly Library, Indiana University Libraries, Bloomington.

face. In an interpretive sense, the word "type*face*" is strikingly appropriate. A (type)face can be manipulated to express myriad messages while yet remaining a face. The various typefaces found in four centuries of printing the King James Bible testify that typography does more than simply combine to signify various words. Typography can connect its text to numerous levels of historical, cultural, and intellectual discourse. One wonders if all the debates over how various words

FIGURE 25. Illuminated word containing theological commentary in the Golden Cockerel Press's 1931 *The Four Gospels,* page 66. Courtesy of The Lilly Library, Indiana University Libraries, Bloomington.

FIGURE 26. Illuminated word that spreads outside the margin, invoking hand-drawn illuminated letters found in early printed books and manuscripts, in the Golden Cockerel Press's 1931 *The Four Gospels,* page 37. Courtesy of The Lilly Library, Indiana University Libraries, Bloomington.

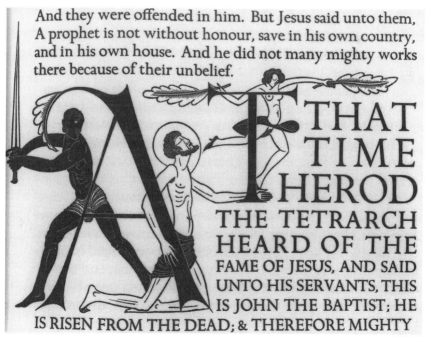

have been changed from one biblical translation to the next might be reflected in some measure in the incredibly diverse ways publishers have chosen to depict those seemingly changeless words using a multitude of typefaces. The interpretative power of type should constantly be kept in mind as one reads and interprets the biblical text. The constantly shifting use of typefaces in Bible production stands as a vivid testimony that it is often as important to read the means to the message as it is to read the message itself.

Bridge One

Paul Gutjahr's "The Letter(s) of the Law" describes typography as "the means to the message" of a text, a means whose own semiotics must be deciphered if one is to understand the message fully. The following essay, by Sarah A. Kelen, discusses a book whose typography needed to be deciphered in a different way: the dense and archaic blackletter typeface of Thomas Dunham Whitaker's 1813 edition of *Piers Plowman* was an interpretive obstacle for its readers. The introduction to this collection of essays notes that typography is too often "invisible" to the reader; in Whitaker's text, the problem is just the reverse.

As Gutjahr's essay on Bible printing clarifies, the choice of blackletter or roman face had significant interpretive ramifications in the early modern period. Blackletter was traditional in Bible printing because it recalled monastic scribal production and thus staked a claim to authority through that textual tradition: God speaks in blackletter. This is often still the case in typographic semiotics: while Bibles (like most other books) are now printed in a roman face, the title "Holy Bible" on spine or book cover is frequently still printed in the "sanctified" blackletter.

By the nineteenth century, roman type had superseded blackletter for almost every purpose, and blackletter was used only for ornamental or "marked" text. For Whitaker to publish a long narrative poem in a blackletter face was conservative to the point of idiosyncrasy, a fact not missed by the volume's uncharitable reviewers. Whitaker's use of an archaizing typeface had the opposite effect from that of the 1611 blackletter King James Bible, in which typographic conservatism had signaled the continued and changeless truth of the text. Two centuries later, Whitaker's archaizing typography relegates his work explicitly to the past, foregrounding the poem's historical alterity.

Unlike the four centuries of Bible printers surveyed by Gutjahr, who used typography to signal their catholicism (small c), Whitaker used typography to repudiate Catholicism (big C). For Whitaker, the Romishness of the medieval text had to be safely relegated to England's past, because (like many Anglo-Protestants of the early nineteenth century) he feared the legal emancipation of England's Catholics, an act that was currently under debate in Parliament. Readers' complaints that Whitaker's text was egregiously obscure were thus accurate, but still missed the point: Whitaker insisted on the text's obscurity because he did not want to allow the text's medieval Catholicism into his modern (Protestant) world.

Chapter Two

Peirs Plouhman [*sic*] and the "formidable array of blackletter" in the Early Nineteenth Century

SARAH A. KELEN

At the risk of revealing a trade secret, I will confess that a fair number of medieval-ists are afraid of *Piers Plowman*. William Langland's late fourteenth-century alle-gorical dream vision is just a little too convoluted, a little too resistant to tidy theorizing, a little too *hard*. There are, of course, a number of serious Langland scholars; those of us outside of that circle are rather afraid of them too. Never-theless, even the most cowardly medievalist recognizes the tremendous literary import and impact of Langland's brilliant (if frustrating) poem.[1] The standard editions of the poem do everything they can to aid the puzzled reader: they give extensive glossaries of words particular to the poem's western dialect (much harder for the modern reader than Chaucer's London English);[2] they translate the poem's many Latin quotations and indicate their sources; they gloss particularly difficult passages; and they print the text in a modern, roman typeface, something Langland himself would never have seen.[3]

The printing of medieval texts in a modern typeface is no new innovation. The earliest printed books sought scrupulously to reproduce the look of manu-scripts, even printing on parchment in some cases.[4] However, even the sixteenth-century blackletter type (which no longer resembled contemporary handwriting)

---

1. Or rather his *poems,* since *Piers Plowman* is generally said to exist in three distinct versions: the (in-complete) first version, the A-text; the B-text; and the (revised) C-text. Some have also argued for the existence of a fourth (and earliest) version, the so-called Z-text; Charlotte Brewer and A. G. Rigg, eds., *Piers Plowman: The Z version* (Toronto: Pontifical Institute of Mediaeval Studies, 1983). The traditional ordering of the versions has recently been challenged by Jill Mann who argues that the A-text is a condensa-tion of the earlier (and more Latinate) B-text for a nonclerical audience: "The Power of the Alphabet: A Reassessment of the Relation between the A and the B Versions of *Piers Plowman,*" *Yearbook of Langland Studies* 8 (1994): 21–50.

2. None of the surviving manuscripts is close enough to Langland himself to be considered independent evidence of his dialect (as medieval scribes often imposed their dialects onto the works they copied). But M. L. Samuels concludes from various internal and external evidence that Langland's poem was originally written in a southwest Worcestershire dialect: "Langland's Dialect," *Medium Ævum* 54 (1985): 244.

3. Langland's quotations of Latin Bible verses are, however, typically printed in an italic face in modern (roman face) editions.

4. D. C. Greetham, *Textual Scholarship: An Introduction* (New York: Garland, 1994), 226.

fell out of use in the eighteenth century. Despite the literary conservatism inherent in the act of editing (and thus conserving) works of medieval literature, by the nineteenth century, editors did not generally assume that their audience expected typographical conservatism as well. In fact, Thomas Jefferson refers to a tradition of printing late medieval works in a roman typeface in his appeal for a similar typographical modernization of Anglo-Saxon literature. In a letter of November 1825, Jefferson proposes that an editor of Anglo-Saxon literature should "vest it in the roman type which we have adopted instead of our English blackletter, reform its uncouth orthography, and assimilate its pronunciation, as much as may be, to the present English, just as we do in reading Piers Plowman or Chaucer."[5]

Jefferson clearly believed that the goal of the editor of older English poetry should be to make those works accessible through a process of "reformation" and "assimilation," not to fetishize their "uncouth" antiquity.[6] But Jefferson's assumption that *Piers Plowman* is best dressed in the modern garb of a roman typeface was not shared by the poem's then most recent editor. Twelve years before Jefferson wrote, a blackletter edition of the poem had been published in London by Thomas Dunham Whitaker.[7] Whitaker's choice of a blackletter typeface may seem to manifest a simple nostalgia or some notion of formality in what was a large and expensive edition—and I do not mean to rule these out as motivations—but for Whitaker the blackletter typeface also has a distinct ideological and religious import. The blackletter type Whitaker uses for his edition visibly antiquates *Piers Plowman*. This serves two purposes: it foregrounds the edition's scholarly credentials in presenting the poem as an artifact of English literary history; and it distances the poem's discomfiting Catholicism from England's now (officially) Protestant reading public. The antiquating gesture of using a blackletter type thus accommodates the national intellectual continuity implied by the work of editing medieval texts to the theological discontinuity caused by England's conversion to Protestantism.

Before Whitaker's edition, *Piers Plowman* had a rather sporadic history of appearances in print. Unlike the works of Langland's contemporary Chaucer, which were published separately by William Caxton (England's first printer) in the late fifteenth century, reissued by Wynkyn de Worde in the early sixteenth century, and edited together as a collection of Works in 1532 by William Thynne, and which have remained in print ever since, *Piers Plowman* was not published until

5. Jefferson to J. Evelyn Denison, 9 November 1825, in *The Writings of Thomas Jefferson,* ed. A. E. Bergh et al., 20 vols. (Washington, D.C.: Thomas Jefferson Memorial Association, 1905), 16:131. Quoted in Vincent DiMarco, *Piers Plowman: A Reference Guide* (Boston: G. K. Hall, 1982), item 1825.1.

6. Allen Frantzen provides a political analysis of Jefferson's Anglo-Saxonism in the context of Jefferson's desire to model American democracy on the social organization of Anglo-Saxon England and on Anglo-Saxon law: *Desire for Origins: New Language, Old English, and Teaching the Tradition* (New Brunswick, N.J.: Rutgers University Press, 1990), 204.

7. Thomas Dunham Whitaker, *Visio Willi de Petro Plouhman, item visiones ejusdem de Dowel, Dobet, et Dobest. Or, the vision of William concerning Peirs Plouhman, and the visions of the same concerning the origin, progress and perfection of the Christian life* (London: J. Murray, 1813).

1550.[8] The late appearance of *Piers Plowman* in print is surely not due to the fact that no one was reading it; the manuscript tradition is extensive, and of the fifty-four surviving manuscripts of *Piers Plowman,* seven are from the late fifteenth and early sixteenth centuries.[9] Furthermore, as John Bowers notes, "several fifteenth-century copies, such as BL Cotton Vespasian B.xvi, have been supplied with sixteenth-century annotations," which attests to a continued readership.[10] The delay in printing this widely known poem was most likely a result of the poem's satirical and reformist content.

In the works that he did print, Caxton carefully and consistently names his aristocratic patrons in the prefaces to his editions; the implied audience for Caxton's works is one, as Bowers puts it, "defined as 'courtly' in its orthodoxies if not consistently in rank."[11] *Piers Plowman's* often sharp criticism of clerical abuses, and its political satire (as in the fable of the belling of the cat in B. Pro. 146–210 and C. Pro. 165–216) might well have been unattractive to Caxton's desired market of readers.[12] The output of Caxton's successor de Worde consisted largely of reissues of works from Caxton's press, so it is perhaps unsurprising that he did not choose to produce an edition of *Piers Plowman.* In the early to mid-sixteenth century, when the English printing industry was expanding, the crises of religion caused by Continental Lutheranism, and later Henry's own break with the Church of Rome, led to legislation against the printing or importation of books discussing religion.[13]

Under the reign of Henry's son, the Protestant Edward VI (1547–53), *Piers Plowman's* controversial subject matter, which had presumably hindered its early publication, came to define the poem's value. When *Piers Plowman* was finally printed in 1550, by the Protestant propagandist and printer Robert Crowley, it was actually issued three times within the same year—this seems to suggest a significant readership for the poem.[14] Because Langland had criticized the clergy, Protestant polemicists read him as a forerunner of their own break with Rome. And the poem's reference to a coming king who shall:

8. William Langland, *The Vision of Pierce Plowman* (London: Robert Crowley, 1550).

9. A. I. Doyle, "Remarks on Surviving Manuscripts of *Piers Plowman,*" in *Medieval English Religious and Ethical Literature: Essays in Honor of G. H. Russell,* ed. Gregory Kratzmann and James Simpson (Cambridge, Eng.: D. S. Brewer, 1986), 36.

10. John Bowers, "*Piers Plowman* and the Police: Notes toward a History of the Wycliffite Langland," *Yearbook of Langland Studies* 6 (1992): 37.

11. Ibid., 36–37.

12. Citations of the B-text and C-text of the poem are to: William Langland, *The Vision of Piers Plowman: A Complete Edition of the B-Text,* ed. A. V. C. Schmidt (London: J. M. Dent, 1978), and *Piers Plowman, an Edition of the C-text,* ed. Derek Pearsall (Berkeley: University of California Press and York Medieval Texts, 1978).

13. David Wilkins, *Concilia Magnae Britanniae et Hiberniae, a Synodo Verolamiensi A. D. CCCCXLVI ad Londinensem A. D. MDCCXVII,* 4 vols. (London: Sumptibus R. Gosling, 1737), iii, 706—7; iii, 719–24; iii, 737–39.

14. John N. King, "Robert Crowley: A Tudor Gospelling Poet," *Yearbook of English Studies* 8 (1978): 227–28.

> confesse yow religiouses,
> And bete yow, as the Bible telleth, for brekyng of youre rule,
> And amende monyals [nuns], monkes and chanons [canons],
> And puten hem to hir penaunce   (B. X. 314–17)

was read as a prophesy of Henry VIII's dissolution of England's monasteries. Langland was (incorrectly) deemed a Lollard, and thus a proto-Protestant. In his overview of English literary history, the *Illustrium maioris Britanniae scriptorum . . . summarium,* John Bale claimed that the poem was written by John Wycliffe himself; he later revised that opinion in his *Catalogus,* and attributed it to "Robert" Langland, one of the first disciples of Wycliffe—"ex primis Ioannis Vuicleui discipulis unu[s]."[15] Thus Langland's anticlericalism became a mark of his Wycliffism and (in the mind of the sixteenth-century reader) consequently his proto-Protestantism. In 1561, Owen Rogers issued what was effectively a reprint of Crowley's edition, with the Lollard poem *Pierce the Ploughman's Crede* appended to it.[16] The juxtaposition of these two poems (the latter obviously written in imitation of the former) demonstrates the long-standing association of *Piers Plowman* with Lollardy; and in practical terms it also may have helped Rogers sell more copies of what was, in effect, an old edition.

These four mid-sixteenth-century printings of the poem remained the only complete texts available until 1813, when Thomas Dunham Whitaker reedited the poem as the *Visio Willi[am] de Petro Plouhman. . . . Or the Vision of William concerning Peirs Plouhman.* Whitaker's edition is an impressive (and weighty) work: the text of the poem is in a blackletter typeface, with proper names and Latin phrases in a matching redletter. (See figure 27, where "Malverne" in line 6 is printed in redletter.) Whitaker also preserves the Middle English characters thorn (þ) and yogh (ȝ) rather than normalizing spelling into a modern orthography ("th" and "y," respectively), and uses several medieval scribal abbreviations, for instance "oþr" for "other" in line 9 of Passus 2. (See figure 28.) At the bottom of each page is a summary of that page's contents, headed PARAPHRASE in a smaller-size, roman type. Whitaker also includes a lengthy "Introductory Discourse," to which I will return. The text of the poem takes up 412 pages and is followed by eighteen pages of explanatory notes and a thirty-one page glossary.[17]

---

15. John Bale, *Illustrium maioris Britanniae scriptorum . . . summarium.* ("Ipswich": John Overton, 1548); and *Scriptorvm Illustriu[m] maioris Brytanniæ quam nunc Angliam & Scotiam vocant . . . Catalogus* (Basel: Oporinum, 1557), 475. The name "Robert" Langland seems to derive from scribal misinterpretation of B. VIII. 1: "Thus yrobed in russet I romed aboute" as "Thus Y, Robert, . . . " The now-conventional attribution of the poem to William Langland is based on both an external manuscript note of about 1400 and a number of references within the poem to the protagonist as "Will": Anne Middleton, "Introduction: The Critical Heritage," in *A Companion to Piers Plowman,* ed. John A. Alford (Berkeley: University of California Press, 1988), 6–7.

16. William Langland, *The vision of Pierce Plowman newlye imprynted after the authours olde copy. Wherevnto is also annexed The crede of Pierce Plowman, neuer imprinted with the booke before* (London: Owen Rogers, 1561).

17. Despite his archaizing gestures in typeface, orthography, and abbreviation, Whitaker does intend to clarify the poem, which is (in his words) "altogether the most obscure in the English language" (xix). He

Whitaker's edition, unlike that of Crowley, was based on a C-text manuscript, although the distinct versions of the poem had not yet been identified as such. Whitaker thus believed Crowley's (B-text) edition to be full of errors, and he did not use it as an aid. In fact, Whitaker discusses at length his belief that Crowley must have used a faulty manuscript as an exemplar (xxxi–xxxv).

Portions of *Piers Plowman* had been printed in various anthologies of English poetry before Whitaker's massive undertaking, but an early nineteenth-century reader who wished to read the poem in its entirety would have had to find a 250-year-old copy of one of Crowley's or Rogers's editions.[18] Perhaps the relative inaccessability of the poem should not be a surprise; literary tastes do change, and, of course, the language of medieval literature makes it that much more difficult for modern readers to appreciate its merits. While antiquaries and editors of the late eighteenth century did much to preserve and disseminate medieval literature, they focused primarily on ballads and short romances.[19]

One of the handful of literary anthologies to excerpt *Piers Plowman* between the editions of Rogers and Whitaker is Joseph Ritson's *English Anthology* (1793– 94).[20] Ritson claims in the Advertisement to volume I of the *Anthology:* "The public is here presented with a selection of English poetry, in a chronological series" (1:i). However, that is not entirely true. The first item in the *Anthology* is Sir Thomas Wyatt's early sixteenth-century poem "My Lute Awake." The *Anthology* is divided into four parts, each internally chronological. The first, and by far the longest (filling more than half of the *Anthology*'s three volumes), consists of English poetry by male authors from the sixteenth century to the present; the second part contains English poetry by women. The third part (the only part whose organizing principle is explicit) is "Poems By Uncertain Authors"; and the fourth part contains a variety of English poetry (both complete poems and

---

offers as aids to the readers not only his glossary and paraphrase but also a passus-by-passus "attempt at an analysis of the whole work" (xix). This allegoresis takes up pages xix–xxx of Whitaker's Introductory Discourse.

18. In chapter 2 of *Editing Piers Plowman,* Charlotte Brewer surveys the poem's partial appearances in the two centuries between the complete edition of Rogers and that of Whitaker: *Editing Piers Plowman: The Evolution of the Text* (Cambridge: Cambridge University Press, 1996).

19. Arthur Johnson, *Enchanted Ground: The Study of Medieval Romance in the Eighteenth Century* (London: Athlone Press, 1964), 3–6. A well-known case in point is Thomas Percy's ballad collection, the *Reliques of Ancient English Poetry,* which first appeared in 1765 and was reprinted in different editions throughout the eighteenth and nineteenth centuries: *Reliques of Ancient English Poetry: consisting of Old Heroic Ballads, Songs, and other Pieces of our earlier Poets (chiefly of the Lyric kind) Together with some few of later Date,* 2 vols. (London: J. Dodsley, 1765).

20. Joseph Ritson, *The English Anthology,* 3 vols. (London: C. Clarke, for T. and J. Egerton, 1793–94). Ritson's *Anthology* had been preceded by his own ballad collection, *Ancient songs: from the time of King Henry the Third, to the Revolution* (London: J. Johnson, 1790); later editions have the title *Ancient Songs: from the time of King Henry the Second to the Revolution.* Ritson was a hyperconservative editor, and he maintained archaic orthography in his ballad collection; furthermore, he was a vociferous critic of those whose editorial principles differed. In particular, he carried on a lengthy battle with Percy over the radical emendations (or inventions) of verse in Percy's *Reliques.* On Ritson as both a scholar and a critic of others' scholarship, see Bertrand H. Bronson, *Joseph Ritson: Scholar-at-Arms,* 2 vols. (Berkeley: University of California Press, 1938). Johnson also has chapters on both Percy and Ritson (*Enchanted Ground,* chaps. 3 and 5 respectively).

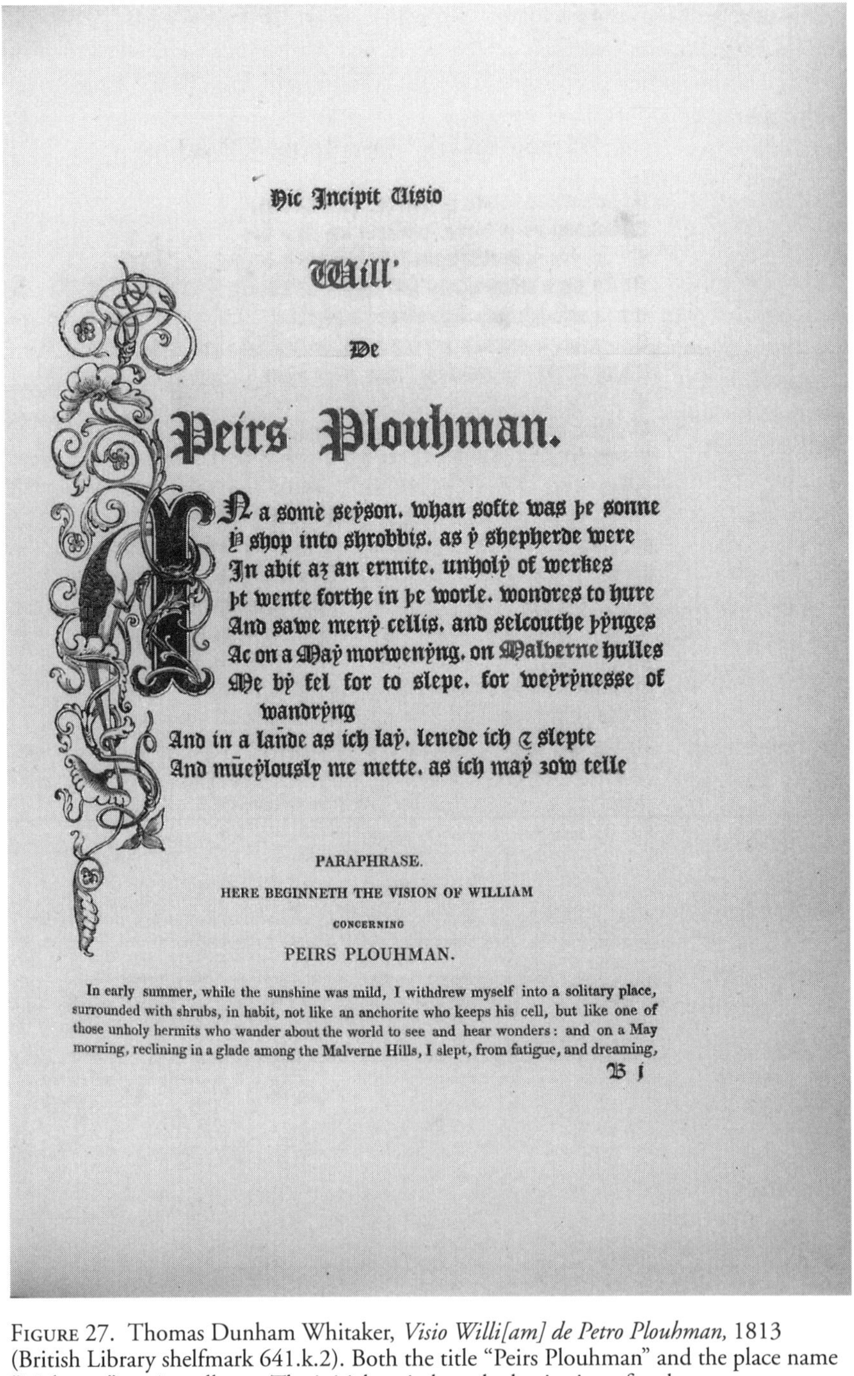

Hic Incipit Visio

Will'

De

Peirs Plouhman.

I
N a some seyson. whan softe was þe sonne
Þ shop into shrobbis. as ý shepherde were
In abit aȝ an ermite. unholý of werkes
þt wente forthe in þe worle. wondres to hure
And sawe mený cellis. and selcouthe þýnges
Ac on a May morwenýng. on Malverne hulles
Me bý fel for to slepe. for weýrýnesse of
wandrýng
And in a lande as ich laý. lenede ich ⁊ slepte
And mueýlously me mette. as ich maý ȝow telle

PARAPHRASE.

HERE BEGINNETH THE VISION OF WILLIAM

CONCERNING

PEIRS PLOUHMAN.

In early summer, while the sunshine was mild, I withdrew myself into a solitary place, surrounded with shrubs, in habit, not like an anchorite who keeps his cell, but like one of those unholy hermits who wander about the world to see and hear wonders: and on a May morning, reclining in a glade among the Malverne Hills, I slept, from fatigue, and dreaming,

B j

FIGURE 27. Thomas Dunham Whitaker, *Visio Willi[am] de Petro Plouhman*, 1813 (British Library shelfmark 641.k.2). Both the title "Peirs Plouhman" and the place name "Malverne" are in redletter. The initial capitals at the beginning of each passus are similarly fanciful, invoking medieval manuscript production.

Incipit passus secundus.

Þat þe montaýne bý meneþ. and þe merke dale
And þe feld ful of folke. ich shall ȝow faýre shewe
A loveliche ladý of lere. in lýnnen þ clopid
Cam down fro þat castel. and calde me bý name
And seide Wille slepest þow. sýrt þow þis puple
Þow busý þai ben. about þe mase
The most þtie of þe puple. þat passeth on þis erthe
Haved þei worship in þis worlde. þei willen no betere
Of oþ. hevene þan here. þei holden no tale
Ich was aferd of hure face. thauh hue faire were
And saide mcý ma dame. wat maý þis be to mene
The tour up on toft quaþ hue. treuthe þs þer þnne
And wolde þat ȝe wrouhte. as hus worde techeþ
ffor he is fader of faith. and formour of alle
To be faith ful to hým. he ȝave ȝou fýve wittes
ffor to worshepen hým þ with. wile ȝe lýven here
Werfore he het þe elemens. to helpe ȝow alle týmes

PARAPHRASE.   13

What is meant by the mountain, the dark valley, and the field full of people, I will now explain. A fair-complexioned lady, clothed in linen, came down from the castle, and calling me, said, William! why sleepest thou? Seest thou these people so busy, each about his own fancies. They represent the greatest part of the people of this world, who, had they worship (honour) here, would desire no other heaven. Notwithstanding her beauty, I was afraid, and cried to her, Mercy, Madam, what may this mean. The tower on the hill, saith she, is the abode of Truth, who would have you to do as he teacheth; for he is the Parent of Faith, and the Maker of all Things. To this end he hath given you five senses, with which to worship him. Wherefore, also, he commanded the elements to produce for

C iij

FIGURE 28. Thomas Dunham Whitaker, *Visio Willi[am] de Petro Plouhman.* The medieval characters and abbreviations are attempts to reproduce medieval scribal practice.

excerpts from longer works), beginning with a Chaucer excerpt and continuing through two pieces by Sheridan. The *Piers Plowman* excerpt (the Confession of the Sins, B. V. 1–441) follows the General Prologue of the *Canterbury Tales* in part IV of Ritson's *Anthology* (3:35–58). The excerpt from Chaucer's poem is clearly meant to be the central text of part IV, as the title page of this part shows the Canterbury Pilgrims heading off on their journey. (See figure 29.)

Ritson feels compelled to include some early works in his anthology, but not to include them with the "real" content of part I. Interestingly, the illustration that precedes part I depicts a group of male poets in archaic (mostly Renaissance) dress facing a female allegorical figure who holds a laurel garland (perhaps a representation of Poetry); Chaucer holds a central position in this illustration, despite the fact that his poetry does not appear in part I. (See figure 30.) Ritson's ambivalence toward the inclusion of pre-Renaissance poetry is manifest in the Advertisement that begins volume I of the *Anthology,* where he laments disingenuously: "It were, perhaps, to be wished, that the collection could have commenced at an earlyer period." He then resolves this mock complaint with a justification of the exclusion of early English poetry based on the fact that "the editor is sufficiently familiar with the poetical productions of preceding centuries to pronounce with confidence, that no composition of a moderate length is to be found, prior to the year 1500, which would be thought to deserve a place in these volumes" (1:v). Ritson's displacement of early literature to the later parts of his *Anthology* balances his desire for completeness against his reluctance about including works he considers "unworthy."

But Ritson refuses to shoulder all of the blame for his principle of selection, ending his explanation by demonstrating that early poetry is unworthy of inclusion not only because of its own faults, but because of the narrowness of current literary tastes: "the nicety of the present age [is] ill disposed to make the necessary allowances for the uncouth diction and homely sentiments of former times" (1:v).[21] By claiming that his editorial choices are driven by *both* his personal expertise *and* contemporary standards of taste, Ritson avoids the possibility of criticism from readers who would defend the value of medieval literature. In fact, he had always planned to have at least one selection from "prior to the year 1500," as the Advertisement refers to the *Anthology's* inclusion of "an extract from Chaucer, from the latter part of the fourteenth [century]" (1:i). This extract is, however, deferred until the last volume.

Given the "nicety" of later eighteenth-century tastes, and the "uncouth diction" of Middle English poetry, as described by Ritson, perhaps it should be more surprising that Whitaker finally *did* choose to produce a new edition of *Piers Plowman* than that no one had edited the poem for over two centuries before him. In the "Introductory Discourse" of his edition, Whitaker makes it clear that

21. Ritson's publication of early ballads demonstrates clearly that he did not himself find the "uncouth" diction of medieval poetry to be distasteful.

THE

ENGLISH ANTHOLOGY.

PART THE FOURTH.

EXTRACTS.

" THE

CANTERBURY TALES

OF

[GEOFFREY] CHAUCER."*

THE PROLOGUE.

Whanne that April with his fhourés fote
The droughte of March hath perced to the rote;

---

* *Born* 1328 ; *dyed* 1400. *The peculiarity of this au-*
thors metre feems to juftify the accents introduced in this

Vol. III.   A

FIGURE 29. Joseph Ritson, *The English Anthology,* 1793–94 (British Library shelfmark
82.b.3). In this illustration of the Canterbury Pilgrims setting off, Harry Bailey
(initiator of the tale-telling game) is at the center of the composition; the figure
immediately to the left of his hand appears to be Chaucer himself.

THE

ENGLISH ANTHOLOGY.

PART THE FIRST.

THE LOVER COMPLAINETH OF THE UN-
KINDNESS OF HIS LOVE.

BY SIR THOMAS WYATT. *

My lute, awake; perform the laſt
Labour that thou and I ſhall waſt,
 And ende that I have now begunne;
And when this ſong is ſong and paſt,
 My lute, be ſtyll; for I have done. 5

 * Born 1503; dyed 1541. — To diſtinguiſh him from
another of the name, he is uſually called Sir Thomas Wyatt
the elder.

Vol. I.   A

FIGURE 30. Joseph Ritson, *The English Anthology.* Chaucer stands at the center of a group of poets paying homage to an allegorical figure, perhaps Poetry, or the Muse, who holds a laurel garland.

he values *Piers Plowman* for the poem's age and distance from the modern reader, but he does not conclude that these make the poem inaccessible. He notes that "the æra of these Visions is now ascertained to have preceded the great work of Chaucer by twenty years," and thus that "the author must be considered as the first English poet: for that he was a poet, and a great poet, will be denied by few, who have taken pains to understand him. He was also . . . the first English satirist" (xxxvi).[22] Whitaker does not attempt to reduce the distance between his medieval text and its modern reader, as had Crowley in his emphasis on Langland's proto-Protestant Reformism. Langland is, for Whitaker, a point of origin in the literary history of England, but his antiquity does not prohibit studious readers from appreciating his verse.

In fact, Whitaker's interest in marking the poem's distant origins (more distant, even, than those of the *Canterbury Tales*) drives his choice of the blackletter typeface, despite its difficulty for a readership accustomed to roman type:

> [the editor] may be permitted to hope that, even in the present appetite of mankind for easy and dissipating objects of literary pursuit, there are some readers who will be happy in an opportunity of being introduced to the spirited and vigorous Father of English Poetry, if not divested of all his difficulties, and still clad in the formidable array of blackletter, yet more familiar and accessible than in the rugged and repulsive garb in which he was left by the former editor. (xli)

The "difficulties" of the medieval text are indeed obstacles for the modern reader, but only those frivolous readers who prefer the "easy and dissipating objects of literary pursuit" will balk at the challenge. The "formidable array of blackletter" is, for Whitaker, what Langland *ought* to wear, although Whitaker's editorial proficiency and judicious selection of a manuscript exemplar do allow Langland to remove the "repulsive garb" of Crowley's textual errors—Whitaker shares with Jefferson the metaphor of typefaces as a text's clothing. Presumably Whitaker was also aware that his preservation of an archaic orthography using thorn and yogh, rather than their modern equivalents, was as "formidable" to a nineteenth-century reader as his use of a blackletter typeface.

Whitaker's clothing metaphors demonstrate his awareness that his choice of a blackletter typeface is just that: a choice. All four of the previous editions of the poem had been printed in a blackletter typeface; however, the use of blackletter was common in the sixteenth century, while it was decidedly anachronistic in the nineteenth. In the middle of the sixteenth century, the choice between a blackletter and a roman typeface was largely determined by subject matter (humanist or

22. Current scholarship dates *Piers Plowman* and Chaucer's major poetry as more nearly contemporary: Langland seems to have worked on *Piers Plowman*'s different versions ca. 1367–87, with the C-text revision begun after the Rising of 1381. Chaucer's major works are primarily from the 1380s (*Troilus and Criseyde, The Legend of Good Women*) and 1390s (*The Canterbury Tales* in their latest forms, although some individual tales were composed earlier).

classical works were almost always printed in a roman face).[23] By the beginning of the nineteenth century, blackletter fonts were almost entirely out of use. As John Johnson notes in his *Typographia* (1824), before the advent of modern black typefaces, it might have been "reasonable to conclude that [blackletter] would, ere this, have been banished from every office and consigned to rest in oblivion's tomb."[24] But in 1815, Vincent Figgins's type book introduced the first modern "fat" blackface.[25] These fat faces (and there were several of them from different families) were purely decorative, used, for example, on title pages for contrast.[26] But in 1813, when Whitaker printed his edition of *Piers Plowman,* even this innovation had not yet entered the nineteenth-century English printshop; his choice of a blackletter font is not merely conservative (in that it approximates the typeface of the earlier editions), it is idiosyncratic.

Chaucer's works had first been printed in a whiteletter typeface almost a century earlier, in 1721. That edition had been projected and advertised as a blackletter edition, but when it finally appeared (after the death of its original editor, John Urry), it was printed in a roman typeface.[27] Furthermore, the typographical innovation of the Urry Chaucer was preceded by Dryden's influential modernizations of some of the Canterbury Tales in his *Fables Ancient and Modern* (1700); these modernizations, too, were printed in a roman typeface.[28] Urry's intention of printing his Chaucer edition in a blackletter typeface suggests that such a typeface was still considered appropriate for a work of early poetry at the beginning of the eighteenth century. However, the eventual publication of the work in a roman typeface proves that blackletter was no longer *necessary* in printing early works. And by the time of Whitaker's edition of *Piers Plowman,* Chaucer had been divested of his "formidable array" for nearly a century, as had Langland— for when *Piers Plowman* was excerpted in eighteenth-century anthologies, it was

23. The reverse was, however, no longer always true. The Geneva Bible of 1560 was printed in a roman typeface (the roman face having been adopted for vernacular works earlier on the Continent than in England); however, the Bishops' Bible of 1568, the one officially sanctioned by the English government, was printed in a blackletter typeface. The Geneva Bible circulated widely enough in England that an English reader of the late sixteenth century would have been familiar with the Bible in both roman and blackletter typefaces: S. H. Steinberg, *Five Hundred Years of Printing,* new ed., rev. John Trevitt (London: The British Library, 1996), 77. As Paul Gutjahr discusses in chapter 1, Robert Barker's 1611 King James Bible is also printed primarily in a blackletter typeface, although it uses roman and italic letters for headings, notes, and commentary.

24. John Johnson, *Typographia, or the Printer's Instructor,* 2 vols. (London: Longman, Hurst, Rees, Orme, Brown & Green, 1824), 2:10.

25. Nicolete Gray, *XIXth Century Ornamented Types and Title Pages* (London: Faber and Faber, 1938), 26, 168. Michael Twyman, *Printing 1770–1970: An Illustrated History of Its Development and Uses in England* (London: The British Library, 1970), 69.

26. Figure 16 in Paul Gutjahr's essay demonstrates this use of blackletter type.

27. The advertisement for this edition notes that "A new Black Letter, Accented, has been cast on purpose for this Work, for the ease of the Reader." The newly cast type will presumably "ease" the reader, insofar as any blackletter type extant in 1721 would be quite worn. W.E.A.A., "Chaucer," Advertisement for Urry's Chaucer, reprinted from the *Monthly Catalogue,* January 1714–15, *Notes and Queries,* fifth ser., 3 (2 January 1875): 7.

28. William L. Alderson and Arnold C. Henderson, *Chaucer and Augustan Scholarship* (Berkeley: University of California Press, 1970), 55.

printed in each anthology's standard (whiteletter) typeface. This must be the form in which Jefferson knew *Piers Plowman,* to judge by his assumption that both Chaucer and Langland wear modern dress. In such an anthology, the poem's antiquity would be visible in its diction and orthography, but not in its typeface.[29]

Whitaker's use of a blackletter face thus marks Langland's poem with a visible antiquity. A concern for maintaining the poem's identity *as* antique is manifested as well in the title that Whitaker gives to his text:

> Visio Willi[am] de Petro Plouhman, Item Visiones ejusdem de Dowel, Dobet, et Dobest. Or, The Vision of William concerning Peirs Plouhman, and The Visions of the same concerning the Origin, Progress, and Perfection of the Christian Life. Ascribed to Robert Langland, a secular priest of the County of Salop; and written in, or immediately after, the year MCCCLXII. Printed from a MS. contemporary with the author, collated with two others of great antiquity, and exhibiting the original text; together with an introductory discourse, a perpetual commentary, annotations, and a glossary.

In addition to remarking on the antiquity of the manuscript exemplar, Whitaker's title page explicitly notes the poem's date of composition (a date some twenty years earlier than modern critics give Whitaker's C-text). And Whitaker first offers the poem's Latin title, a gesture that both formalizes and antiquates the poem. Even the English title that he gives this English poem is noteworthy, for Whitaker uses a kind of *faux* Middle English in his spelling of the title character's name: "Peirs Plouhman." Crowley's edition had titled the poem *The Vision of Pierce Plowman,* a spelling preserved by Ritson. The impressive, and in its own way formidable, title that Whitaker chooses for his massive edition thus echoes the antiquating strategy inherent in his selection of an archaic typeface.

In fact, Whitaker's decision to print the poem in blackletter does not seem to have been well received. Whitaker's editing practice as a whole was widely criticized, from his selection of a manuscript exemplar to his fidelity to that text. A scathing review of the edition in the *Gentleman's Magazine* for April 1834 acidly turns Whitaker's own words (and dubious editorial theory) against him, noting that his choice of a manuscript exemplar was not only hampered by his limited access to the poem's many manuscripts, but skewed by his nostalgic and jingoistic

---

29. In fact, Ritson not only normalizes early poetry to a roman face in his *Anthology* (see figure 29), but critiques the eighteenth-century practice of using an italic face generously within the roman: "It must be confessed that the use, or rather abuse, of Italic types and capital letters has proved a source of constant discouragement and vexation. To have entirely preserved these frivolous distinctions, of which, in many instances, it was utterly impossible to discover the reason, would have been perfectly ridiculous; to omit them altogether appeared an act of violence. The editor, therefore, has not the vanity to hope that either the retention or the omission will satisfy the more critical reader; being utterly unable to discover any principle which will justify either the one or the other. It is however to be wished that, except in fixed and given instances, they could be entirely laid aside; being no more necessary, one would think, to the works of Pope or Swift than to those of Virgil or Horace" (1:iii). For Ritson, a vociferous defender of *orthographic* conservatism in printing earlier texts, the *typographic* features of eighteenth-century texts are "frivolous," though he recognizes it as an act of textual "violence" to remove them altogether.

preference for one whose "orthography and dialect . . . approach very near to that Semi-saxon jargon, in the midst of which [the editor] was brought up, and which . . . he continues to hear daily spoken on the confines of Lancashire, and the West Riding of the county of York" (xxxii), a motivation the reviewer rightly derides as "capricious."[30] Whitaker's claims to have repaired the text from the damage that Crowley had allegedly inflicted on it were also rejected by his learned readers; the *Gentleman's Magazine* review begins by asserting: "There is no monument of the literature of our semi-Saxon forefathers, next to the works of Chaucer, which so well deserves a good edition, and which has always met with a fate so contrary to its desert, as the Visions of Piers Plowman."[31]

A few years later, Isaac D'Israeli reiterated this criticism of Whitaker in a lengthy note to his own analysis of the poem (whose title he spells *Piers Plough-man*) in his *Amenities of Literature*. D'Israeli notes that Whitaker often omits sections of the text, attributing this to the fact that Whitaker's "delicacy of taste unfitted him for this homely task; the plain freedom of the vigorous language is sometimes castrated, with a faulty paraphrase and a slender glossary; and passages are slurred over with an annihilating &c."[32] Furthermore D'Israeli singles out for criticism Whitaker's choice of an archaic (and difficult) typeface: "For the general reader I fear that 'The Visions of Piers Ploughman' must remain a sealed book. The last edition of Dr. Whitaker [is] the most magnificent and frightful volume that was ever beheld in the black letter." The volume's magnificence was clearly reflected in its price, as D'Israeli complains: "Much was expected from this spendid edition; the subscription-price was quadrupled, and on its publication every one would rid himself of the mutilated author."[33]

According to D'Israeli, Whitaker's edition has not lived up to its billing or its expense; Whitaker has not fulfilled his goal of producing the definitive edition of *Piers Plowman*. Indeed, D'Israeli seems to call for a *new* edition to correct Whitaker's editorial faults, both typographical and orthographical, for Whitaker "has not assisted the reader through his barbarous text interspersed with Saxon characters and abbreviations, and the difficulties of an obscure and elliptical phraseology in a very antiquated language. Should ever a new edition appear, the perusal would be facilitated by printing with the white letter."[34] Ironically, then, D'Israeli considers Whitaker to have over- *and* underedited his text (not to mention overcharged his readers).

D'Israeli rejects Whitaker's choice of a chronologically alien typeface for a

---

30. "The Visions of Piers Plowman," review of Whitaker's edition, *Gentleman's Magazine* 155 (April 1834): 386. This review is anonymous, but DiMarco identifies the reviewer as Thomas Wright.

31. Ibid., 385. The naming of the population of late medieval England as "semi-Saxon," a term that the reviewer may have picked up from Whitaker's own use of it, seems to reflect not only a nineteenth-century interest in Indo-Germanic history, but a submerged anti-French sentiment. If the people and language of fourteenth-century England were "semi-Saxon," they were equally "semi-Norman."

32. I[saac] D'Israeli, *Amenities of Literature*, 3 vols. (London: Edward Moxon, 1841), 1: 304.

33. Ibid., 303–4.

34. Ibid., 304.

poem that was itself chronologically, religiously, and linguistically alien to its nineteenth-century readership. But Whitaker insists on highlighting the historical distance between Langland's poem and its modern readers; this is evident not only visually in his choice of typeface, but also in his rejection of the sixteenth-century notion that Langland's criticism of the Church marks him as a kind of proto-Protestant: "The Reformers of the sixteenth century claimed as their own the Author of these Visions; but surely on no good grounds," Whitaker grouses (xvii). Langland was critical of various abuses, but he was, without a doubt, still Catholic in both temperament and historical circumstance. That is, he was neither a Lollard nor a Protestant:

> Yet in the midst of darkness and spiritual slavery, his acute and penetrating understanding enabled him to discover the multiplied superstitions of the public service, the licentious abuse of pilgrimages, the immoral tendency of indulgences, the bad effects upon the living of expiatory services for the dead, the inordinate wealth of the papacy, and the usurpations of the mendicant orders, both of the rights of the diocesans and of the parochial clergy. These abuses, Langland, with many other good men who could endure to remain in the communion of the church of Rome, saw and deplored; but though he finally conducted his pilgrim out of the particular communion of Rome into the universal church, he permitted him to carry along with him too many remnants of his old faith, such as satisfaction for sin to be made by the sinner, together with the merit of works, and especially of voluntary poverty; but, above all, the worship of the cross; incumbrances with which the Lollards of his own, or the Protestants of a later age, would not willingly have received him as a proselyte. (xviii)

Langland is trapped by history, the "darkness and spiritual slavery" of pre-Protestant England. While Whitaker seems rather bemused by the idea that there actually were "good men who could endure to remain in the communion of the church of Rome," he insists on Langland's Catholicism, settling for the idea that Langland was imaginatively able to transcend that flawed institution when "he finally conducted his pilgrim out of the particular communion of Rome into the universal church." Of course, Langland would not have been able to make such a fine distinction, living in a time when the Catholic Church *was* the Universal Church.

Although Whitaker makes a point of arguing that Langland was Catholic, the poet's Catholicism is clearly troubling enough to him that he feels compelled to distance himself from it. He notes (without an actual apology) that he is "unable to trace" Langland's references to "the schoolmen . . . my own knowledge of those forgotten writers, the great lights of their own and the following ages, scarcely extending beyond a small portion of Aquinas" (xxxix). However, the deficiencies in Whitaker's knowledge of medieval theology are not to be counted as failures of editorial effort. Indeed, he assures his readers that he is "not unacquainted with scholars," but that "I should be at a loss to apply to any one, in the hope that he would be able to point out to me a reference to Scotus or Peter Lombard" (xxxix). Whitaker is further unable to explain some of the poem's literary, cultural, or proverbial allusions; and he notes: "A wider acquaintance with the legendary knowledge of the middle ages would also have been useful in elucidating some ridiculous stories of those times, alluded to by the author" (xxxix).

But Whitaker is not really concerned by his inability to gloss the poem further; his deficiencies of learning are no embarrassment. Quite the contrary, in fact. His unfamiliarity with "those forgotten writers," the medieval scholastics, marks his theological discrimination as higher than that of a medieval reader. For even the "scholars" with whom Whitaker is acquainted are, apparently, uninterested in such writers as John Duns Scotus or Peter Lombard, major figures in medieval theology who are, apparently, irrelevant to a modern, Protestant age. Medieval Catholic theology, like "the legendary knowledge of the middle ages," is beneath a modern reader's concern. The implication of Whitaker's discussion here is clear: anything the modern reader of Whitaker's text loses because of the editor's own lack of knowledge is probably not worth knowing.

In carefully identifying Langland's Catholicism as entirely separate from England's modern Protestantism, Whitaker explicitly rejects one of the tenets of the early modern editions of *Piers Plowman*. And, as Crowley's and Rogers's were the only available editions of the full poem, Whitaker effectively redefines the poem's identity, for those editions had emphasized Langland's supposed prescience in anticipating Protestantism.[35] Whitaker is particularly scornful of the sixteenth-century belief that Langland prophesied the dissolution of the monasteries. Langland clearly saw the widespread corruption among members of the religious orders; but, Whitaker notes, given the distribution of political power in medieval England, he could only have imagined the eventual correction of the clergy as coming from a monarch. If it were a true prophecy, Whitaker argues, it would have been more specific in its prediction. "Ther shal come a king and confesse yow religiouses, / And bete yow" (B. X. 314–15) is hardly a clear reference to Henry VIII: "from what [Langland] had seen of the conduct of a spirited and vigorous Monarch, in pillaging the religious houses at pleasure, he would naturally be directed to a King as the probable instrument of their destruction. The evil would increase, correctives would lose their effect, and extermination would naturally follow. Meanwhile the prediction was couched in general and guarded terms: but genuine prophecy dares to be particular" (xxxviii). In Whitaker's mind, the evidence is clear: Langland was not a Protestant himself, and he did not predict the rise of Protestantism in England.

But Whitaker is not content to let the matter rest with a simple explanation that Langland's cryptic verse is too vague to be a true prophecy; he goes further

---

35. John N. King, "Robert Crowley's Editions of *Piers Plowman:* A Tudor Apocalypse," *Modern Philology* 73 (1976): 342.

in his denial that Langland's poem was prophetic, and this further elaboration manifests an anxiety that in some way seems to underlie much of Whitaker's project in editing *Piers Plowman:*

> What, for example, if some dreaming bard at present should fortel that a King would arise, who should strip the church of its remaining revenues, or what, in the present lethargy of Protestantism, is quite as likely, that Popery should once more become the established religion of this country, the fulfilment of such a prediction at a distant period would add little to his reputation as a seer into futurity: whereas, if he foretold that all this should fall out in the reign of George the Eighth, or Edward the Ninth . . . the fulfilment of his prophecy, under a Prince of the very name and number foretold, would certainly go far towards vindicating his memory from the charge either of insanity or imposture. (xxxviii–xxxix)

Whitaker, writing under the Regency of George IV, names the reigns of "George the Eighth, or Edward the Ninth" as representative of a now unimaginably distant future (the last Edward had been Edward VI in the mid-sixteenth century). The unlikely events he proposes as the topic of "some dreaming bard's" prophecy, a prophecy that might earn him "the charge either of insanity or imposture," are the disendowment of the Church of England and the return of Catholicism to the position of established religion; that is, the reversal of Henry's break with Rome, which was itself the topic of Langland's alleged prophecy.

A prediction of these events might seem insane to a nineteenth-century reader, but Whitaker does not seem as certain of their impossibility as he would like to be. The disendowment of the Church is unlikely, and the reestablishment of Catholicism as the national religion is, as Whitaker asserts, "quite as likely." But if Protestantism is, as Whitaker claims, in a "present [state of] lethargy," how unlikely *is* the reestablishment of Catholicism? Both of Whitaker's examples of improbable occurences have to do with the failure of English national Protestantism, suggesting that his concern over the "present lethargy of Protestantism" is rather deeper than he might like to admit.[36] In fact, Whitaker's apparent anxiety about the reestablishment of Catholicism manifests a common English fear in the early nineteenth century.

In the shadow of the Act of Union, which incorporated Ireland into Great Britain in 1800, Catholic emancipation was a divisive political issue. Already by the late eighteenth century, popular support for emancipation was growing, although it was answered by a considerable amount of political backlash in the form of both anti-Irish sentiment and a more locally English anti-Catholicism.[37] The union with Ireland was effected without the full emancipation of Catholics

---

36. Disunity among Protestant sects might also have been a source of consternation for Whitaker, although his comments here focus on Catholicism as the primary threat to the Church of England.

37. Linda Colley, *Britons: Forging the Nation, 1707–1837* (New Haven: Yale University Press, 1992), 329–31.

that many had hoped for, and that Pitt had hinted at as a likely consequence of union. George III was, however, intransigent in his opposition to emancipation.[38] Despite the king's refusal to consider it, emancipation was debated popularly and in Parliament for almost the next thirty years. Relief from the anti-Catholic laws was repeatedly (though unsuccessfully) raised in Parliament from 1805 onward. The supporters of the continued exclusion of Catholics from full participation in civic life had ever diminishing numbers until Parliament finally voted for Catholic emancipation in April 1829.[39]

In the second decade of the nineteenth century, worried English Protestants might well have foretold the return of Catholicism to the position of national religion. The union of Ireland and England ensured that the Catholic Irish would not form another "union," allying with Catholic France, should Napoleon invade Ireland.[40] But protecting against an external enemy opened Great Britain to the threat of an internal enemy: those English and Irish Catholics who were believed to be loyal to the pope and the Roman Church, rather than to king and country. Anti-Catholic English Protestants waged a propaganda war (ultimately unsuccessful) to prevent emancipation, arguing that any liberties that Catholics were allowed could permit them not only to overthrow Protestantism but to return to a practice of martyring English Protestants, as they had, notoriously, done under Queen Mary, the last time that they had been given such an opportunity.

This anxiety shows up notably in a reprint of John Foxe's sixteenth-century masterpiece of Protestant propaganda, the *Acts and Monuments,* often referred to as the *Book of Martyrs.* Foxe's massive work was a best-seller from the sixteenth through the nineteenth centuries. In America and Great Britain, there were about ten separate editions of the work in the late eighteenth to mid-nineteenth centuries, each of which was reissued or reedited several times. One edition, that of the Reverend Charles A. Goodrich, was published first in Hartford in 1830; reissued there in 1831, 1832, 1833, and 1836; printed in Middletown in 1832 and 1833; printed in Philadelphia in 1833 and 1835; printed in New York in 1832; and printed in Cincinnati in 1832. A brief survey of the hundreds of entries under Foxe's name in the National Union Catalogue attests to the widespread readership of this work well into the late nineteenth century.

An English edition of the *Acts and Monuments* almost precisely contemporary with Whitaker's edition of *Piers Plowman* expresses its editor's particularly topical concern in bringing this work to press. John Malham's prefatory letter, dated Dec. 18th, 1813, from his 1814 London edition of what he calls "Fox's" *Book of Martyrs,* seeks to explain the utility of this edition in light of England's current parlia-

38. G. I. T. Machin, *The Catholic Question in English Politics, 1820 to 1830* (Oxford: Clarendon, 1964), 12. Bernard Ward, *The Eve of Catholic Emancipation, Being the History of the English Catholics during the First Thirty Years of the Nineteenth Century,* 2 vols. (London: Longmans, Green, 1911), 1:37.

39. Colley, *Britons,* 328.

40. And this must have seemed a real possibility: in the 1790s the Society of United Irishmen actively encouraged such a French invasion. Machin, *Catholic Question,* 11.

mentary debates over emancipation. Malham warns his readers: "We may assure ourselves, that the present depressed state of popery in England is no proof that its leading principle has been abandoned, though this assertion has often been sounded in our ears." Malham is unconvinced by the rhetoric of emancipation that stressed either Catholic loyalty or Catholic impotence: "That popery has now become an innocent thing, and perfectly harmless, is a sentiment which, we acknowledge, we cannot persuade ourselves to subscribe to."[41] And Malham casts Foxe's work as a corrective to any arguments that would deny Catholicism's inherent danger to Protestant England. The "unthinking politicians" who might mistakenly allow English Catholics their liberty would do well to learn the lesson implicit in Foxe's work: that Catholicism poses an unquestionable threat. And while "some of our hereditary legislators, and of the representative counsellors of the nation" might be deluded into thinking emancipation safe, any reader who has "attentively perused the contents of this volume (part of the First Book, and thence through all the other Books to the close, wholly consisting of the persecutions of protestants by the papists)" will "in their conscience" know otherwise (A*).

Interestingly, Malham assures his readers that "popery" is in a "depressed state"—like the "lethargy" Whitaker ascribed to contemporary Protestantism—but Malham is far from convinced of Catholicism's impotence. He concedes that Anglo-Catholicism may now appear nearly dead, but it is like a dark ember on the edge of the hearth; the mortal threat it poses to English Protestants could at any time be fanned into a blaze: "We cannot possibly doubt of its still lurking on the hearth in obscurity, in readiness to blaze out on stirring of the embers; and that it only wants a fostering-hand to blow up the coals, and to rekindle the sparks into an over-powering flame" (A*). That Malham sees such a persecutory and anti-Protestant conflagration as the necessary result of Catholic emancipation is clear from the reflection he asks of his readers. Once they have "attentively perused the contents of this volume," his readers are "to lay their hands on their hearts, and tell us whether, in their conscience, they can really entertain an opinion that the tenets of the latter are so very innocent, as some unthinking politicians would induce them to believe." A judgment on the wisdom of emancipation can be made, Malham suggests, only with a full awareness of the history and "ancient tenets of popery as contained in our pages proved." The persecution of Protestants was not an aberration, but is a principle of Catholic doctrine—its "leading doctrine," no less. Such persecution of Protestants is even an inbred characteristic of the Catholic individual. What could be more dangerous than giving any power to "persons so constituted" (A*)? Malham is in haste to point out his liberalism: "Persecution we detest as much as any persons," he claims. And he insists that the government does have a duty to "Protect [Anglo-Catholics] in

41. John "Fox" [i.e., Foxe], *The Book of Martyrs or the Acts and Monuments of the Christian Church, Being a Complete History of Martyrdom from the Commencement of Christianity to the present time, Revised and Improved by the Rev'd. John Malham* (London: Thomas Kelly, 1814), A*.

their private capacity as subjects of the state." But anti-Catholic laws are, in his assessment, a matter of national and religious self-preservation, not persecution; they are all that prevent the "[subversion] of the government" by papists (A*).[42]

This, then, is the political and religious climate in which Whitaker produced his edition. Whitaker's apparent anxiety over the possibility of a reinvigorated Anglo-Catholicism, emblematic of a more general Protestant anxiety in the early decades of the nineteenth century in England, demonstrates what is at stake in his distancing of *Piers Plowman* from its modern readers. Whitaker highlights Langland's Catholicism, denying the work's proto-Protestant prescience, and he visibly antiquates the text on the page through his typography and orthography. The visual effect of this book, with its "formidable" blackletter typeface is, in D'Israeli's phrase, "magnificent and frightful" (210); the book thus visually reinforces the historical distance between the medieval Catholic text and its modern Protestant reader that Whitaker so insists on in his "Introductory Discourse." Since Whitaker's sense of doctrinal accuracy demands that *Piers Plowman* be divested of its false identity as a proto-Protestant work, he must further insist on the text's historical distance from its modern audience.

Whitaker clothes the text in its blackletter garb to authenticate and enforce a distinction between Catholicism and modernity. *Piers Plowman*'s ultimate orthodoxy, despite its anticlerical complaint, certainly separates it from the anti-Romishness of (Whitaker's) Protestantism. However, the poem is not so theologically different from the beliefs of some of its potential audience: those Anglo-Catholics with rising political power who so worry Malham and Whitaker. Whitaker's insistence on the poem's historical distance ensures that Catholicism stays safely in England's past. Any "dreaming bard" who should foresee the reestablishment of Catholicism in the land must be charged with "insanity or imposture." As medieval theologians are "forgotten writers" whom even scholars can afford to ignore, Catholicism itself should, Whitaker implies, be left behind by

42. Interestingly, parts of this preface are borrowed and reworked in Goodrich's American edition: John "Fox," *A History of the Lives, Sufferings, and Triumphant Deaths of the primitive as well as protestant martyrs: from the commencement of Christianity to the latest periods of pagan and popish persecution. . . . Originally composed by the Rev. John Fox, M. A., and now improved by important alterations and additions, by Rev. Charles A. Goodrich* (Hartford: Philemon Canfield, 1830). Goodrich asserts, like Malham, that "the present depressed state of Popery, both in England and on the continent, is no proof that its leading principles have been abandoned" (iii). He, too, makes the distinction between persecution and self-destructive license: "We wish not, indeed that papists should be persecuted; we would say, protect them in their private capacity, wherever they exist in the land; but beware of so encouraging them, as to bring the American people under their temporal and spiritual dominion" (iv).

Despite its borrowings, Goodrich's preface is distinctly American in focus, and Goodrich sees Catholicism as posing a distinct threat to the [Protestant] American population: "To the American people, this subject presents itself with peculiar interest. Within a short period, the attention of the Pope of Rome has been directed to North America, and systematic efforts are now making, under his immediate patronage, and at his expense, to introduce and establish this corrupt system, in various parts of our land. . . . The question presents itself to the American people: 'shall this system find encouragement in the land of the pilgrims?' " (iii). Foxe's text seems infinitely transferable: as Catholicism is (in the minds of anti-Catholic polemicists) unchanging in its threat to Protestants, Foxe's book is, despite its chronological (and here geographical) distance, continually relevant and admonitory.

modernity. The blackletter garb in which he clothes *Piers Plowman* (not to mention *Peirs Plouhman,* clothed in Whitaker's gratuitously "medieval" spelling) visually asserts that Langland's Catholicism is irreparably distant from nineteenth-century English life. The monkish, and even monstrous, blackletter typeface of Whitaker's *Piers Plowman* edition of 1813 marks Catholicism as properly belonging only to England's past.

Bridge Two

One of the comfortable truisms in printing history is that the transition from scribal book production to mechanical printing with metal type both simplified and standardized letterforms. Because familiar, regularized letterforms were easier to recognize and read than individual scribes' handwriting, the notion runs, printing from type slowly helped to democratize literacy, to pave the way for expanded literacy among those with little or no formal education. By the nineteenth century, thanks to industrial as well as economic and social and cultural developments, the printed word had become ubiquitous throughout most parts of Europe and America. Type, we are told, made those printed letterforms universally legible.

Both the preceding essay by Sarah Kelen and the following essay by Megan Benton argue, however, that type can be an instrument used to limit readerships as much as to expand them. Both authors describe how, in a century in which literacy approached "mass" proportions, encompassing working-class and other culturally marginalized communities, publishers used type selection to narrow—not broaden—their prospective audiences for particular books. Along with price, edition size, marketing and sales channels, and other production and commercial decisions, choice of type style could impede or discourage the "wrong" audience from reading the book.

Kelen explores the deliberate decision by early nineteenth-century printer Thomas Whitaker to use blackletter type to underscore the medieval Catholicism of the early English poem *Piers Plowman,* thus defusing its potentially politically volatile interpretation by contemporary readers as a proto-Protestant document. The blackletter type rendered the poem not only visibly "antique" and historically distant but also much harder for modern eyes to read. Better-educated, sophisticated initiates accustomed to medieval texts could manage nicely, but others who might wish access to the poem would be turned away by its archaic presentation on the page.

Benton investigates a similar dynamic at the end of the nineteenth century when again printers used type to narrow rather than expand a book's audience. Equating the familiar "modern" typefaces with the largely female reading markets of the day, printers and publishers revived older, preindustrial type styles that evoked eras in which book culture was still the elite province of relatively privileged men. This revival of historical typographic forms was ostensibly intended to restore the aesthetic quality of books considered cheapened by industrial production techniques. It also, however, rejected as vulgar and tasteless the "weak" and "feminine" type of the day, spurning as well the women who, thanks to vast numbers of books printed by machines in large, affordable quantities, had risen to dominance in Western book culture. Both Kelen and Benton thus demonstrate that type can be a powerful tool for manipulating not only how a printed text is read, but even who reads it.

Chapter Three

Typography and Gender:
Remasculating the Modern Book

MEGAN L. BENTON

Toward the end of the nineteenth century, William Morris and others in England and America felt they could no longer endure the material and aesthetic debasement they perceived in contemporary, machine-made books. In proclaiming the tenets of what was soon considered the era's great typographic renaissance or revival, they used gendered terms to describe both the faults of modern (that is, conventional nineteenth-century) types and the merits of the preindustrial type forms they advocated. They deplored the former as fussy, pale, and "feminine," calling for a return to darker, heavier, more "robust" letterforms, which they argued would restore vigor and "virility" to the printed page. In 1892 Theodore Low De Vinne, widely regarded as America's leading printer of the era, expressly heralded this reform as a long-overdue return to "masculine printing."[1]

 As the bookmaking industries became nearly fully mechanized in the nineteenth century, many worried that the machine had usurped the essential human elements of production so vital to the nature of books. They feared that men had become little more than operators of the machines. Type styles, for example, no longer bore any traces of the hand-formed letter; they had become distilled emblems of mechanical speed, economy, artifice, and precision. But many men felt that they had lost control over books in another sense as well, as women authors and readers seemed to dominate what had once been a mostly masculine world.[2]

1. Theodore Low De Vinne, "Masculine Printing," *American Bookmaker* 15 (November 1892): 140–44. Subsequent references to this source are given parenthetically in the text.

2. The nineteenth-century printing trade itself, although still dominated by male labor, had begun to witness some feminine—even feminist—inroads. Most notable was the work in England of Emily Faithfull (1835–95), who founded the Victoria Press in 1860 to give women training and employment in the printing trades, particularly type composition. Although barred from joining the unions, Faithfull and her female employees secured some important contracts and enjoyed moderate success for a time. See William E. Fredeman, "Emily Faithfull and the Victoria Press: An Experiment in Sociological Bibliography," *The Library* 29 (1974): 139–64.

 It should also be noted that women occasionally played roles in the modern typographic revival, although they usually contributed skilled handcraft labor, under the direction of and in service to a father, husband, or brother active in revivalist publishing, rather than editorial or typographic decision-making. Among the most well known are Elizabeth and Lily Yeats, whose Dun Emer and Cuala presses in Dublin

Reformers believed that the machine had enabled a commercial pandering to this new mass, largely female, audience, whose tastes were reflected in the "effeminate" typography that characterized most books of the day.

This essay looks at reform-minded efforts to "rescue" texts typographically from their conventional "feminized" nineteenth-century presentations. It focuses on treatment of two particular texts: Chaucer's *Canterbury Tales* and Walt Whitman's *Leaves of Grass* were among the texts whose power and meanings were felt to have been constrained by the modern feminine forms in which they were usually produced. Considering various editions of these two texts, ranging from pre-revival ordinary formats to craft-based deluxe editions of each produced in the early 1930s, I examine the interpretive environments created both by the discredited feminine typographic page and by the heralded "masculine" alternative. I contend that reformers, in exalting preindustrial type forms and production methods, were also implicitly invoking the superiority of a past in which men (not machines, and not women) dominated book culture itself.

My assertion is grounded in a closer look at what Jerome McGann calls bibliographical codes—the typographic and material forms that make a text visible and physically manifest.[3] Those forms shape readers' perceptions of a text's import and meaning much as, for example, an actor's voice and gestures interpret even as they convey a dramatic text. Furthermore, such codes embody the social, commercial, and ideological frameworks in which the books are produced, which in turn inform how they are read, and even by whom. De Vinne's objection to feminine printing, then, was fundamentally an objection to the material and aesthetic environment in which modern readers encountered texts. To De Vinne and other reformers, what had once been men's domain, the printed word, had become emasculated, made feminine. How did such emasculation work? Why was it such a threat? How was it to be resisted? This essay explores the ways in which printers understood and answered these and other questions.

De Vinne detected a feminization of books in three senses: in type design, in printing technology, and in consumer tastes. First, he characterized as feminine two separate but related styles of type prevalent in Victorian England and America. One was the most commonly used book or text face of the century, generically called "modern," which featured a relatively small surface area, compressed forms with shortened ascenders and descenders, pronounced contrast between the thick and thin strokes of the letters' form, and very sharp, hairline serifs (figure 31). Although De Vinne portrayed this style of type as a "miserably weak and ineffective" aberration, by the 1880s it had become not only the most commonly used but the most widely admired style of type; it was generally regarded throughout both England and America as the century's highest achievement in

---

produced fine editions of literature of the Irish Renaissance as selected (and often written) by their brother W. B. Yeats. In the United States, Bertha Goudy was a skilled typesetter who assisted her husband, the prolific type designer and fine printer Frederic Goudy.

3. Jerome McGann, *The Textual Condition* (Princeton: Princeton University Press, 1991), 13.

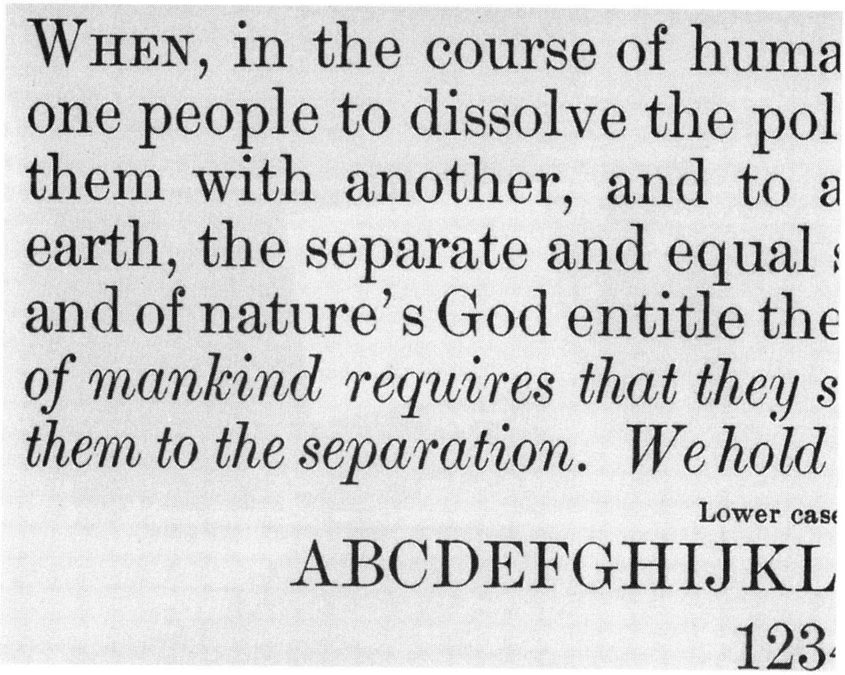

WHEN, in the course of huma
one people to dissolve the pol
them with another, and to a
earth, the separate and equal ;
and of nature's God entitle the
of mankind requires that they s
them to the separation. We hold

Lower case

ABCDEFGHIJKL

123.

FIGURE 31. Close-up of the "modern" typeface shown in the American Type Founders specimen catalog, 1906.

typographic art. Its hairline serifs and sharp contrast in the weight of the letter-forms' vertical and horizontal strokes highlighted what many particularly admired about so-called modern type, the ability of the machine to achieve a fineness of line that eluded the pen stroke. Most nineteenth-century typographic critics praised modern type as graceful, sensitive, and exquisite, viewing its fine detail as evidence of technological refinement, an emblem of the Victorian marriage of intricate form and industry.

The use of modern types also made for a light, open page. Not only had the letters been pared down to relatively sharp, small forms, but they needed plenty of space around them to be readable. This encouraged the practice of leading—inserting extra strips of lead between the lines of type—and of putting wide spaces between words and especially between sentences. In figure 32, for example, the type of this typical, mass-produced nineteenth-century novel is of standard size (twelve-point) but another four points, a third of the type's body size, of leading have been added. (By comparison, books for adult readers today are commonly composed in ten- or eleven-point type with one additional point of leading, a proportion reflecting the subsequent prevalence of reformist principles.) Furthermore, nineteenth-century printers commonly positioned each text block in the center of its page, so that margins on both left and right were roughly

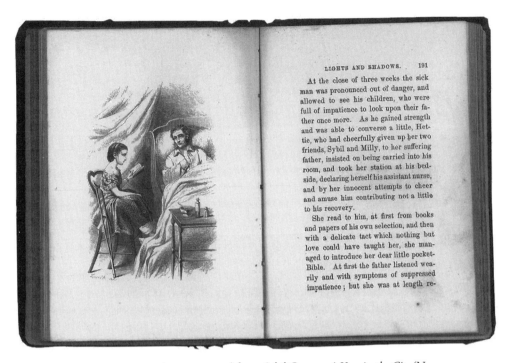

FIGURE 32. Representative page spread from *Sybil Grey; or, A Year in the City* (New York: American Tract Society, 1866), illustrating conventional nineteenth-century typography.

equal. This created an especially open space in the center of the book where the two inner (or gutter) margins combined. This widespread typographic practice was not merely a Victorian fashion; it culminated what French cultural historian Henri-Jean Martin calls the "triumph of white over black" on the printed page.[4] Over the course of the preceding centuries of print production, the growing use of white space around and even within text blocks acknowledged the growing proportion of relatively unskilled readers, whose eyes were less able to navigate dense blocks of closely set type. Nineteenth-century feminine type and typography in part reflected this accommodation to unprofessional readers.

The other typographic fashion De Vinne labeled as feminine was the abundance of ornamented faces that flourished during the century. Intended for display and embellishment rather than text composition, ornamented types showcased both the Victorian taste for decoration and the era's mechanical prowess in creating complex, detailed designs that no human hand could engrave with such precision and uniformity. The proliferation of ornamented type, particularly toward the end of the century, signaled to most printers a luxurious array of decora-

4. Henri-Jean Martin, *The History and Power of Writing*, trans. Lydia G. Cochrane (Chicago: University of Chicago Press, 1994), 329.

tive vocabulary with which they could create treasuries of attractive and valued printed work.

The 1860 edition of *Leaves of Grass,* for example, was widely admired for its ornate typography. One reviewer praised the "sumptuous elegance" of the book's design and declared it "one of the richest specimens of taste and skill in book-making, that has ever been afforded to the public by either an English or an American publisher." Another readily admitted that "nothing can be more taste-ful than its paper and typography," even if he regarded the text it adorned as "pure unmitigated trash."[5] The book's decorative and light typography was regarded as a masterpiece of taste and beauty. Stout as a hymnal, the volume sought to impart the aura of parlor respectability that Whitman wanted for his work in this edi-tion, the look of a valued, even revered, book by a nationally recognized and beloved poet. Significantly, however, it marked a striking typographical shift from that of the first edition, published five years earlier. The frontispiece portrait and facing title page typography of the 1855 edition announce a self-proclaimed "rough." A young Whitman slouches in his shirtsleeves, throat bare to his under-wear, hat tilted rakishly on his head. The facing text is equally insolent in its forthright simplicity; the typography here introduces perfectly the revolutionary style and substance of Whitman's poems (figure 33). Yet the book met a mostly dubious critical reception, not least because many claimed they didn't know what it was—chants? songs? aphorisms? inchoate thoughts that stretched across the wide page? All subsequent editions made sure the reader recognized it not only as poetry, but poetry to be taken seriously in mid-Victorian America. The 1860 frontispiece presents a Whitman suitable for any Sunday parlor, hair and beard neatly combed, soft scarf at his throat, forehead furrowed in contemplation. Fac-ing this sensitive fellow is a title page to match, calligraphic letterforms sprouting wispy tendrils and light, decorative flourishes (figure 34). The book's interior typography has been similarly "feminized," replete with a wide assortment of adornments that rendered it an acclaimed triumph of the nineteenth-century printer's art (figure 35).[6]

In criticizing such design, De Vinne's 1892 manifesto defied the prevailing typo-graphic tastes of the day. Typography that others praised as preeminently artistic and cultured he deplored as weak, feeble, and fussy—feminine. William Morris went even further in his invective, denouncing the "sweltering hideousness" of

5. [Henry Clapp (?) or Walt Whitman (?)], "Walt Whitman: Leaves of Grass," New York *Saturday Press,* 19 May 1860, 2; untitled, unsigned review, London *Critic,* 14 July 1860, 43–44. Both reviews are re-printed in Kenneth E. Price, ed., *Walt Whitman: The Contemporary Reviews* (New York: Cambridge Uni-versity Press, 1996), 81, 97. That Whitman may have written the effusive review cited above has little bearing on its typographic reception; although he may have spoken in particularly enthusiastic terms about it, most reviewers similarly remarked on the book's attractive appearance, even if sometimes it was the only aspect of the publication they could countenance.

6. For a study that looks at the some "bibliographical codes" of the editions of *Leaves of Grass* that appeared during Whitman's lifetime, many of which Whitman designed or helped to produce, see Michael Feehan, "Multiple Editorial Horizons of *Leaves of Grass,*" *Resources for American Literary Study* 20, no. 2 (1994): 213–30.

FIGURE 33. Frontispiece and title page of the first edition of Walt Whitman's *Leaves of Grass*, 1855.

Bodoni, the progenitor of nineteenth-century modern type designs, and pronouncing it the "most illegible type that was ever cut, with its preposterous thicks and thins."[7] Scorning the fashion for what he called "letters that seem to have been modeled by a teacher of school girl penmanship or by an engraver of visiting cards," De Vinne warned fellow printers that their taste had been "perverted" by the feminine style, that the modern hairline serifs had "thoroughly emasculated" book types (142). He urged his fellow printers to rouse themselves from their aesthetic beguilement and practice masculine printing instead, which he characterized as "noticeable for its readability, for its strength and absence of useless ornament" (140).

De Vinne's assignment of gender values to these two contrasting styles of type and typography was hardly original. It had long been commonplace to associate decorative and finely detailed form with feminine taste and to align darker, simpler forms with masculine taste. Equally ingrained in Western culture is a tendency to devalue decorative embellishment as "useless," as De Vinne called it, to

---

7. William Morris, "The Ideal Book" (1893), in *The Ideal Book: Essays and Lectures on the Arts of the Book by William Morris,* ed. William S. Peterson (Berkeley: University of California Press, 1982), 69.

FIGURE 34. Title page of the third edition of Whitman's *Leaves of Grass*, 1860.

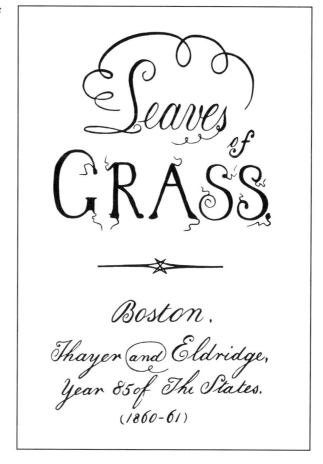

regard it as an inessential quality that diffuses or obscures the power and clarity of the pure form. To De Vinne ornamented type thus performed a kind of visual ekphrasis, interrupting the formal function of the letterform by elaborating upon it. He and others deemed this impulse toward ornamentation peculiarly feminine, perhaps suitable for some texts but altogether not for those with more masculine origins or audiences. "Laces and jewels are proper adornments for a woman and they compel our admiration," he allowed, but "what is proper adornment to a woman is not to a man. You will certainly agree with me that lace and jewels and silks and velvets are not becoming to the man" (141). As the critic Grant Scott explains of this familiar gendered opposition, "The mistrust of finery and ornament at least in part . . . stems from a fear of its origins in the feminine unconscious. To embellish is to do women's work, to declare plainly and straightforwardly [is] to further the 'manly' cause. This dichotomy derives from a debate

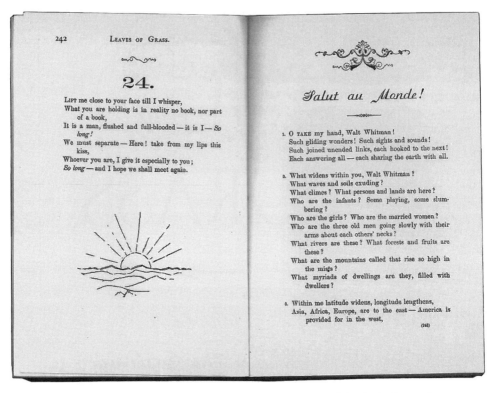

FIGURE 35. Typical interior pages, with decorative elements, of the third edition of Whitman's *Leaves of Grass,* 1860.

between clarity and sophistry deeply embedded in Western thought."[8] Little wonder that reformers objected to the presentation of "masculine" texts in ornamented forms, likening such treatment to draping them in an oppressive "florid effeminacy" of style.

Yet the gendering of book production was rooted in more than the look of the page; it derived from methods of printing as well. To explain reformers' qualms about modern mechanized printing techniques, it is necessary first to clarify that letterpress printing is a relief process, wherein the raised surface of the type's face is inked, then pressed against a sheet of paper to transfer the ink to it, creating an image of the letterform. From Gutenberg's day until the early nineteenth century, paper was traditionally dampened or moistened before printing in order to soften its fibers and allow a better impression—the slight depression caused when the

8. Grant F. Scott, "The Rhetoric of Dilation: Ekphrasis and Ideology," *Word & Image* 7, no. 4 (1991): 305. Although Scott uses the concept of ekphrasis primarily in its conventional literary context, I think that nineteenth-century ornamented type similarly "frustrates linear progression and offers an alternative poetics of space and plenitude" (302)—creating precisely the sort of spatial, visual disruption that De Vinne deplored as effeminate.

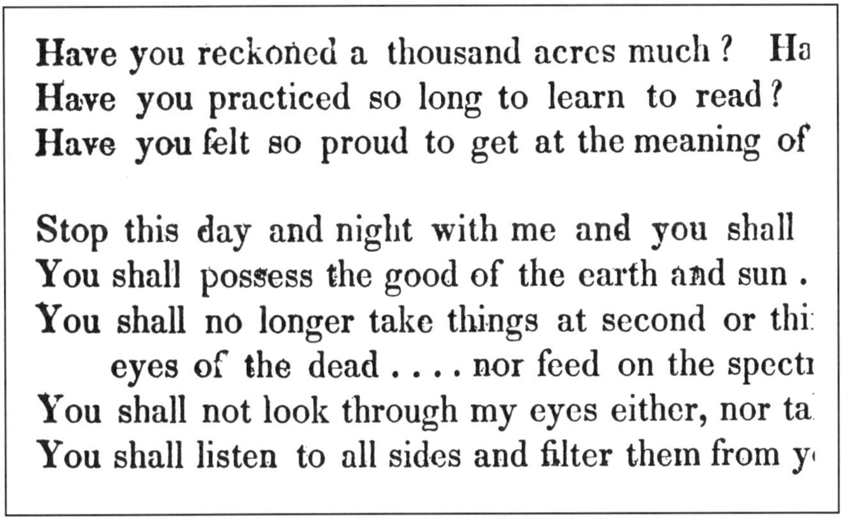

Have you reckoned a thousand acres much ?   Ha
Have you practiced so long to learn to read ?
Have you felt so proud to get at the meaning of

Stop this day and night with me and you shall
You shall possess the good of the earth and sun .
You shall no longer take things at second or thi:
    eyes of the dead . . . . nor feed on the specti
You shall not look through my eyes either, nor ta
You shall listen to all sides and filter them from y‹

FIGURE 36. Close-up of type in the first edition of Whitman's *Leaves of Grass*, 1855.

inked type sinks slightly into the paper. Traditional letterpress printing thus has a natural three-dimensional quality that today's offset lithography, based on surface-only chemical differences, does not.

The modern types that prevailed through most of the nineteenth century were well suited for mechanized printing. Their thin forms and hairline serifs required (or allowed) only the slightest moment of contact with the paper during the high-speed printing process, and their minimal surface area was well suited to the thinned inks that enabled the automated machine presses to run most efficiently. Anything more than the slightest pressure damaged them, or caused their shapes to fill with ink. And a corresponding shift at midcentury to machine-made papers only compounded the situation; De Vinne decried the cheap new woodpulp book papers for their hard, smooth "surface that resists ink almost as effectually as a plate of glass" (143). The result was the "thoroughly feminine" page that De Vinne deplored, a "weak and misty style of printing" that is "practically invisible to the ordinary reader, who has to guess at each word" (143). The slight forms of feminine type, then, worked in tandem with feminine printing, yielding pages that looked to reformers either anemic, their texts a furtive gray that seemed to float impermanently on the surface of the paper, or blotchy, marred by pools of ink and smudged or broken letterforms. Figure 36, a close-up from the 1855 first edition of *Leaves of Grass,* illustrates the problems.

By contrast, De Vinne pronounced that good printing was masculine printing. He meant that in two senses: in the design qualities of the type and typography, and in the printing process itself, or presswork. A good printer, he attested, "re-lies most upon the plainness of his type, the simplicity of his composition, the blackness of his ink, and the solidity and readability of his presswork . . . his work must be simple, direct, manly or masculine" (141). Type design was central to his notions of reform. Pointing to a few of the faces recently used by William Morris as exemplary "practical protests against the effeminacy of modern types," De Vinne applauded their "masculine" qualities—more traditional tapered serifs, larger surface areas, and more moderate contrast in the weight of their thick and thin strokes. One of the first such faces to be manufactured was called Jenson, a name that highlighted its radically antimodern allegiance to the very early roman type designed by Nicolas Jenson in the 1470s. Modeled after Morris's private, proprietary type, Jenson exemplified the new sorts of types that, De Vinne promised, were superior for their strength and legibility. They would hold up well in the modern pressroom, delivering a firm, palpable impression when printed into good-quality papers.

De Vinne thus contended that feminine type and presswork were simply less legible and in dubious taste, that ornamental and pale pages impeded rather than enhanced a text's presentation, particularly if that text had some "masculine" qualities (however vaguely defined) or was presumably destined for male audiences. But typographic taste and legibility are less universally self-evident and more culture-bound than De Vinne assumes. Bibliographical theorists are increasingly adamant on this point: Karl Gerstner notes that "it is not possible to determine which is the most legible face of all, [because] the function of reading is based on subjective habits rather than on objective conditions," and David Greetham states bluntly that "there is no inherent physical display of text and apparatus that is more natural to a specific work than any other."[9] De Vinne's call for printers to resist feminine printing stems from more than a devotion to typographic clarity, which he characterizes as masculine. The reform impulse had deeper grievances, and it went well beyond clarity and simplicity.

Lurking subtly throughout De Vinne's essay are references to the true culprit of feminization, the vague tyranny of consumers who prefer such things. "We allow customers who pay the least to select fragile and useless types, and to compel us to absurd imitations of lithography and copperplate [engraving]," he complained. Printers foolishly defer to such "false standards of light and delicate presswork," he groused, "in disregard to the general preference for strong and readable workmanship" (144). "We keep ourselves poor in buying letters that *our best customers* do not want, that wear out quickly, and that make composition difficult. . . . We allow our compositors to waste their time over feminine composition that is unprofitable and highly distasteful to *men of business*. . . . I think it time to call a halt, and to . . . make some renewed efforts to be masters of our business in all its details" (142–44, italics added). He resented that printers' better sense and indeed their professional integrity had been subverted by feminizing

9. Karl Gerstner, *Compendium for Literates* (Cambridge: MIT Press, 1974), 132; D.C. Greetham, "Editorial Theory and Critical Theory: From Modernism to Postmodernism," in *Palimpsest*, ed. George Bornstein and Ralph G. Williams (Ann Arbor: University of Michigan Press, 1993), 14.

commercial forces, especially when those customers "pay the least." Even worse, he felt that the sensible, tasteful preferences of the "best customers, . . . men of business," had been overwhelmed and suppressed in the widespread capitulation to feminine taste in book design.

It is worth repeating that what De Vinne scorned as feminine—in both its ordinary and its fancy forms—was in fact the typographic style of the great majority of ordinary books, periodicals, newspapers, and other publications in the nineteenth century. Just as machine production had changed (or feminized) the look and feel of most printed texts, so had it dramatically altered the nature of book production and consumption. Simply put, mechanization had enabled many more books to be produced in a fraction of the time and at a fraction of the cost of preindustrial methods. A skilled printer with a handpress could produce no more than about 250 impressions an hour, an output dwarfed by the eight to ten thousand or more that flew from the jaws of mechanized presses. The resulting relative accessibility of reading material in turn fostered a profound shift in literary cultural consumption, from elite and predominantly masculine to popular and increasingly feminine. Figure 32, from the anonymously written novel *Sybil Grey* published in no-doubt large quantities by the American Tract Society in 1866, illustrates this social shift as well as the book design habits that De Vinne scorned. The drawing depicts a bedridden man, unable to hold a book himself, being read to by his young daughter. With "delicate tact," we are told, the child has stopped reading the material her father requested and shifted instead to "her dear little pocket-Bible." The man is powerless to resist; decisions about what and how he reads are literally in the young girl's hands. Printers' and publishers' best customers may have been those well-bred men of business, but they were neither the most influential nor the most numerous customers, as Melville, Hawthorne, and others had so plaintively noted.

De Vinne's complaints about typography are part of a larger chorus of voices lamenting the feminization of American cultural and intellectual life. Feminine typography seemed but a symptom of a larger cultural phenomenon; to reformers it embodied what Janice Radway has described as "the rise of a commercial mass culture aimed at a broad audience of immigrants, laborers, women, and the minimally educated."[10] Radway and others have identified a variety of high culture zones that were demarcated in the latter half of the nineteenth and early decades of the twentieth centuries in defensive response to this emerging mass culture. I believe that the reform hailed as masculine printing was part of this effort to stratify cultural production and consumption; it was a peculiarly gendered effort to sacralize the *well-printed* word as both emblem and agent of an elitely framed

10. Janice Radway, "Books and Reading in the Age of Mass Production: The Book-of-the-Month Club, Middlebrow Culture, and the Transformation of the Literary Field in the United States, 1926–1940," paper presented at NEH seminar, "Print Culture in America," Chicago, July 1996, 18. See also Lawrence W. Levine, *Highbrow/Lowbrow: The Emergence of Cultural Hierarchy in America* (Cambridge: Harvard University Press, 1988), and Richard Brodhead, *Cultures of Letters: Scenes of Reading and Writing in Nineteenth-Century America* (Chicago: University of Chicago Press, 1993).

sense of Culture. The historian Lawrence Levine provides context, analogies, and even a governing metaphor for this masculinizing reform when he describes "what happened to culture toward the turn of the century" in America.

> When Shakespeare, opera, art, and music were subject to free exchange, as they had been for much of the nineteenth century, . . . the manner of their presentation and reception was determined in part by the market, that is, by the demands of the heterogeneous audience. They were in effect "rescued" from the marketplace, and therefore from the mixed audiences and from the presence of other cultural genres; they were removed from the pressures of everyday economic and social life, and placed, significantly, in concert halls, opera houses, and museums that often resembled temples, to be perused, enjoyed, and protected by the initiated—those who had the inclination, the leisure, and the knowledge to appreciate them.[11]

Reforming printers aimed to rescue the "serious" book from the marketplace forces that threatened to cheapen, vulgarize, and feminize it. To put it more accurately, they sought ways to visually distinguish the important books for serious readers from the swarms of ephemeral, cheap, and light books that dominated the popular market. Masculine printing thus constructed a kind of typographic temple for the "better" book, sacralizing it and separating it from its more ordinary, mainstream cousins.

Reform-minded typographic productions assaulted virtually everything that feminization implied. Most centrally, reformers' distaste for contemporary society and culture led them to valorize the preindustrial past. They quickly championed largely forgotten typographic models of past centuries, proclaiming them exemplars of a lost but timelessly right aesthetic. "High standards of quality . . . are the by-products of good taste," one printing critic explained, "and good taste is the result of long study of . . . the work of old masters."[12] Both Morris and De Vinne were among the reformers who consequently invested a good measure of their energies in the scholarly retrieval and reconstruction of printing history.[13] By invoking and aligning themselves with the pre-Victorian past, reformers cast an authoritative glow of tradition over their own work and effectively excluded the typographic developments of the industrial nineteenth century from that historical lineage. As Rita Felski has observed, turn-of-the-century efforts to locate the modern in relation to the past "repeatedly positioned women in a zone of ahistorical otherness," thereby seeking "to minimize their agency, contemporaneity, and humanity."[14] Modern "feminine" printing, in other words, was consid-

11. Levine, *Highbrow/Lowbrow,* 230.

12. W. Arthur Cole, *The Influence of Fine Printing* (Pittsburgh: Carnegie Institute of Technology, 1929), 34.

13. Morris wrote several essays on medieval and early modern printing and typography, and De Vinne published a widely respected treatise, *The Invention of Printing* (1876), among other historical studies.

14. Rita Felski, *The Gender of Modernity* (Cambridge: Harvard University Press, 1995), 210.

ered aberrant, an enervating disruption in the cultural tradition that reformers sought to revive.

Blaming mechanization for an aesthetic and hence cultural impoverishment of the modern book, reformers revived medieval and Renaissance typography and glorified handcraft as the production ideal. They translated this historicized aesthetic into a proclaimed refusal to compromise with such contemporary realities as popular taste and the market, twin forces of feminization. In short, reformers effaced the modern age by subordinating it to the seemingly eternal rightness, elegance, and above all taste of historical models. Their work soon encompassed a subtle spectrum of social, political, and ideological dimensions that went well beyond matters of legibility or beauty. At its heart, the reform agenda implicitly resisted the feminization of American book culture itself.

It was William Morris who most memorably championed the rejection of machine-made cultural goods, on moral as much as aesthetic grounds. Inspired by John Ruskin's belief that workers in medieval society were allowed some expressive scope in their craft, Morris contended that, if allowed to wield tools rather than merely to operate machinery, modern workers would be able to express the "roughness and majesty of their souls" (in Ruskin's words) and escape the brutality of Victorian factory labor. Like Ruskin, Morris believed that modern industrialization divorced workers from the products of their labor, destroying a source of self-definition while yielding a spiritually sterile product. More particularly, Morris at times described his fears about mechanization in gendered terms that echo De Vinne's. He equated machine production, and the capitalist system it served, with the "effeminacy of luxury and waste," while he aligned craftwork with manliness. Contrasting the "useful work" of craftsmanship with the "useless toil" of factory labor, he declared it "manly to do the one kind of work, and manly also to refuse to do the other."[15]

Few forms of labor, it seemed, were more closely linked to the soul than the making of books—the very embodiment of human thought, wisdom, and spirit. The last five years of Morris's considerable energies were devoted to what he called his "typographical adventure," the production of books at his private Kelmscott Press. He explained that he "felt that for the books one loved and cared for there might be attempted a presentation . . . which should be worthy of one's feelings. . . . The ideas we cherish are worth preserving, and I fail to see why a beautiful form should not be given to them."[16] Embodying his medieval ideals, Morris's books were printed by hand on a press little changed from what Gutenberg had used, on dampened papers custom-made by hand to Morris's specifications. And just as mechanization characterized mainstream nineteenth-century typography,

15. Eileen Boris, *Art and Labor: Ruskin, Morris, and the Craftsman Ideal in America* (Philadelphia: Temple University Press, 1986), 12; William Morris, "Useful Work versus Useless Toil," in *The Collected Works of William Morris with Introductions by his Daughter May Morris,* 24 vols. (London: Longmans, Green, 1915), 23:99.

16. "The Kelmscott Press: An Illustrated Interview with Mr. William Morris" (1895), in *The Ideal Book,* ed. Peterson, 107.

I grante thee lyf, if thou kanst tellen me
What thyng is it that wommen moost desiren;
Be war, and keep thy nekke·boon from iren.
And if thou kanst nat tellen it anon,
Yet shal I yeve thee leve for to gon
A twelfmonth and a day, to seche and leere
An answere suffisant in this mateere;
And suretee wol I han, er that thou pace,
Thy body for to yelden in this place.
O was this knyght, and sorwefully he
siketh;
But what! he may nat do alas hym liketh;
And at the laste, he chees hym for to wende,
And come agayn, right at the yeres ende,
With swich answere as God wolde hym purveye;

FIGURE 37. Close-up of type, designed by William Morris and produced for his exclusive use, from the Kelmscott Press edition of *The Complete Works of Chaucer* (1896).

so Morris's antimodern assertions about labor and art were mirrored in the Kelmscott types and typography. If most people in the 1880s viewed delicate, fine-lined letterforms as "a hallmark of refinement—a more advanced state of civilization," Morris saw the thin-serifed modern types as a "symptom of modern decadence."[17] He could not proceed with his plan to produce books until he had first produced radically different new types.

For what many regard as his greatest book, his 1896 edition of the complete works of Chaucer, Morris designed a neogothic new type, modeled on fifteenth-century faces, and commissioned its limited, exclusive production (figure 37). The resulting book startled and usually awed its first viewers (figure 38). Both the type and the typography—close spacing between words, little or no leading between lines, woodcut illustrations by the Pre-Raphaelite artist Edward Burne-Jones, broad outer and bottom margins filled with decorative imagery or radiant in their vast expanses of crisp, watermarked, deckle-edged paper, deep impressions, and majestic proportions (11 by 16 inches)—bespoke a time and culture radically distant from that of Victorian ladies' parlor books. The heavy, pigskin-bound volume might have been slipped proudly among the treasured books in a medieval nobleman's library.

Typographic reform flourished initially among so-called private presses, through which talented and committed visionaries like Morris produced beautiful books

17. William S. Peterson, "Introduction," *Ideal Book,* xx–xxi.

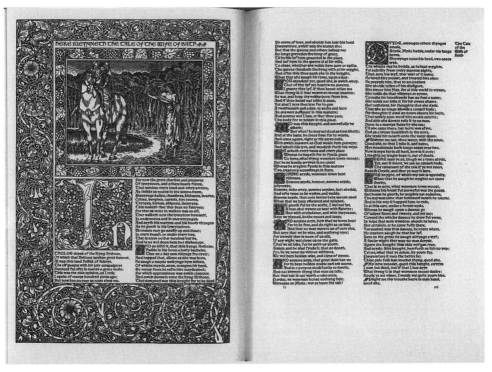

FIGURE 38. Page spread from the Kelmscott Press edition of *The Complete Works of Chaucer* (1896), designed by William Morris and illustrated by Edward Burne-Jones.

with little concern for the significant material and labor costs involved, since their primary objective was to produce specimens of ideal bookmaking. The books were essentially exercises in and assertions about bookmaking principles; they were not "published" in a fully commercial sense and so their producers made no efforts to address the larger market considerations essential to most publishing businesses.[18] By the 1920s, however, typographic reformers had deliberately moved into the public sphere. Resolved to improve mainstream book production by modeling reformist tenets, a new generation of professional printers and publishers in both England and America produced thousands of deluxe or "fine" editions expressly destined for the marketplace. In Britain the Nonesuch Press led the way in defining this new vein of books published (and purchased) chiefly for the merits of their typography, and in America several publishers—including Random

18. By the turn of the century, a few trade publishers in America had begun to embrace the revival's typographic reforms. Most notably, in Boston Houghton Mifflin's Riverside Press imprint won considerable acclaim for the work of the designer Bruce Rogers, and D. B. Updike's nearby Merrymount Press similarly modeled the new look and ethic of high-quality bookmaking. Other publishers achieving comparable recognition for revivalist typography in the 1890s include Copeland and Fay, Stone and Kimball, and Way and Williams. The single best account of this early and influential activity is Susan Otis Thompson, *American Book Designers and William Morris,* 2d ed. (New Castle, Del.: Oak Knoll Books, 1996).

House, Covici-Friede, Crosby Gaige, Fountain Press, and Spiral Press—special-ized in fine editions. Their activity, both in their publications and in extensive public pronouncements calling for higher standards of bookmaking, echoed the spirit of private press typographic reform and much of its impetus.

It was not coincidental, for example, that just as the allure of fine books reached almost frenzied proportions in the dozen or so years following the First World War, the denouncements of national cultural effeminacy grew more bitter. In 1922, Harold Stearns wrote a memorable polemic on the subject for a volume assessing American civilization, a term he considered something of an oxymoron. "Things of the mind and the spirit have been given over, in America, into the almost exclusive custody of women," he declared, culminating in the nation's "intellectual anaemia or torpor."[19] Men who seem to share in cultural and intel-lectual pursuits have in fact only been feminized, he contended, blighted by what George Santayana had dubbed the "genteel tradition." Men have been disabled, Stearns wrote, by an "essentially American (and essentially feminine) timorous-ness before life itself." He added that his essay might bear the subtitle "A Study in Sterility."[20]

Sterility was precisely the diagnosis of what ailed popular typography as well. Inspired by Morris and his contemporaries, resistance to, or at least vigilant wari-ness toward, machine production remained a benchmark of typographic quality and taste well into the twentieth century. Postwar reformers passionately con-tended that "printing at its best" could derive only from hand processes of type casting and setting, papermaking, printing, and binding. Carl Rollins, longtime printer at Yale University Press and a leading advocate of high standards of typo-graphic quality, insisted in 1923 that "to pretend that more machinery . . . is the way of salvation is to blaspheme the eternal verities . . . and the more we rely on these inhuman machines the less scope we offer to man's soul." In something of a manifesto published in 1929 in his weekly column in the *Saturday Review of Literature*, Rollins blasted the bland, suffocating sameness of machine-made books. Only handcraft truly preserved the human spirit, he argued, through the "minute irregularities" introduced by an individual's labor. The handcrafted book was both more interesting and more attractive, he proclaimed, because in its occa-sional roughness and imperfections lay what he called its *virility*.[21]

One of the best examples of the typographic virility Rollins admired is the monumental fine edition of *Leaves of Grass* published in 1930 by Random House. The printers, Edwin and Robert Grabhorn, were considerably frustrated in their typographic efforts because they felt that their initial designs proved too weak, too feminine. Edwin Grabhorn later testified that their dilemma ended only

19. Harold Stearns, "The Intellectual Life," in *Civilization in the United States: An Inquiry by Thirty Americans* (New York: Harcourt, Brace, 1922), 141, 135.

20. Ibid., 147–48.

21. Carl Purington Rollins to E. G. Gress, 19 December 1923, in the Edmund G. Gress Papers, Rare Books and Manuscript Division, New York Public Library; Rollins, "Printing at Its Best," *Saturday Review of Literature*, 2 November 1929, 356–57.

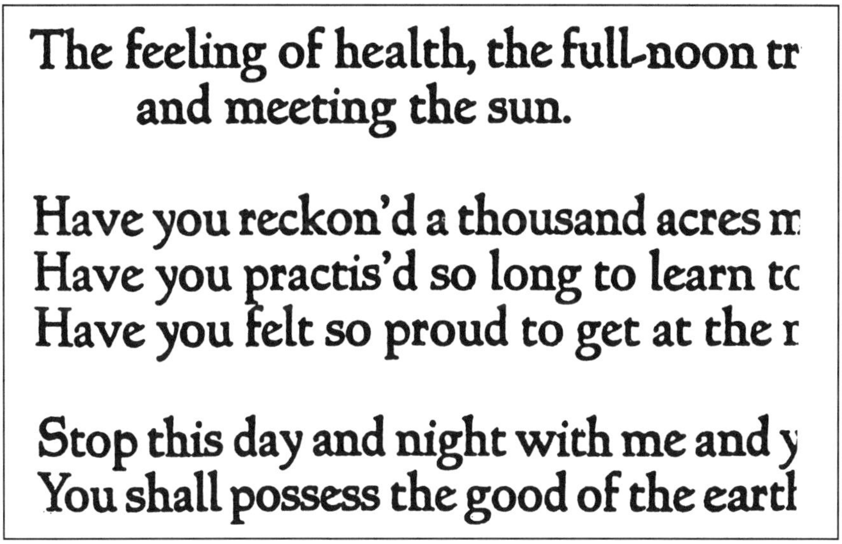

The feeling of health, the full-noon tr
and meeting the sun.

Have you reckon'd a thousand acres m
Have you practis'd so long to learn tc
Have you felt so proud to get at the r

Stop this day and night with me and y
You shall possess the good of the eartl

FIGURE 39. Close-up of the Goudy Newstyle type, designed by Frederic Goudy, used by Edwin and Robert Grabhorn for the Random House edition of Walt Whitman's *Leaves of Grass* (1930).

when they composed a few pages in a sturdy, revival-inspired typeface named Goudy Newstyle, designed by the eminent American type designer Frederic Goudy, that lay forgotten among their typecases (figure 39). Grabhorn proclaimed that in the resulting pages he saw "something the machine had discarded; he saw strength: he saw the strong, vigorous lines of Whitman. . . . He saw strong, vigorous, simple printing—printing like mountains, rocks and trees, but not like pansies, lilacs and valentines."[22] Reminiscent of the Kelmscott masterpiece *Chaucer* thirty years before, the Grabhorn *Leaves* featured large folio pages (9½ by 14 inches), woodcut illustrations, handmade papers and bindings, and spacious margins.

The book was a masterful specimen of masculine bookmaking in its presswork as well. The type was printed with such force that it left deep sculptural impressions in the thick, dampened handmade paper; this heavy impression was by then a trademark feature of Grabhorn printing that commonly thrilled critics. James Hart particularly praised it as part of the "strong masculine approach" of the Grabhorns: as he put it, they "did not merely let the type kiss the paper lightly and discreetly but instead embedded it in a forceful embrace that could be felt by fingers as well as seen by eyes." The Grabhorns' bold typography, in both design and production, gave their books what Hart termed "integrity and virility."[23]

22. Edwin Grabhorn, "The Fine Art of Printing" (1933), in *Books and Printing: A Treasury for Typophiles,* ed. Paul A. Bennett, rev. ed. (Cleveland: World, 1963), 232.

23. James D. Hart, *Fine Printing: The San Francisco Tradition* (Washington, D.C.: Library of Congress, 1985), 25–26.

The phallic implications that color Hart's language resonate with a familiar gender dichotomy. As J. Hillis Miller writes in his exploration of the interplay between text and image, "In the traditional gendering of acts that are like the sex act, the act of fissuring a surface with a stick, engraving a furrow, the art of scratch, is seen as male; the act of weaving some fabric as a cover for nakedness is seen as female."[24] Masculine printing often exaggerated the degree to which the letterpress printing process drives type into paper, and it frequently featured woodcut or wood engraving illustrations printed by similar relief techniques. The pale, anemic, mass-produced page disdained by De Vinne and others was thus feminine in a physical as well as visual sense: the modern type and the litho-graphic images that accompanied it were not only finely detailed and decorative but printed with imperceptible pressure. They rested barely on the surface of the paper, a tapestry of fine threadlike lines laid upon rather than driven into it.

These few examples have suggested the most obvious technical and aesthetic differences between masculine and feminine printing. But remasculating the book went beyond dark, archaic letterforms and forceful presswork. In other ways as well the historicized typography invoked cultures of book reading and owner-ship vastly different from that of the modern day. One essential feature was the revival of medieval and Renaissance layout arrangements, which regarded facing pages as a single visual unit: type blocks were positioned toward the upper, inside corners of the pages, so that the gutter and top margins were relatively small, the outside margin roughly twice the width of the gutter, and the bottom margin the widest of all. Based on formulas derived from fifteenth-century Venetian print-ing, these margins could sometimes reach extravagant proportions: as much as three or four inches at the foot of a folio edition, for example. Other features revived from historical models—second and third colors of ink for important elements, unusually large type sizes and page dimensions, and a colophon, or statement describing the book's material production—similarly ensured that the book imparted a sense of stately grandeur.

Those much-vaunted standards of material quality and aesthetic beauty for which reformers are admired today also, however, systematically rendered good bookmaking an elite—and even in some ways misogynist—commodity. For one thing, the extravagant design (multiple colors, large margins, and so on), coupled with the use of hand production methods and fine materials—handmade or at least all-rag papers (and sometimes even vellum), cloth or leather bindings—made fine books unquestionably expensive. The Kelmscott *Chaucer* cost 33 pounds for a copy printed on paper and bound in tooled pigskin and 120 guineas for a copy printed on vellum. And in 1930, when a skilled worker earned about forty dollars a week (if employed), and an ordinary trade book cost two to three dollars, the Grabhorn edition of *Leaves of Grass,* bound in mahogany boards with a leather spine, cost one hundred dollars.

24. J. Hillis Miller, *Illustration* (Cambridge: Harvard University Press, 1992), 78.

These breathtakingly high prices were accepted, and sometimes even embraced, as the necessary and natural consequences of adherence to the highest ideals of bookmaking. If books were "more arduously come by," reasoned the enthusiast Richard Le Gallienne in 1894, they would be deemed more precious by those who owned them. He declared it better that books aspire to the highest standards of quality and remain expensive treasures "than that any sacrilegious hand should fumble them for threepence."[25] On the other hand, Morris was no doubt genuinely grieved to realize that, even in his lifetime, his books appealed most to the "swinish rich" who could afford to buy them, and did so avidly. But when asked by a journalist in 1891, "Is it not better to give [the millions] books with small type, which they can buy cheap, than to prevent them from reading at all, which would be the case if there were no small type and consequent cheap editions?" Morris replied that the solution would be a socialist government; until things changed politically, he conceded, "if they have not money enough to buy [my books] they must go without." Two years later he reiterated, "I wish indeed that the cost of the books was less, only that is impossible if the printing and the decoration and the paper and the binding are to be what they should be."[26]

The standards that defined what a fine book's typographic and material nature "should be" rendered it elite in a second sense as well. Edition sizes were always explicitly limited. A colophon both helped to cast this second aura of eliteness and justified it. That is, stating the number of copies amid other information about type, materials, methods of production, and so on (information most intelligible to those schooled in the printing history that gave it all meaning) implied that the edition size had been naturally limited by the conditions of production, rather than arbitrarily kept low to increase scarcity and snob appeal, as was sometimes irreverently suggested.[27] While certainly some publishers did exploit the "conspicuous consumption" appeal of fine books and shrewdly plan edition sizes accordingly, a more common and more subtle function of the limited edition size, and the colophon that announced it, was to distance fine books from the popular marketplace.

Ideally, access to fine books was limited to sympathetic insiders, members of a tacit community of those whose education or social background prepared them to recognize and appreciate the aristocratic Western cultural tradition that the books so vividly valorized. Carefully construed as patrons rather than consumers, this audience was define by taste more than by wealth. It constituted a typographical

25. Richard Le Gallienne, "The Philosophy of Limited Editions," in *Prose Fancies* (New York: G. P. Putnam's Sons, 1894), 121, 122. "Let us not vulgarize our books," he exclaimed. "Let us, if need be, make our editions smaller and smaller, our prices increasingly 'prohibitive,' rather than that we should forget the wonder and beauty of printed dream and thought, and treat our books as somewhat less valuable than wayside weeds" (125).

26. "The Poet as Printer" (1891) in *Ideal Book,* 92; " 'Master Printer Morris': A Visit to the Kelmscott Press" (1893), in ibid., 98.

27. See, for example, Thorstein Veblen's trenchant remarks on Kelmscott revival typography in *The Theory of the Leisure Class: An Economic Study of Institutions* (1899; New York: New American Library, 1953), 115–17.

equivalent of what Irving Babbitt had in mind when he wrote in 1927 that "the hope of civilization lies not in the divine average but the saving remnant."[28] Unlike the masses, deemed dangerously susceptible to economic, social, and political manipulation, this saving remnant in theory resisted those modern forces. The consumption of fine printing was thus figured in opposition to and unswayed by the popular marketplace, ostensibly driven instead by Kantian disinterested judgments of beauty and value.

Fine books were certainly elite. But I have also suggested they carry misogynist implications. Is this based simply on De Vinne's light/dark dichotomy or his construction of mass or popular consumer tastes as feminine and more selective, judicious consumption as masculine? No, although reformist typography's aversion to popular market tastes conveyed a "critique of capitalism" that, as Felski notes, "provided an alibi for the expression of misogynist attitudes toward women."[29] In content as well as in form, fine editions remasculated the book. Like the material forms in which they were housed, the content of most fine editions tended to both honor and replicate the values associated with preindustrial worlds of privilege and refinement. The books were reprinted classics and other works from the past deemed important enough to distinguish from the ordinary, or they were new work that was ideologically compatible with, if not overtly sympathetic to, bibliophilia's antipopular impulses.[30] A distinctly masculine aura resulted.

"Classics" were usually selected from the core of authors and texts whose reputations for quality had been distilled over time. Most were familiar texts encountered through genteel educations: works by Dante, Shakespeare, Pope, Voltaire, and others. They emerged from a fairly unrigorous, passively canonical understanding of literature, identified by generations of teachers and critics as the best work embodying the Western literary tradition. Few women authors from that literary past were honored with such ennobling editions; Christina Rossetti and Elizabeth Barrett Browning were among the usual rare exceptions (this bias is partly explained, however, by the predominance of poetry over prose).

It is worth noting that, by taking American writers like Whitman under their bibliophilic wing, reformers played a subtle but significant role in escorting them into the status of classics. They were thus typographically canonized, lifted from the dubious crowd of nineteenth-century American writers and placed on a finely

28. Irving Babbitt, *Democracy and Leadership* (Boston: Houghton Mifflin, 1924), 278.

29. Felski, *Gender of Modernity*, 88.

30. Various scholars have noted the affinity between the era's avant garde modernist writers and fine book publishing. Yeats, Pound, Eliot, Woolf, and others sought the distinction imparted by fine editions. In his discussion of Eliot's efforts to publish *The Waste Land* in a fine format, for example, Lawrence Rainey explains that "the limited edition established a kind of special productive space insulated from the harsh exigencies of the larger marketplace. It . . . addressed a prosperous minority with a luxury good that emphasized innovation and was produced in small quantities. . . . It enacted, in other words, a return to an essentially precapitalist structure, an artisanal economy producing luxury goods in limited quantities for aristocratic consumption" ("The Price of Modernism: Publishing *The Waste Land*," in *T. S. Eliot: The Modernist in History*, ed. Ronald Bush [Cambridge: Cambridge University Press, 1991]: 114–15).

printed pedestal. American publishers, in particular, felt a need to invest their talents and resources in establishing the nation's literary status on a par with its newly emergent political, military, and economic predominance. When Chicago's Lakeside Press determined in the mid-1920s to produce four fine illustrated editions, for example, the company president, George Littell, insisted that they stick to "books of American literature that were interesting to read to the normal American business man."[31] His comments reflect both a Babbittlike iconoclasm toward the Anglo-European literary tradition and a confidence that the tastes of "the normal American business man" would steer him to the most appropriate selections. Throughout the decade, works of Poe, Hawthorne, Melville, Twain, and others joined Whitman's in the rank of literature deemed worthy of what one printer termed "monumental" presentations. Significantly, none of the newly asserted American classics were written by women, although the works of contemporary writers Willa Cather, Edna St. Vincent Millay, and Elinor Wylie did merit fine editions.

Subject matter also invoked interests and occupations redolent, sometimes in strikingly anachronistic ways, of an aristocratic gentleman's lifestyle. Exuding an affinity with past eras of privilege, privacy, and refinement, fine editions offered textual oases amid the modern commercial and industrial society in which bibliophiles lived and worked. A good example is the spate of sporting books devoted to foxhunting, fly-fishing, equestrian subjects, and so on. One New York publisher, the Derrydale Press, was entirely devoted to fine editions of such titles as *Hounds and Hunting through the Ages* and *Gentlemen Up,* stories and illustrations of steeplechase riding.

A third category of content that signaled a mainly masculine audience was a vein of exotic, somewhat decadent, and often droll texts that Donald Friede, a publisher of fine editions, discreetly termed "polite erotica."[32] These were unexpurgated editions of such texts as the Song of Solomon, the Satyricon, and works of Rabelais, Balzac, Oscar Wilde, James Branch Cabell, and Pierre Louÿs. They nearly always featured stylishly erotic illustrations by such artists as Rockwell Kent, Eric Gill, and Alexander King. For example, the 1931 Golden Cockerel edition of the *Canterbury Tales* featured a sensuous Eric Gill nude reclining languorously beneath the opening title (figure 40). These were editions clearly destined for the private libraries of affluent men, editions whose fine formats helped them skirt the attention of censors, since—their publishers argued—they were unlikely to encounter the nation's vulnerable readers, its youth and women. These editions well distanced their owners from the "feminized" moral and cultural climate of the era, the world of the Scopes trial, women's suffrage, prohibition, and Emily Post.

31. Littell to William Kittredge, 17 January 1930, William A. Kittredge Papers, Newberry Library, Chicago.
32. Donald Friede, *The Mechanical Angel: His Adventures and Enterprises in the Glittering 1920s* (New York: Knopf, 1948), 84.

FIGURE 40. Eric Gill's part-title illustration for *The Canterbury Tales*, published by the Golden Cockerel Press, 1930. Courtesy of the Harry Ransom Humanities Research Center, The University of Texas at Austin.

In short, the presumed gender of the audience for reformers' books was signaled in the form of the books as implicitly as was that of their "feminine" counterparts. Masculine bookmaking created studied replicas of the books whose content, stature, rich materials, and traditional styles gave substance and elegance to that fabled refuge of aristocratic manhood, the gentleman's library. Just as the library was often regarded as the last domestic territory not controlled by feminine taste, so the fine book became a sort of masculine retreat. In America the equivalents of the English gentry library and the gentleman's club were the several prestigious book collecting clubs established between the 1880s and the 1920s.

In all but a few cases, their charters limited membership to bibliophiles of means and taste, and to men. Today the clubs' posh quarters and elegant activities continue to venerate the fine book, although most now admit "qualified" women.

Much the same might be said about the subsequent story of masculine printing. As with so many of the illusions lost by the end of the 1920s, most printers realized that resistance to modern technology and social realities was futile. Although in 1924 Carl Rollins likened the Linotype machine to "a wild beast—obedient under the trainer's whip, but a wild jungle beast at heart," he reluctantly came to terms with machinery. "Much as I dislike slavery," he wrote, "I much prefer that the machine should be my slave than my master."[33] Reformers conceded that handcraft was an unmanageable standard to maintain, but they held firmly to historicized "masculine" typographic values and transferred their energies to achieving thus-defined good design with machine composition and printing. Their efforts yielded the now-digitized stalwarts of better book composition today, typefaces revived from or inspired by those preindustrial centuries: Bembo, Centaur, Times Roman, Garamond, Caslon, Baskerville, and many others. Although they eventually lost their elitist and misogynist ideological edges, the tenets of typographic reform now lie at the core of modern Anglo-American book design principles.

That reform, moreover, constitutes a remarkable moment in the history of the printed word. Galvanized in resistance to the machine-made, popular, and "feminine" qualities of the ordinary modern book, reforming printers tacitly recognized the powers of typography to characterize the interpretive environment of a text. They then shrewdly deployed those powers to construct books whose typographic gestures of cultural and social otherness rendered an elitely remasculated reading experience. However moderated by eventual concessions to the technological and social realities of modern publishing, those reform design strategies—preindustrial letterforms, Renaissance page design and proportions, ostensible devotion to aesthetic principles unsullied by market demands or economic costs—remain the still-recognizable legacy of masculine printing.

33. Carl Rollins, *Fine Printing and the Small Shop* (Los Angeles: Plantin Press, 1935), 8.

Bridge Three

As this volume's introduction asserts, modern Western book-making and publishing practices often assume that typography is (or at least ought to be) a neutral, invisible conveyer of a text's message. In the previous essay, Megan Benton argues that typography—spacing, illustration, and especially type font—is often anything *but* neutral. In fact, she contends that it is knit into the larger epistemological structures governing the way Westerners have been taught to see difference. In other words, typographical elements emerge from and contribute to an era's normative notions of, for example, gender and social class.

For Benton, turn-of-the-century printing theory and practice reflected growing anxieties about changes in these norms, particularly the democratization, industrialization, and feminization of England and America. Decrying weak, frothy, and "misty" types designed for mechanized printing, for example, reformers resurrected older type faces such as the eighteenth-century Caslon and sixteenth-century Garamond, fonts that to them exuded the solid, "virile," aristocratic masculinity of a lost preindustrial age that invigorated a resurgent style of modern cultural "manliness." Because connotations surrounding typefaces are culture-bound, Benton notes, time has obscured the ideological edges of the reactionary Anglo-American reformers for most late twentieth-century readers. Even so, she concludes, the tenets espoused by those reformers "now lie at the core of modern Anglo-American book design principles." Readers would do well, Benton implies, to heed the implications and consequences of those principles, as well as the role that type plays in textual meaning more generally.

In the following essay, Beth McCoy makes Benton's implicit exhortation explicit by asking scholars and other readers to recognize typography as a maker of meaning, much as they would consider any other textual (e.g., diction) or paratextual (e.g., chapter heading) device. McCoy explores how changes to a text's typography may shift the way readers over time come to understand that text, not only as an object in itself but also in relation to other texts. In particular, McCoy narrates the print history of *Passing,* a novel by the Harlem Renaissance author Nella Larsen. When first published by Knopf in 1929, *Passing* was set in Caslon and thus, ironically, it played a part—

however unwitting—in the nostalgic yearnings Benton finds in the turn-of-the-century typographical reform movement. When republished eventually by Rutgers University Press, however, *Passing* was reset into the modern font Perpetua, a typographical shift that correlates with a surge in Larsen criticism. This surge, McCoy argues, suggests that the new font played a part in shifting *Passing* from a novel that looked stodgy, prim, and old-fashioned to one whose appearance connoted sophisticated ambiguity ripe for contemporary critical inquiry. That typographical shift also, however, removed *Passing* from its historical specificity as a Harlem Renaissance text that responds to the difficulties of maintaining interracial friendships across lines of institutionalized inequity. McCoy suggests that scholars must attend to both the benefits *and* the liabilities that emerge when texts undergo typographical change and technological advancement.

Chapter Four

Perpetua(l) Notion: Typography, Economy, and Losing Nella Larsen

BETH McCOY

In 1929, at the height of the aesthetic and political movement called the Harlem Renaissance, Nella Larsen published *Passing,* her second novel. *Passing* recounts both the return of blond, light-complected Clare Kendry to the black Harlem she abandoned years previously and how that return disrupts the illusion of black middle-class security—complete with husband, children, and racial uplift philanthropy—behind which Clare's old friend Irene Redfield hides her insecurities and personal desires. The novel begins with such disruption already in progress, as Irene sits shocked and overwhelmed by Clare's surprise letter:

> It was the last letter in Irene Redfield's little pile of morning mail. After her other ordinary and clearly directed letters the long envelope of thin Italian paper with its almost illegible scrawl seemed out of place and alien. And there was, too, something mysterious and slightly furtive about it. A thin sly thing which bore no return address to betray the sender. Not that she hadn't immediately known who its sender was. Some two years ago she had one very like it in outward appearance. Furtive, but yet in some peculiar, determined way a little flaunting. Purple ink. Foreign paper of extraordinary size.[1]

Here, the novel reveals itself as intimately concerned with a message's medium, in this case, the graphical form of a handwritten letter. In this initial scene, Irene conflates textual form with textual meaning: Clare's "alien," "mysterious" handwriting stands for Clare herself, who becomes, according to Irene's point of view, supposedly "alien" and "mysterious." Continuing this process throughout *Passing,* Irene will later equate Clare's simultaneously "flaunting" and "furtive" form (i.e., a black woman whose blonde beauty permits her to pass audaciously for white) with ostensible behavior that Irene interprets as both flaunting and furtive (e.g., Irene imagines that Clare is having an affair with her husband right in front of

<hr />

1. Nella Larsen, *Quicksand; and, Passing,* ed. Deborah McDowell (New Brunswick, N.J.: Rutgers University Press, 1986), 143. Subsequent references to this source are given parenthetically in the text.

her disbelieving eyes). Larsen suggests that the problem with Irene's repeated slides from "form" to "content" lies not so much with the slides themselves as with the fact that Irene executes them with little apparent readerly self-awareness or self-criticism. Indeed, as Deborah McDowell has observed, Irene is "the classic unreliable narrator" who is "not always fully aware of the import of what she reveals to the reader."[2]

By *Passing*'s end, Irene's lack of readerly self-awareness becomes intricately correlated with Clare's death: at the very moment that Clare's white husband discovers the "truth" of his wife's blackness, Irene rushes to her side. In the next instant—an instant that "Irene Redfield never afterwards allowed herself to remember" (239)—Clare plunges fatally from an upper-story window. "Vital" and "glowing" but also isolated and disconnected, Clare dies, Larsen strongly suggests, as a result of Irene's violent inattention and inaction. Her failure to be critically aware of how she reads functionally kills Clare, a formally beautiful (according to "white" physical norms) text whose form is isolated from what might have been a nourishing "black" context. At one level, *Passing*'s inter- and intraracially violent denouement says much about how the uncritical acceptance of the epistemology of skin color functions in an America governed by the construct of race, a pseudoscientific fiction that nevertheless holds the material power of a social fact (indeed, throughout this essay, when I use the terms "black," "white," and "race," I acknowledge these terms' status as artificial concepts that nevertheless have real effects).[3]

At the same time, however, *Passing*'s violence has much to say about the study of books, those classic literary objects, for the correlation between Irene's uncritical apprehension of graphical form and Clare's eventual death reminds us, as readers, to be actively and critically aware of what Jerome McGann, following Gérard Genette, defines as the paratext, where "meaning invests a work at the level of physical appearance and linguistic signifiers."[4] Under this definition, paratextual elements such as prefatorial material, chapter headings, and—most important for this essay's purposes—type font constitute significant but often overlooked formal "thresholds" (Genette's term, translated from the French *seuils*) that help to create meaning before a reader has even read a literary work's first formal word.[5]

Examining *Passing*'s various typographical permutations in this essay, I urge a more conscious critical attention to the paratext by exploring how typography intersects both with notions of racial difference and with the processes by which literary works are valorized within the academic economy. Most specifically, ex-

2. Deborah McDowell, "Introduction," *Quicksand; and, Passing,* xxiv, xxv.

3. For a lucid account of race's "fiction," see Stephen Jay Gould's often-cited *The Mismeasure of Man* (New York: Norton, 1996).

4. Jerome McGann, *Black Riders: The Visible Language of Modernism* (Princeton: Princeton University Press, 1993), 12.

5. Gérard Genette, *Paratexts: Thresholds of Interpretation,* trans. Jane E. Lewin (Cambridge: Cambridge University Press, 1997).

ploring *Passing*'s typographies may allow scholars of the Harlem Renaissance to explore more consciously their own responses both to *Passing* itself and to Larsen's complicated relationship to her white 1920s contemporary Carl Van Vechten. More generally, exploring the typography of *Passing* can help illuminate larger concerns, including the connections among advances in typographical technology, academic efforts to make the literary canon more inclusive, and larger shifts in cultural attitudes regarding racial integration. Such considerations, which question both what is gained and what is lost when typographies change, become especially important when the text in question is one produced by an author rendered "other" within U.S. structures of domination.

Passing was published by Alfred A. Knopf in 1929. The book world into which the novel emerged was a vibrant one, for during the 1920s, a continued craving for fiction and a thriving postwar economy invigorated the U.S. publishing industry. As John Tebbel has documented thoroughly, Knopf played a particularly important role in that invigoration by serving as a "transitional" figure linking such venerable, still-powerful publishers as Henry Holt and younger, upstart ones such as Bennett Cerf, Alfred Harcourt, and Donald Brace. Creating milestones for what has proved to be the house's long and influential life, Knopf began to issue anniversary collections; titled *Borzoi* after the Russian wolfhound he chose as the house's icon, these collections featured writings by and about Knopf authors (the tenth-anniversary *Borzoi 1925,* for instance, featured essays by Joseph Hergesheimer and Julia Peterkin). When Blanche Knopf joined the firm in 1928 to serve as both vice-president and editorial director, the house became the first U.S. publisher ever run by a husband-and-wife team. In the 1920s, the firm made concerted efforts not only to sustain a small, high-quality list but also to achieve new breadth and depth within that list. To this end, Alfred and Blanche sought new writers abroad. Admittedly, it was hardly new for a U.S. publisher to court international authors (Tebbel notes that "the practice was as old as modern publishing"), but the Knopfs took further steps; not only did they plumb overlooked European territory (Denmark and Norway) in search of new and meritorious authors, but they also forged into South America.[6]

Not all of the Knopf diversity came from outside U.S. borders, however. In fact, by working to broaden and deepen the quality of the list within the United States as well, Knopf served once again as a sort of transitional figure, helping to mediate the color line that W.E.B. Du Bois had years earlier predicted as "the problem of the twentieth century."[7] For during the 1920s, the house of Knopf brought on board not only Nella Larsen but also other black authors such as Langston Hughes, James Weldon Johnson, Rudolph Fisher, and Walter White; additionally, the house hired the black visual artist Aaron Douglas to illustrate Knopf books and promotional materials.

6. John Tebbel, *A History of Book Publishing in the United States,* vol. 3: *The Golden Age between Two Wars, 1920–1940* (New York: R. R. Bowker, 1978).

7. W.E.B. Du Bois, *The Souls of Black Folk,* ed. Henry Louis Gates Jr. (New York: Bantam, 1989), 76.

Of course, Knopf was hardly the only white publisher to court, showcase, and otherwise utilize black art during the 1920s. Encouraged by Urban League and NAACP literary contests (contests that themselves were developed and adjudicated by interracial coalitions) targeting and promoting black poets and novelists, white houses such as Macaulay, Harper, and Boni and Liveright published the work of African American writers including George Schuyler, Countee Cullen, Jean Toomer, and Jessie Redmon Fauset. During this time, black writers gained access to the wide distribution and massive publicity that such prominent houses could offer, but they also found themselves having to negotiate all-too-familiar territory as black people affiliated with white institutions—however liberal those institutions were—that held virtually all the power, money, and access. Forging into such territory, though, was a risk that Harlem Renaissance artists and thinkers were willing to take for both personal and communal progress. As David Levering Lewis notes, some influential black intellectuals hypothesized that the arts constituted one of the few remaining paths to economic and political parity for African Americans. "If the road to the ballot box and jobs was blocked," Lewis writes, black thinkers such as Charles Spurgeon Johnson "saw that the door to Carnegie Hall and New York publishers was ajar."[8] With Knopf prestige underwriting her novels, Nella Larsen was able to play a part in keeping that door ajar.

It was not only prestige, however, that recommended Larsen's books and those by other Borzoi-affiliated authors—it was also the Knopf passion for books as objects. During the 1920s, the Borzoi colophon came to emblematize the house's growing aesthetic interest in how its books felt to the hand and looked to the eye. Both Knopfs (but especially Blanche) carefully selected distinctive, high-quality paper and boards for the house's rigorously selected and edited volumes. And in 1926, the publisher began a practice that stands as Knopf tradition today: each book included at the end "A Note on the Type in Which this Book Is Set."[9] This practice itself constituted a form of mediation, allowing readers—bibliophiles and tyros alike—to gain insight not only into the choice of font but also into the publisher's reason for the choice.

According to its "Note on the Type," *Passing* is set in what Knopf called at the time a "modern adaptation" of Caslon, an adaptation that features no lower serif on the capital C, for example, but preserves the scallop in the apex of "A" by which any version of the font may be recognized.[10] By 1929, Caslon was already an old typeface, having been cut by its namesake William Caslon early in the eighteenth century, and this historicized authority is no coincidence, for Knopf appears to have chosen the font precisely because of its venerable "old-style" echoes: "it is of interest," the note reads, " . . . that the first copies of the Declaration

8. David Levering Lewis, *When Harlem Was in Vogue* (New York: Oxford University Press, 1989), 48.
9. Tebbel, *A History of Book Publishing*, 3:115.
10. Alex Brown, *In Print: Text and Type in the Age of Desktop Publishing* (New York: Watson-Guptill, 1989), 40.

of Independence and the first paper currency distributed to the citizens of the new-born nation were printed in this type face."

Caslon was the first type designed and produced in England, and in the 1920s under Knopf's aegis, this expression of nascent English nationalism becomes an expression of ascendant American nationalism. Both drawn into the Knopf fold and set in the now-patriotic Caslon, *Passing*'s first edition can be read as literarily and typographically fulfilling a central tenet in the strain of Harlem Renaissance thought that believed both that "each book, play, poem, or canvas by an Afro-American would becomes a weapon against the old racial stereotypes" and that Americans of African descent would finally be recognized as "American" by the white countrymen with whom they had fought for democracy overseas.[11] In 1929, then, the Knopf *Passing* looked visibly authoritative, powered by both the publisher's name and the modernized Caslon.

Ironically, the visually authorized *Passing* appeared just as Larsen began the slow process of unauthorizing herself, for, as Thadious Davis's biography demonstrates, she began to withdraw slowly from the New York literary and cultural scene during the 1930s.[12] She never published another novel; eventually poor health, a plagiarism scandal, and a deteriorating marriage added further to the pressures that finally pushed Larsen back into her nursing career and away from the sophisticated, highly visible milieu in which she had circulated. Larsen's own disappearing act coincides with what is understood generally as a shift in black arts and letters as the 1930s began, a shift understood most often as tied to the Depression that took its toll on white disposable income and philanthropy, decimated the economic state of many black communities, and dismantled much of the programmatic visibility that the Harlem Renaissance seemed to have acquired.[13]

During this time, Larsen's work fell out of print and thus remained largely unavailable to the bulk of the reading public—that is, until much later in the twentieth century when the academy began finally to register the hard-won political gains of the Civil Rights struggle and the attendant Black Aesthetic and Black Arts movements by instituting black studies programs and bringing back into print "lost" work by black authors.[14] *Passing* was one rediscovered novel: it reappeared in no fewer than three new editions during the 1960s and 1970s. One was a small, cramped Collier/Macmillan paperback (1971) set in Caledonia, part of an African/American Library series. Two other editions (from Arno [1969]

11. Lewis, *When Harlem Was in Vogue*, 48.

12. Thadious Davis, *Nella Larsen, Novelist of the Harlem Renaissance: A Woman's Life Unveiled* (Baton Rouge: Louisiana State University Press, 1994).

13. Why—and if—the Harlem Renaissance declined remains a matter of vigorous scholarly disagreement. Contrast, for example, Lewis's assiduously documented *When Harlem Was in Vogue* with George Hutchinson's equally well documented *The Harlem Renaissance in Black and White* (Cambridge: The Belknap Press of Harvard University Press, 1995).

14. Davis, *Nella Larsen*, xv.

and Negro Universities Press [1969]) merely reproduced the Knopf Caslon *Passing,* issuing facsimile editions between new covers.

During these years, critics who sought to write about *Passing* relied of necessity either on some version of the Knopf Caslon edition or the Collier Caledonia edition. Appearing during the 1970s and early 1980s in such venues as *Black American Literature Forum* and *Afro-Americans in New York Life and History,* this criticism emerged as part of a larger black feminist/womanist project to recover and assert the value of "lost," neglected, forgotten, or derided work by black women. In this effort, such now well-known black feminist critics as Cheryl Wall and Claudia Tate combated multiple obstacles, including the lack or untrustworthiness of biographical information about Larsen and others, and the relative paucity of venues and institutional recognition for scholarly work about African American women writers.[15]

Around 1986, however, the critical road to Larsen's work got smoother when, as part of its growing American Women Writers series, Rutgers University Press published *Passing* in a one-volume omnibus with *Quicksand,* Larsen's first novel (published by Knopf in 1928). The arrival of the Rutgers edition seemed to spark a veritable explosion of critical interest in Larsen's novels, asserting her larger importance to critical investigations of American and African American literary and cultural studies. Certainly the cachet and market access provided by affiliation with Rutgers, a major university press, accounts for at least some of that increased critical attention. Indeed, it would make sense to assume that, finding both *Quicksand* and *Passing* to be available for the first time in one volume at a reasonable price, scholars began to see Larsen's work with a frequency that made the novels look like appropriate objects for studies narratological, psychoanalytical, and pedagogical, to name only a few.

The pre-1986 criticism had appeared primarily (though not exclusively) in venues explicitly identified with exploring black literature and culture. And, indeed, the post-1986 Larsen criticism continued to appear in such African American–affiliated publications as *Black American Literature Forum* (which later be-

---

15. See, for example, Mary Mabel Youman, "Nella Larsen's *Passing:* A Study in Irony," *CLA Journal* 18, no. 2 (1974): 235–41; Cheryl A. Wall, "Passing for What? Aspects of Identity in Nella Larsen's Novels," *Black American Literature Forum* 20 (1986): 97–111; Hortense Thornton, "Sexism as Quagmire: Nella Larsen's *Quicksand,*" *CLA Journal* 16, no. 3 (1973): 285–301; Claudia Tate, "Nella Larsen's *Passing:* A Problem of Interpretation," *Black American Literature Forum* 14 (1980): 142–46; Priscilla Ramsey, "Freeze the Day: A Feminist Reading of Nella Larsen's *Quicksand* and *Passing,*" *Afro-Americans in New York Life and History* 9 (January 1985): 27–41; and Mary Helen Washington, "Nella Larsen: Mystery Woman of the Harlem Renaissance," *Ms.* (December 1980): 44–50.

The importance of this germinal work cannot be overestimated, for it accomplishes much of the recovery necessitated by the oversights of both the masculinist-identified Black Arts/Aesthetics movement and the white-identified Anglo-women's movement (the response to such oversight is best emblematized by the title of Gloria Hull's book, *All the Women Are White, All the Blacks Are Men, but Some of Us Are Brave*). For instance, spurred by mystery surrounding Larsen's life and work, Thadious Davis began in the 1970s the long process of researching and writing her monumental biography of the writer. As Davis notes in the biography's preface, Hortense Thornton's 1973 essay "rekindled" her interest in engaging those mysteries (xvi). Davis's biography also provides a first-rate version of the history I have reconstructed here.

came *African American Review*) and *CLA* [College Language Association] *Journal.* Yet—and this is significant in a culture that still constructs "black" as deviant or adjunct (e.g., those who receive "special rights") and "white" as normative—work on Larsen after 1986 also began to appear with some frequency and visibility in what are reputed to be high-prestige, mainstream journals such as *PMLA, Narrative, Journal of the History of Sexuality,* and *College English,* and in major book-length studies such as Judith Butler's *Bodies That Matter.*[16] Nearly all of these post-1986 critics use as their primary text the 1986 Rutgers University Press edition for the American Women Writers series.

At the risk of understatement, there are, of course, more than a few plausible explanations for the apparently sudden increased critical interest in Nella Larsen's work.[17] For instance, Larsen's intensified critical visibility can be credited to cumulative growth in interdisciplinary work impelled by the institutionalization of programs in African(a), African American, women's, and cultural studies. Additionally, the cachet afforded by both the press's status and the American Women Writers series' success certainly informed the apparent "choice" of Larsen's work as befitting what mainstream academics would consider a wide (as opposed to "narrow" or "limited," as black-centered studies are still often called) range of intellectual approaches. Further, Larsen's apparent vogue in mainstream journal articles written quite often (as Ann DuCille has recorded ambivalently) by white women can be taken as evidence that black feminists not only investigated Larsen's work and life rigorously and ethically but also spurred Anglo-feminist critics to stop ignoring black women writers' work.[18] And, undeniably, Deborah E.

16. See, for example, Ann E. Hostetler, "The Aesthetics of Race and Gender in Nella Larsen's *Quicksand,*" *PMLA* 105 (January 1990): 35–46; Jennifer DeVere Brody, "Clare Kendry's 'True' Colors: Race and Class Conflict in Nella Larsen's *Passing,*" *Callaloo* 15, no. 4 (1992): 1053–65; Pamela L. Caughie, " 'Not Entirely Strange, . . . Not Entirely Friendly': *Passing* and Pedagogy," *College English* 54 (November 1992): 775–93; Mary Condè, "Europe in the Novels of Jessie Redmon Fauset and Nella Larsen," *Difference in View: Women and Modernism,* ed. Gabriele Griffin (Bristol, Pa.: Taylor and Francis, 1994), 15–26; Ann DuCille, "Blue Notes on Black Sexuality: Sex and the Texts of Jessie Fauset and Nella Larsen," *Journal of the History of Sexuality* 3, no. 3 (1993): 418–44; T. S. McMillan, "Passing Beyond: The Novels of Nella Larsen," *West Virginia University Philological Papers* 38 (1992): 134–46; Corinne E. Blackmer, "African Masks and the Arts of Passing in Gertrude Stein's 'Melanctha' and Nella Larsen's *Passing,*" *Journal of the History of Sexuality* 4, no. 2 (1993): 230–63; Peter J. Rabinowitz, " 'Betraying the Sender': The Rhetoric and Ethics of Fragile Texts," *Narrative* 2 (October 1994): 201–13; Jacquelyn Y. McLendon, "Self-Representation as Art in the Novels of Nella Larsen," in *Redefining Autobiography in Twentieth-Century Women's Fiction: An Essay Collection,* ed. Janice Morgan and Colette T. Hall (New York: Garland, 1991): 149–68; Judith Butler, "Passing, Queering: Nella Larsen's Psychoanalytic Challenge" in her *Bodies That Matter: On the Discursive Limits of 'Sex'* (London: Routledge, 1993); and Lauren Berlant, "National Brands/National Body: *Imitation of Life,*" *Comparative American Identities: Race, Sex, and Nationality in the Modern Text,* ed. Hortense J. Spillers (New York: Routledge, 1991).

17. Even my characterization of this development as "sudden" and an "explosion" is, of course, problematic, for it fails to unpack the fact that black feminist critics had been examining Larsen and her work for a long time. For example, Thadious Davis began her biography in the 1970s, and Hazel Carby, whose important *Reconstructing Womanhood* was published in 1987 by Oxford University Press, had obviously been at work on the volume several years before the appearance of the Rutgers *Quicksand and Passing.*

18. As one of the most visible examples of such exhortation, see Deborah McDowell, "New Directions for Black Feminist Criticism," in *The New Feminist Criticism,* ed., Elaine Showalter (New York: Pantheon, 1985). By 1997, Ann DuCille was rigorously examining her own ambivalences about the relative flood of

McDowell's ground-breaking introduction to the Rutgers volume, which asserted the multiple interpretive possibilities revealed by reading *Passing* as a text about desire between women, played a large part both in that self-identified black feminist effort and in the general opening out of Larsen criticism.

But I suspect that the expansion of critical interest in Larsen cannot be fully explained by these reasons. I suspect that any attempt at narrating Larsen's rise to mainstream critical visibility must acknowledge that there may have been something else at work here, something so intrinsic to how Larsen's work "looked" in the new edition that perhaps few critics were aware of it when they read the novels and decided they could produce something about them. For in the process of making *Quicksand* and *Passing* into part of the American Women Writers series, the books were not merely reprinted but were, in fact, reset in the font Perpetua, a change that may have made this black woman's text look more stylish to other scholars, perhaps particularly to those who did not identify themselves primarily as "African Americanists." More than mere bibliographic detail or publishing history anecdote, this typographic shift can help explain how some critics have come to understand and articulate Larsen's work, in itself but also in relation to other writers and texts within American literary and cultural history.

When Rutgers reset *Quicksand* and *Passing* in Perpetua (like the rest of the texts included in the American Women Writers series), it was a historically accurate move for Larsen's work, since the type was first used for an edition of *The Passion of the Saints Perpetua and Felicity* published in 1928, precisely when Larsen's novels first appeared in print.[19] Designed by Eric Gill, Perpetua's "strongly sculptured" face "hints at Gill's background as a stonemason," according to Roy Brewer, and provides a font combining strong readability with what Clive Lewis calls a "typeface personality" that now connotes slimness, elegance, and sophistication.[20] And, indeed, that sense of sophistication brings the typographical form of *Passing* more visually in line with its content. For although Knopf chose Caslon to provide both contemporary power and historical depth to modernist cultural production, it can be argued that, by the beginning of the twenty-first century, that which connoted both modernity and history in the 1920s now connotes archaism.[21] In contrast to its Caslon ancestor, Perpetua retrieves *Passing* from the slow, cumbersome bulkiness that Caslon might now evoke for a late twentieth-century reader and suddenly renders the novel more akin to the "sly, slim thing"

white women writing about the previously overlooked or ignored black women's literature that critics such as McDowell pointed out. See DuCille, "The Occult of True Black Womanhood: Critical Demeanor and Black Feminist Studies," in *Female Subjects in Black and White: Race, Psychoanalysis, Feminism,* ed. Elizabeth Abel, Barbara Christian, and Helene Moglen (Berkeley: University of California Press, 1997): 21–56.

19. Roy Brewer, *Eric Gill: The Man Who Loved Letters* (Totowa, N.J.: Rowman and Littlefield, 1973), 47.

20. Ibid., 46. Clive Lewis and Peter Walker, "Typographic Influences on Reading," *British Journal of Psychology* 80 (May 1989): 241–57.

21. As Clive Lewis notes, the "connotative capacity" of a typeface "may undergo modification through historical change and [is] therefore subject to temporal instability." Lewis and Walker, "Typographic Influences," 243.

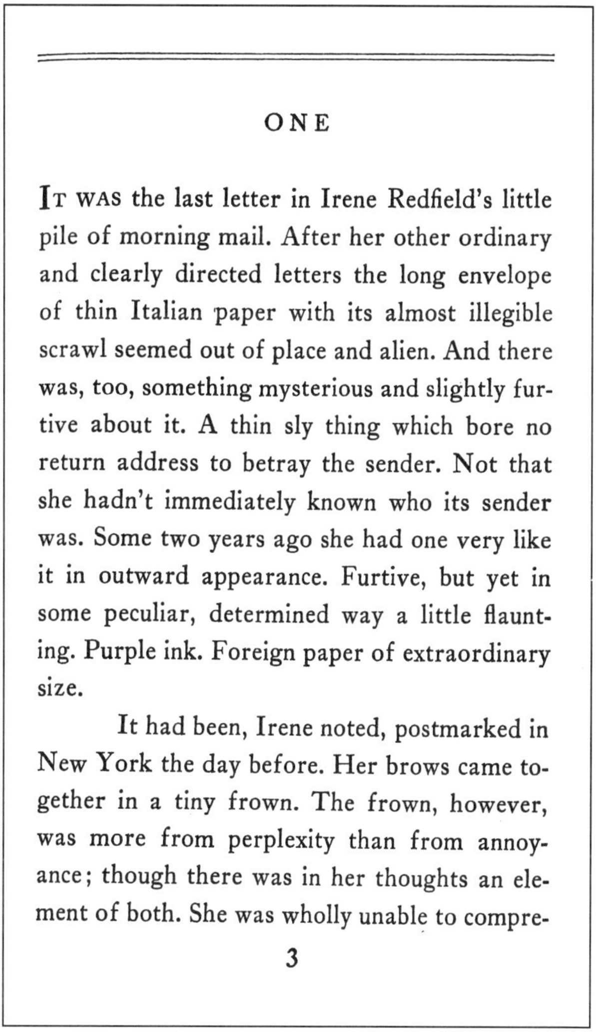

FIGURE 41. The 1929
Knopf edition of Nella
Larsen's *Passing,* set in
Caslon.

ONE

IT WAS the last letter in Irene Redfield's little
pile of morning mail. After her other ordinary
and clearly directed letters the long envelope
of thin Italian paper with its almost illegible
scrawl seemed out of place and alien. And there
was, too, something mysterious and slightly furtive about it. A thin sly thing which bore no
return address to betray the sender. Not that
she hadn't immediately known who its sender
was. Some two years ago she had one very like
it in outward appearance. Furtive, but yet in
some peculiar, determined way a little flaunting. Purple ink. Foreign paper of extraordinary
size.

It had been, Irene noted, postmarked in
New York the day before. Her brows came together in a tiny frown. The frown, however,
was more from perplexity than from annoyance; though there was in her thoughts an element of both. She was wholly unable to compre-

3

that fascinates Irene in the opening paragraph. For example, in the Knopf Caslon
version (and, of course, in the Arno and Negro Universities Press reprints), *Passing* totals 216 pages, and its first chapter, which recounts Irene's memories of
Clare Kendry sparked by the surprise letter, takes eight and one-third pages to
complete. The first paragraph occupies nearly two thirds of a page, not only because of the type itself but because substantial leading adds a prodigious amount
of white space between lines (figure 41). The Collier Caledonia edition, while a
bit more compact and cramped than the Caslon, still spends five pages on the
first chapter.

Set in Perpetua, however, *Passing* encompasses a mere 103 pages while still enjoying substantial margins; the first chapter occupies three pages. Perpetua allows more of *Passing* to fit on each page, thus highlighting the narrative's ambient fluidity and coherency—qualities obscured by the often awkward page breaks that Caslon and Caledonia occasioned. For example, the Caslon edition breaks the novel's first page in the middle of "comprehend" in the sentence: "She was wholly unable to comprehend such an attitude towards danger as she was sure the letter's contents would reveal; and she disliked the idea of opening it and reading it." The Caledonia edition breaks the first page at the same sentence, but in the middle of "contents." On the other hand, the Perpetua edition breaks no words in the transition from first to second page and breaks the fourth paragraph rather than the second one. The overall effect: set in Perpetua, *Passing* is presented as a more coherent, more smoothly flowing narrative than the stop-and-start readings (punctuated by frequent page-turnings) that Caslon and Caledonia invite (figure 42).

But why ought critics to take into account the font in which a text appears? If resetting *Passing* in a font connoting sophisticated modernity to a late twentieth-century readership raises the novel's critical and pedagogical stock, why complicate things by demanding more self-conscious investigation of type fonts' roles in the interpretive enterprise? Why ask for *more* analysis? One possible response to such questions lies in the intertextual relationship between *Passing* and *Nigger Heaven* (1926), a commercially successful novel written by Larsen's friend Carl Van Vechten, a white journalist, music critic, photographer, and all-around bon vivant known as the white master of Harlem's 1920s revels. By the mid-1920s, Van Vechten had become a fixture at many Harlem social functions; he judged drag balls, led white forays to cabarets, and attended and hosted interracial soirees. So ubiquitous was Van Vechten's tall, pale presence around Harlem that Andy Razaf's popular song "Go Harlem" referred to "goin 'inspectin' like Van Vechten."[22] The novel, an ostensibly sociological look at the lives of middle-class Harlemites, sold astoundingly well, enjoyed fourteen printings, and was translated, in the words of one scholar, "in almost every country where American literature circulated."[23]

For many black people, however, including some prominent members of the black intelligentsia, *Nigger Heaven* caused some concern, both because of its title epithet and because the portrait of Harlem street life decorating the book's bourgeois core seemed, to many observers, to recommend a sort of exotic primitivism as essential to American black life. W.E.B. Du Bois, for one, advised readers of the NAACP's *Crisis* to "drop the novel into the grate," and anti–Van Vechten rallies were held around New York (one gathering even burned him in effigy).[24]

22. Bruce Kellner, *Carl Van Vechten and the Irreverent Decades* (Norman: University of Oklahoma Press, 1968), 198.

23. Ibid., 220.

24. Robert F. Worth, "*Nigger Heaven* and the Harlem Renaissance," *African American Review* 29, no. 3 (1995): 463; Lewis, *When Harlem Was in Vogue,* 194.

ONE

IT WAS the last letter in Irene Redfield's little pile of morning mail. After her other ordinary and clearly directed letters the long envelope of thin Italian paper with its almost illegible scrawl seemed out of place and alien. And there was, too, something mysterious and slightly furtive about it. A thin sly thing which bore no return address to betray the sender. Not that she hadn't immediately known who its sender was. Some two years ago she had one very like it in outward appearance. Furtive, but yet in some peculiar, determined way a little flaunting. Purple ink. Foreign paper of extraordinary size.

It had been, Irene noted, postmarked in New York the day before. Her brows came together in a tiny frown. The frown, however, was more from perplexity than from annoyance; though there was in her thoughts an element of both. She was wholly unable to comprehend such an attitude towards danger as she was sure the letter's contents would reveal; and she disliked the idea of opening and reading it.

This, she reflected, was of a piece with all that she knew of Clare Kendry. Stepping always on the edge of danger. Always aware, but not drawing back or turning aside. Certainly not because of any alarms or feeling of outrage on the part of others.

And for a swift moment Irene Redfield seemed to see a pale small girl sitting on a ragged blue sofa, sewing pieces of bright red cloth together, while her drunken father, a tall, powerfully built man, raged threateningly

FIGURE 42. The 1986 Rutgers University Press edition of Nella Larsen's *Quicksand; and, Passing,* set in Perpetua. Reprinted with permission of Rutgers University Press.

As many scholars, however, hurry to point out, not all black intellectuals decried Van Vechten's Harlem novel. James Weldon Johnson and Langston Hughes, for example, publicly and privately supported the book. Nella Larsen also supported her long-time friend amid the public tumult, not only writing Van Vechten letters full of praise and "flattery" about the novel, as Davis notes, but also keeping a collection of *Nigger Heaven* book reviews.[25] Such documented and thus seemingly uncontrovertible flattery has galvanized scholars interested in the era, who have read Larsen's relationship to Van Vechten variously as one of sycophancy and blind worship or one of sincere respect and admiration.[26]

Regardless of one's opinion—pro, con, or ambivalent—about Van Vechten, *Nigger Heaven,* and Larsen's reactions to both of them, it is important to note that such reactions were never and, indeed, could never have been just about an individual [white] man and an individual book. Also at play here was the fact that Van Vechten was one of the most prolific and important Knopf authors. *Nigger Heaven* was published by Knopf, as were ten of his essay collections and all six of his other novels between 1916 and 1930. And Van Vechten was more than just a Knopf author. As Peter Flora has demonstrated, Knopf correspondence archived at the University of Texas reveals that Blanche Knopf depended almost entirely upon Van Vechten's opinion when the press considered black-authored manuscripts. Van Vechten himself remained one of the few channels for an African American–authored work to come to the Knopfs' attention, and black authors who otherwise came to Blanche's attention had to pass Van Vechten's muster anyway.[27]

For Nella Larsen, *Nigger Heaven*'s publication in 1926 came just as she was beginning both to cement her friendship with the increasingly influential Van Vechten and to acknowledge her own writerly ambitions (she was publishing short stories and beginning work on *Quicksand*). Given this intersection of circumstances, any comment she made about *Nigger Heaven* either to Van Vechten or to the acquaintances they conceivably shared would have much riding on it, and not merely good feelings between good friends. Such background complicates, at the very least, Larsen's flattery.

Within *Passing,* however, Larsen appears far more cagey and ambivalent not only about *Nigger Heaven* but also about Van Vechten's rather visible role in promoting and benefiting from Harlem's cultural production. Embedded in Larsen's novel are both a thinly veiled Van Vechten character named Hugh Wentworth

25. Davis, *Nella Larsen,* 213.

26. Hutchinson, for one, belongs to the camp advocating Larsen's admiration and Van Vechten's incontrovertible sincerity. Noting, for example, the shared Scandinavian heritage of each of the two friends, Hutchinson (somewhat astoundingly) asserts: "One of the motives of Larsen's friendship with Van Vechten was apparently to maintain connection with her own ethnic background—with her *mother's* ethnic background. Apparently she felt close to Van Vechten also because he accepted her self-definition. To deny this 'motherless child' her connection with Van Vechten is, in an important sense, to deny her self, her female self, her deep blues" (*Harlem Renaissance,* 445).

27. Peter Flora, "Carl Van Vechten, Blanche Knopf, and the Harlem Renaissance," *Library Chronicle of the University of Texas* 2, no. 4 (1992): 64–83.

and an acknowledgment of the shortcomings of the cross-racial gaze that Van Vechten promulgated so adeptly through his own work and in his advisory capacity for Knopf.[28] Given the African American literary tradition of "signifying" (using words to comment on or critique another text or speaker indirectly), it should not be at all surprising that Larsen could and would use her novel to respond— perhaps critically—both to her influential friend and to his Knopf-sanctioned gatekeeping role while at the same time maintaining their personal friendship. My point in this essay is not to analyze the tenor(s) of that response but to point out that an intertextual link between the two novels would not only be plausible ideologically and theoretically but would also be underscored *visually* by the fact that *Passing* is paratextually commensurable to *Nigger Heaven* (figure 43). Both books were published by Knopf, both were set in Caslon, and thus both books look similarly authoritative and contemporaneous. As a Knopf text set in Caslon, Larsen's novel looks like neither a subordinate nor a supplicant to Van Vechten's.[29] Rather, *Passing* looks equivalent to *Nigger Heaven,* connoting the autonomy of its author's own subjectivity and suggesting that subjectivity's interrelatedness with another across racial and institutional lines.

Yet, since the mid-1980s, the vicissitudes of literary history and publishing technology have functionally conspired to obliterate the visual traces of intertextuality between the two novels. *Nigger Heaven* went out of print during the 1930s and remains so to this day despite some recent efforts to find a new publisher for the book.[30] Scholars must locate a copy of the Knopf edition and thus receive the novel much as it appeared in 1926, as a cog in the Knopf machine. In the process, *Passing's* intertextual connection to the Van Vechten novel with which it was once so closely and obviously associated seems to have been virtually—because visually—elided. The possibility of Larsen's complex response to Van Vechten remains largely hidden, her novel de-historicized, and she herself portrayed by her biographer as under Van Vechten's "spell": a black woman silenced and unable to talk back to the white man who had used his connections to get Knopf to publish her manuscripts.[31]

Thus, it can be argued that once *Quicksand* and *Passing* were set in Perpetua, Larsen (here meaning both the author and her writing) gained a wide and deep critical appeal that has helped her work be discussed more frequently in academic

28. For more detailed analyses of this cross-racial gaze, see Jonathan Weinberg, " 'Boy Crazy': Carl Van Vechten's Queer Collection," *Yale Journal of Criticism* 7 (Fall 1994); James Smalls, "Public Face, Private Thoughts: Fetish, Interracialism, and the Homoerotic in Some Photographs by Carl Van Vechten," *Genders* 25 (1997); and Beth McCoy, "Inspectin' and Collecting: The Scene of Carl Van Vechten," *Genders* 28 (1998).

29. As Megan Benton might observe, however, the extra leading used between the lines of the Knopf *Passing* could be construed as feminizing and thus, perhaps, subordinating the novel to Van Vechten's visually more dense page (such leading would also increase *Passing's* pages and raise the book's price).

30. Marcy Jane Knopf and Elizabeth J. Swanson Goldberg narrate their quest to find a new publisher for Van Vechten's novel in their paper "On Judging Books by Covers: Re-Reading Carl Van Vechten's *Nigger Heaven,*" presented at the 24th Annual Twentieth Century Literature Conference, University of Louisville, 22 February 1996.

31. Davis, *Nella Larsen,* 311.

One

Mary Love closed the door softly behind her, shutting out the brassy blare of the band playing on the floor below, crossed the room, and hesitated before the open window. Unwontedly, she found herself quite ready to cry and she welcomed the salt breeze that blew in from the ocean. When she had consented to spend the week-end with Adora Boniface she had not taken into consideration, she discovered, all that this acceptance would imply. She had met—she should have known that she would meet—people who, on the whole, were not her kind. Adora, in her earlier life on the stage, and in her later rich marriage, had gathered about her—and tolerated—a set which included individuals who would never have been admitted into certain respectable homes in Harlem. There was, for example, Randolph Pettijohn, the Bolito King. Adora had probably invited him because he was rich and good-natured. Mary conceded the affluence and the good-nature. She even tried not to be a snob when she thought of the manner in which he had accumulated his fortune. Hot-dogs, cabarets, even gambling, all served their purposes in life, no doubt, although the game of Numbers was a deliberate—and

[19]

Figure 43. The 1926 Knopf edition of Carl Van Vechten's *Nigger Heaven,* set in Caslon.

journals and appear in new editions (Penguin's Twentieth-Century Classics issued Thadious Davis's edition of *Passing* in 1997) and, conceivably, on classroom syllabi. At the same time, however, Larsen also enters the complexly disturbing realm of the exceptional black woman in the context of the largely "white" American Women Writers Series (according to a flyer issued by Rutgers University Press, Larsen is the series' sole African American author). She becomes a sort of exception among her Harlem Renaissance peers as well, perhaps especially relative to Jessie Redmon Fauset, whose four novels have been reprinted with new covers and new scholarly introductions but with 1920s and 1930s typographies that may look dated to late twentieth-century readers. Rendered typographically sleek and slim rather than clunky and melodramatic, *Passing* (along with *Quicksand*) becomes one of the few texts from the era apparently deemed complex or sophisticated enough to sustain various theoretical readings.

At the very least, it is ironic and curious that Larsen's response to Van Vechten can be rendered typographically silent just as her work enjoys perhaps its widest and most aesthetically appealing distribution. But this is no more curious than other phenomena of the late twentieth century, for what I have speculated here regarding the role of typography in the critical response to Nella Larsen and *Passing* is knit both to larger political structures of technology, economics, and "race" and, concomitantly, what might be called a willed ignorance of how these structures shape everyday academic life. With the release of the long-awaited *Norton Anthology of African American Literature,* for instance, a formidable corpus of work by Americans of African descent has been "nortonized": made, for the first time as a volume, visually comparable with "classic" Norton anthologies already established rather heavily in student backpacks.

This visual homogenization is accomplished through standardized paratextual devices such as biographical/historical prefaces, footnotes, and the anthologies' venerable Electra and Bernhard Modern typefaces. The appearance of this particular volume in the always-changing Norton series might seem to be racial harmony's ne plus ultra, for on any given shelf, such authors as June Jordan, Henry Highland Garnet, and Ed Bullins sit with William Shakespeare, who, to paraphrase W.E.B. Du Bois, winces not.[32]

Yet as the good and necessary thing that is the *Norton Anthology of African American Literature* is both celebrated and sold in the academic marketplace, and as Nella Larsen's work becomes increasingly woven into what is called mainstream American critical discourse, it is imperative to note that these discrete and inclusive phenomena occur amid a critical reevaluation of a certain kind of liberal integration, one assuming that people of color benefit as a whole when a few join the nation's white majority. Voices within and without the academy continue to articulate long-held suspicions that the tools of this kind of integration have been produced by and have resulted in what Robyn Wiegman has called "a vapid fetishization of the visible," where the sight of putatively diversified institutions, commercials, and, for that matter, bookshelves is proffered as a substitute for substantive, structural political change.[33]

This reevaluation of integration manifests itself in ways ranging from the work of Critical Race Theory, an influential branch of legal studies challenging the notion that legal theory and praxis are "color-blind," to battles over school busing

32. Du Bois, *Souls,* 102.
33. Robyn Wiegman, *American Anatomies: Theorizing Race and Gender* (Durham: Duke University Press, 1995).

in which black parents question the need to have their children bused to white schools.[34] Within these struggles, enacted in popular media and academic journals as well as around the water cooler, people of color challenge what has now become a white norm: the assumption that "integration" on these terms and these terms only is what the nation's minority populations want, or *should* want. As Aída Hurtado observes, "The notion that people of Color may have a different 'list' of what a good life is, or what a good person is . . . is not acknowledged in a paradigm in which whiteness reigns supreme."[35]

I must emphasize here that such reevaluations of integration do not reject the possibility or desirability of a truly integrated United States, but they do underscore the need to acknowledge both the gains *and* the losses accrued as the country moved from racial segregation de jure to that particular limited vision of integration de jure. For example, Americans of African descent are no longer prevented by law from entering "white" public spaces, but the advent of such access coincided with the demolition of black communities' economic power centers by such "neutral" moves as the Federal Highway Act of 1956, which bisected black neighborhoods in order to move white, middle-class commuters to and from urban employment and increasingly suburban domiciles.

It may seem a great distance between such bread-and-butter economic issues regarding integration and the apparently more esoteric concerns I have related here regarding typeface. Yet the critical questions remain quite similar: if devices such as typography help to usher Larsen's work into the predominantly white American Women Writers series and to add "African American literature" to the Norton anthology series, what are the gains in such moves? What are the losses? What could possibly be "lost" if, presumably, through the access provided by the Norton name and "look," more American readers are exposed to a wide range of African American writers, traditions, techniques, and subject matters? What could possibly be lost if Larsen's, book through the intervention of Perpetua, becomes distanced from its link with a novel whose title and author alone will cause difficulty in the classroom?

In two articles responding to the *Norton Anthology of African American Literature*'s appearance, Kevin Meehan (1997) and William Lyne (1996) deal specifically with the politics of anthologization and regularization and thus implicitly with the politics of both integration and typography. Meehan (who engages the *Norton* specifically) and Lyne (who surveys generally what happens when African American authors get anthologized) suggest that the various processes of editing down African American literature to fit in anthologies at the end of the twentieth

34. See, for example, Kimberlé Crenshaw, Neil Gotanda, Gary Peller, and Kendall Thomas, eds., *Critical Race Theory: The Key Writings That Formed the Movement* (New York: New Press, 1995), and Richard Delgado, ed., *Critical Race Theory: The Cutting Edge* (Temple University Press, 1995).
35. Aída Hurtado, *The Color of Privilege: Three Blasphemies on Race and Feminism* (Ann Arbor: University of Michigan Press, 1996): 141.

century share one element: a drive to mute critiques of political structures in favor of works dealing with individualized and belletristic concerns.[36]

Though Meehan and Lyne do not deal specifically with typography, its presence can—and indeed ought to—easily be read into their critiques. Extending their arguments, I would like to suggest that *in addition* to modernizing African American texts and thus making them possibly more appealing to contemporary readers, typographical changes that bring volumes such as the Rutgers *Passing* and the *Norton Anthology of African American Literature* into the visual mainstream can also functionally mute structural critique. When typography, along with other tools, is used to normalize the physical presence of African American literature, the sense of the works themselves as artifacts with both individual and cumulative force and aesthetic and political context can be lost, or at least diluted. The type fonts that say "Norton" to student and professorial eyes, for example, can tempt those same eyes to render the condition of African Americans "the same as" that of all other groups currently featured in Norton anthologies: British writers, American writers, poets, and women writers. Such moves are disturbingly similar to narratives currently circulating in American culture at large as a force to dismantle the Civil Rights struggle's hard-won gains. These narratives declare that African Americans now have the "same" opportunities as white Americans, and therefore (in a curious logic), white Americans now suffer "the same as" black Americans (in my classrooms, I have taken to characterizing this homogenizing logic as "the Great Equals Sign [=]"). And typography can shift *Passing* from its status as a very public response to Carl Van Vechten and the institutional power he wielded through Knopf to a series text that, in a sort of cosmetic sisterhood, is putatively "the same as" other recovered texts by white women writers, such as "Behind a Mask," by Louisa May Alcott.[37]

To note these possible links between publishing technologies and what can be read as an anxious drive for sameness is not to recommend that editors and anthologists should necessarily take the route of the Schomburg Library of Nineteenth-Century Black Women Writers, which, under the editorship of Henry Louis Gates Jr. (also one of the *Norton*'s primary editors), has apparently chosen to represent its books as a series while still retaining the nineteenth-century typography of the works' original forms. Nor should any one typographical route necessarily stand as preferable to another. Indeed, as Theodore O. Mason has pointed out in his article on the *Norton Anthology of African American*

36. William Lyne, "Tiger Teeth around Their Neck: The Cultural Logic of the Canonization of African American Literature," *Arizona Quarterly* 52 (Autumn 1996): 99–125; Kevin Meehan, "Spiking Canons," *The Nation,* 12 May 1997: 42–46. I should note that Lyne and Meehan are merely two of the most recent critics of canon formation and African American literature. As Meehan himself observes, anthologies have long been important political and aesthetic tools for black writers, and many writers, such as Ishmael Reed, have been both agents in and critics of the process of anthologization (43).

37. This short story is found in the American Women Writers series volume *Alternative Alcott,* edited by Elaine Showalter.

Literature, rather than finding one technically correct way of packaging and reproducing culture in an attempt to avoid the dilemmas I have pointed out here,
"we might do well to imagine that in the case of an anthology [or, indeed, any
text] we have . . . more likely set the stage for the work that needs to be done in
understanding the conflicts comprising our history."[38]

I suggest, therefore, that teachers, students, editors, and other participants in
the academic economy examine and articulate the ways that typography informs
how meaning is constructed, for to do so is to expand—not shut down—the
rigorous conversations necessary to understand, as Mason says, "the conflicts
comprising our history." For example, to attend consciously to typography in
particular and the paratext in general can help students both to examine the varying connotations that differently typed editions communicate and to critically
interrogate what is at stake in a prohibitive but roundly impossible adage such as
"Don't judge a book by its cover." Students might even be able to interrogate
what is at stake in the dominant idea of "color blindness," a paradoxical desire to
neutralize visible identity categories while at the same time preserving the socio-
political structures based on those very categories. To attend to typography's ostensible invisible neutrality may be to expose that which is invested in maintaining the appearance of invisible neutrality.

38. Theodore O. Mason, "The African-American Anthology: Mapping the Territory, Taking the National Census, Building the Museum," *American Literary History* 10 (Spring 1998).

Bridge Four

Like Beth McCoy in the preceding essay, Steven R. Price examines how the choice of type fonts affects how a text is read. Though separated by race, gender, and the time period in which they wrote, Nella Larsen and Samuel Richardson are nonetheless typographically linked by the Caslon type font—the type used for the Knopf first edition of Larsen's *Passing* (1929) and the primary type used for each of the five editions of *Clarissa* (1748–59) that Richardson printed in his lifetime.

As McCoy and Price both note, Caslon was not without limitations. For Larsen, the use of Caslon made for a text that readers over the course of decades came to view as sluggish and cumbersome. For Richardson, Caslon's generic appearance compromised epistolary verisimilitude, reminding readers that they were reading a work of fiction rather than transcripts of real letters—a significant distinction for an author concerned with producing a didactic text and not a romantic story. Consequently, both *Passing* and *Clarissa* underwent typeface revisions. Larsen's novel was completely reset in 1986 by Rutgers University Press in Perpetua, creating a more accessible text but also one that, McCoy argues, marginalizes and even conceals the novel's important commentary on the Harlem Renaissance. Richardson more subtly juxtaposed Caslon with typographic anomalies, including unconventional use of the pica roman type font and the introduction of a rare script font, thereby visually suggesting the handwritten manuscripts upon which the novel's letters are supposedly based.

Richardson occupied a rare position in the publishing process, however. Unlike most authors, including Nella Larsen and most of his own contemporaries, he controlled all facets of *Clarissa*'s production. As master printer as well as author, Richardson created not only the words on the page but the visual appearance of the page itself; he was able to manipulate typeface selections to accentuate his characterization and plot. Decisions of composition, literary and typographic—whether or not to intensify Lovelace's evilness, to restore a deleted passage, or to use the pica roman or roman small capitals, for example—were all made by Richardson himself. He thus ensured that his epistolary novels would not be altered by compositors' errors, house formatting rules, a publisher's whim, or other kinds of unsolicited typographic mediation. Price contends that reading Richardson's *Clarissa*, then, requires reading the typography as well as the words on the page.

Chapter Five

The Autograph Manuscript in Print: Samuel Richardson's Type Font Manipulation in *Clarissa*

STEVEN R. PRICE

Samuel Richardson (1689–1761), remembered today as an eighteenth-century epistolary novelist, began his career not as an author but as a master printer. Operating a successful shop in London's Salisbury Court during the 1730s and 1740s, Richardson produced a wide range of texts, including financially lucrative papers for the House of Lords and the House of Commons as well as the *Philosophical Transactions* for the Royal Society. Additionally, Richardson's press printed periodicals such as the *Daily Journal* and the *Plain Dealer,* nonfiction works by Daniel Defoe, and a diverse collection of literary works, including Susannah Centlivre's *Gamester,* Thomas Morell's *Canterbury Tales of Chaucer,* and an edition of Jonathan Swift's *Gulliver's Travels.* When Richardson himself began writing in 1734, he did so from a book-trade perspective, compiling (and printing) advice for young printers under the title *The Apprentice's Vade Mecum.*[1]

As a printer, Richardson understood that typographical features can present visual, nonlinguistic meaning that supplements the text's words. For instance, writing to his friend Edward Young in 1754 about a series of sermons Young wished to print, Richardson says of the content, "I see nothing . . . to alter in your dedication." But concerning the material form of the sermons, Richardson then questions, "Print it, you say; but in what size, page, type, &c.?"[2] To ensure that the physical appearance of the work complements the intended meaning, Richardson calls on Young to revise the material details of his sermons. As an author of fiction, Richardson addressed similar typographical concerns, none more important to the content of his epistolary novels than his manipulation of type fonts in *Clarissa; or, The History of a Young Lady.* Richardson published five separate, and in many ways distinct, editions of *Clarissa* during his lifetime, beginning with the first edition of 1747–48 in three installments. However, the

---

1. For the most complete list to date of the works printed by Samuel Richardson, see William Merritt Sale Jr., *Samuel Richardson: Master Printer* (Ithaca: Cornell University Press, 1950), 145–250.
2. *The Correspondence of Edward Young, 1683–1765,* ed. Henry Pettit (Oxford: Clarendon Press, 1971), 405.

rare third edition of 1751—as few as a dozen copies remain extant—is the most significant in terms of materiality and type fonts.[3]

In addition to making hundreds of alterations to the third edition linguistic text,[4] ranging from changes in punctuation and single words to the addition of entire letters, Richardson also revises and accentuates the novel's material features. For instance, he announces in his "Preface" to the third edition that type font sizes have been increased, making the text more accessible to "elderly readers, and . . . some who have weak Eyes."[5] Additionally, Richardson notes in the "Preface" that "it has been thought fit to restore many Passages, and several Letters, which were omitted in the former [editions] merely for shortening sake."[6] He marks the restorations with marginal bullets, or what he refers to as "Full-points,"[7] which visually suggest that the third edition text is definitive and complete. (The marginal bullets are used only in the 1751 third edition.) Finally, Richardson reintroduces into the third edition the complete text of Elizabeth Carter's poem "Ode to Wisdom" and makes significant changes to the engraved musical plate that accompanies the poem.

Using the 1751 third edition of *Clarissa* as my primary text, I will explore the significance that Richardson's role as printer plays in shaping the novel's meaning. Because Richardson functions as both printer and author, a thorough reading of *Clarissa* requires evaluation of its material/textual as well as linguistic features.[8]

3. Samuel Richardson, *Clarissa; or, The History of a Young Lady* (1751), ed. Florian Stuber, Margaret Anne Doody, and Jim Springer Borck, 3d ed., 8 vols. (facsimile rpt; New York: AMS Press, 1990). Future references to *Clarissa* are from this edition and are cited by volume and page number.

For convincing arguments in favor of the third edition as copy-text for scholarly editions, see: Florian Stuber, "On Original and Final Intentions, or Can There Be an Authoritative *Clarissa*?" *TEXT: Transactions of the Society for Textual Scholarship* 2 (1985): 229–44; Stuber, "Introduction: Text, Writer, Reader, World," 1:1–43; and Jim Springer Borck, "Composed in Tears: The *Clarissa* Project," *Studies in the Novel*, special issue, *Editing Novels and Novelists Now* 27 (1995): 341–50.

The third edition of *Clarissa* is particularly difficult to find in North America. The National Union Catalogue lists copies at the Yale Beinecke Library (imperfect) and at the University of Vancouver. Other copies can be found in the Berg Collection of the New York Public Library and in the W. Hugh Peal Collection of the University of Kentucky (this copy, apparently owned by Mirabeau, was used by AMS Press for its facsimile reproduction). See O. M. Brack Jr., "*Clarissa*'s Bibliography: Problems and Challenges. A Bibliographical Essay," in *Letters and Passages Restored,* vol. 2 of *Richardson's Published Commentary on* Clarissa, *1747–1765*, ed. Florian Stuber, Margaret Anne Doody, Jim Springer Borck, and Thomas Keymer, 3 vols. (London: Pickering & Chatto, 1998), 308; Florian Stuber, "Introduction: Text, Writer, Reader, World," in *Clarissa*, 1:1.

4. For a description of Richardson's changes to the third edition, see Shirley Van Marter, "Richardson's Revisions of *Clarissa* in the Third and Fourth Editions," *Studies in Bibliography* 28 (1975): 119–52.

5. 1:ix.

6. Ibid.

7. Ibid.

8. In basing my literary analysis on the examination of material/textual features, I am following the lead of a number of textual critics, including: Jerome J. McGann, *A Critique of Modern Textual Criticism* (Chicago: University of Chicago Press, 1983); McGann, "The Monks and the Giants: Textual and Bibliographical Studies and the Interpretation of Literary Works," in *Textual Criticism and Literary Interpretation*, ed. Jerome J. McGann (Chicago: University of Chicago Press, 1985), 180–99; D. F. McKenzie, *Bibliography and the Sociology of Texts,* The Panizzi Lectures 1985 (London: The British Library, 1986), especially 1–21; Peter L. Shillingsburg, "Text as Matter, Concept, and Action," *Studies in Bibliography* 44 (1991): 31–82; and Shillingsburg, "An Inquiry into the Social Status of Texts and Modes of Textual Criticism," *Studies in Bibliography* 42 (1989): 55–79.

The type font for Richardson is more than a practical tool for imprinting a word on a leaf of paper. Instead, his diversified use of type fonts allows the printer/author to build characterization visually. Additionally, by manipulating type fonts and exploiting typographical conventions, Richardson embellishes the formal realism of his novel. At significant moments throughout the 3,000 pages of *Clarissa,* he creates what I will call the "autograph manuscript in print." That is, given the technological limits of an eighteenth-century print house, Richardson produces typeset pages that visually suggest autograph, handwritten manuscripts of familiar letters. In constructing these metaphoric and metonymic representations, he builds the credibility of his novel's didactic message by raising the possibility that the letters in *Clarissa* could be based on authentic documents.

Three premises inform my typographical reading of *Clarissa*'s third edition. First, Richardson's atypical role in producing *Clarissa* must be acknowledged. Functioning as both author and master printer, Richardson worked in conjunction with, rather than in opposition to, the publishing institution. Thus, unlike most eighteenth-century novelists who lost not only copyrights but also personal control over their texts once printed, he coordinated all facets of *Clarissa*'s production, from creating the words on the page to formatting the pages themselves. With the exception of one volume of the second edition for which he employed two other presses,[9] Richardson oversaw and closely monitored the printing of *Clarissa* in his own shop. He read proofs carefully, and at least once, he stopped his press to correct an error found in the third volume of the first edition.[10] Consequently, typographical gestures in *Clarissa* cannot be dismissed as nonauthorial intrusions of a compositor or print house. Instead, the type fonts chosen by Richardson the printer function as authorial signs that subtly yet significantly influence the meaning of his novel.

Second, the fictional context of *Clarissa* as a text constructed from extant, real letters encourages the reading of material details. Richardson begins promoting his novel's verisimilitude on the third edition title page (figure 44),[11] where he proclaims "CLARISSA" as his primary subject, emphasizing his heroine's name with Caslon double pica roman capitals. In the subtitle, Richardson places his text within the respected and common, for the eighteenth century, genre of a "HISTORY," accentuating the term with the slightly smaller great primer roman capitals often reserved for the primary title and with an exaggerated justification that extends the term to both the left and right margins of the duodecimo page. He builds the credibility of his ostensible historical text with an explanatory note, set in the less emphatic but nonetheless readable pica roman type, announcing that he bases the novel's letters on "Original Manuscripts." The biographical,

9. William Merritt Sale Jr., *Samuel Richardson: A Bibliographical Record of His Literary Career with Historical Notes* (New Haven: Yale University Press, 1936), 53; Brack, "Clarissa's Bibliography," 315.

10. Sale, *Bibliographical Record,* 46.

11. All figures are from Samuel Richardson, *Clarissa; or, The History of a Young Lady,* 3d ed., 8 vols. (London: S. Richardson, 1751), Mirabeau Copy, W. Hugh Peal Collection, University of Kentucky Libraries.

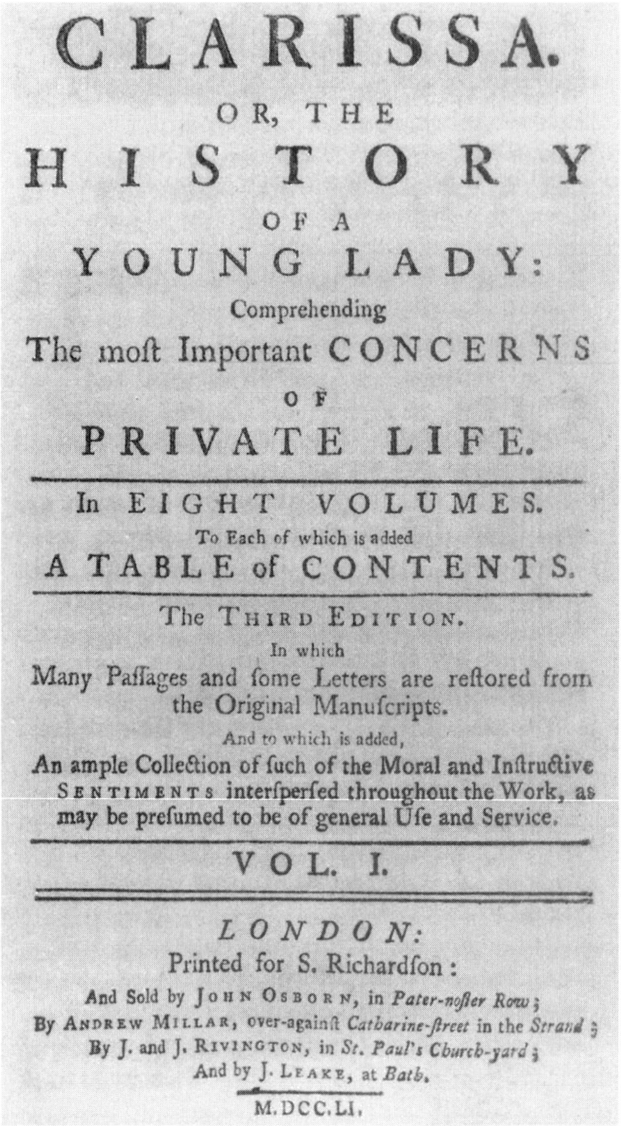
CLARISSA.
OR, THE
HISTORY
OF A
YOUNG LADY:
Comprehending
The moſt Important CONCERNS
OF
PRIVATE LIFE.

In EIGHT VOLUMES.
To Each of which is added
A TABLE of CONTENTS.

The THIRD EDITION.
In which
Many Paſſages and ſome Letters are reſtored from the Original Manuſcripts.
And to which is added,
An ample Collection of ſuch of the Moral and Inſtructive SENTIMENTS interſperſed throughout the Work, as may be preſumed to be of general Uſe and Service.

VOL. I.

LONDON:
Printed for S. Richardſon:
And Sold by JOHN OSBORN, in *Pater-noſter Row*;
By ANDREW MILLAR, over-againſt *Catharine-ſtreet* in the *Strand*;
By J. and J. RIVINGTON, in *St. Paul's Church-yard*;
And by J. LEAKE, at *Bath*.
M.DCC.LI.

FIGURE 44. Title page of Samuel Richardson's *Clarissa; or, The History of a Young Lady,* third edition (1751).

historical narrative based on a recovered manuscript was a common motif in the eighteenth-century novel—*Moll Flanders,* for instance, is purportedly "*Written from her own* MEMORANDUMS," and the first letter in *Humphry Clinker* explains that "the private correspondence of persons still living" will serve as copy-text.[12]

12. Daniel Defoe, *The Fortunes and Misfortunes of the Famous Moll Flanders* (London, 1722), ed. G. A. Starr, (Oxford: Oxford University Press, 1990), first edition title page; Tobias Smollett, *The Expedition of Humphry Clinker* (London, 1771), intro. and notes Thomas R. Preston, textual ed. O. M. Brack Jr. (Athens: University of Georgia Press, 1990), 12.

Unlike Defoe and Smollett, however, Richardson expands the manuscript motif within the novel itself. In *Clarissa,* he includes frequent descriptions of material details which invoke images of the "Original" autograph letters: for instance, Anna Howe describes a note in Clarissa's memorandum book as "written on the extreme edge of the paper"; Clarissa mentions her "trembling pen" following the rape, and her final packet of letters includes "three seals of black wax"; and other letters are distinguished for being "torn in two pieces," "burnt," "creased and rumpled," or "unopened."[13] A zealous letter writer himself, Richardson understood the meaning behind material details, and he frequently asks readers to examine not only the words on his printed pages but also the manuscript features that the words suggest.

Richardson also builds the verisimilitude of the manuscript motif by presenting *Clarissa* as an edited, rather than authored, text. Although he deletes the 1747 first edition title page statement "*Published by the* EDITOR *of* PAMELA" from the third edition title page, he nonetheless builds an editorial apparatus within the third edition. Any additions of at least one full line in length are marked with marginal bullets or "Full-points" (for an example of the editorial apparatus, see figure 49). By noting the supposed restorations,[14] Richardson provides readers with visual cues that extend the autograph manuscript motif. Through the marginal bullets, he implies that he, as editor, consults the manuscripts of Clarissa's historical letters and accepts them as the copy-text for his new edition. After collating the handwritten manuscripts with the first and second editions, where passages had been "omitted . . . merely for shortening sake," Richardson restores the lost passages to the definitive third edition. *Clarissa,* of course, is a fictional text created by an author. However, Richardson's extended gesture toward the possibility of "Original Manuscripts" helps create the formal realism that lends credibility and didactic potential to his novel.

The third premise pertains to the ineffectiveness of Richardson's primary type font—Caslon's pica roman—for presenting the realistic, manuscript-based letters described on the third edition title page. While Caslon's pica roman type font was well received in the mid-eighteenth century, the face struck readers as more practical than aesthetically memorable. For instance, in *The Printer's Grammar* (1755), John Smith offers utilitarian praise for the roman face in general, citing its "true, or rather good shape" and its "uniformity."[15] Today, the roman type

13. 8:222; 7:334; 7:355; 2:88; 3:191; 3:174; 2:88.

14. There is long-standing disagreement over the validity of Richardson's restorations to the third edition. Mark Kinkead-Weekes argues that the additions are not restorations at all, but instead new passages written by the author. T. C. Duncan Eaves and Ben D. Kimpel assert that many of the restorations can be traced back to Richardson's nonextant manuscripts which he circulated among his friends. More than likely, the truth lies somewhere between the two arguments, as Richardson clearly creates some new passages in reaction to the misinterpretations of his readers. See Mark Kinkead-Weekes, "*Clarissa* Restored?" *Review of English Studies* 10 (1959): 156–71, and T. C. Duncan Eaves and Ben D. Kimpel, "The Composition of *Clarissa* and Its Revision before Publication," *PMLA* 83 (1968): 416–28.

15. John Smith, *The Printer's Grammar* (London, 1755), English Bibliographical Sources, Series 3: Printer's Manuals (London: Gregg Press, 1965), 5.

font retains its reputation for being solid though uninspired; Philip Gaskell, for example, specifically describes Caslon's roman faces as "without serious blemish, but also without much life; they were tasteful, subdued, and rather dull."[16] Richardson may have appreciated the consistency and readability of the pica roman type font when printing papers for the House of Commons or the Royal Society. However, for transcriptions of purported autograph manuscripts, the generic appearance of the roman type font undermines the unique, personal features typically found in handwritten letters. In effect, the print form reminds readers that *Clarissa* is a work of fiction, thus compromising the epistolary verisimilitude Richardson develops on the third edition title page, in the characters' repeated references to the materiality of their letters, and through his own editorial apparatus. Richardson overcomes this print limitation by disrupting the uniformity of the roman face.

In *Clarissa,* Richardson sets type fonts with two basic strategies that allow him to exploit the manuscript motif announced on the third edition title page. First, he modifies the standard pica roman line to create visually unique pages which distinguish each letter writer. Four brief examples will illustrate. In Clarissa's letter written immediately after her rape, commonly referred to as Mad Paper X,[17] Richardson sets three passages of small pica roman type with a slanted orientation that upsets the conventional symmetry of the printed page (figure 45). In the letters of John Belford, the reformed rake who befriends Clarissa, Richardson frequently uses small roman capitals to mark his poignant, indirect quotations (figure 46). In the letters of Robert Lovelace, the rake who rapes Clarissa, Richardson disrupts the page with excessive and inconsistently constructed em dashes, randomly set as two (--), three (---), five (-----), and six hyphens (------), and also as a conventional em dash (—), two linked em dashes (——), and three linked em dashes (———) (for a number of the variations, see figures 47 and 48). Finally, in the three letters of the presumptuous Reverend Elias Brand (a precursor to Jane Austen's Mr. Collins), Richardson sets an inordinate number of words in italic letters (figure 49). Although Brand correctly defines excessive underlining or italics as the typographical equivalent of "call[ing] his readers *fools,*" he dismisses his own caution, ignorantly praising his absurd display as "a page distinguished by *different characters,* as a *verdant field* overspread with *butter-flowers* and *daisies,* and other summer-flowers."[18]

In each of the four examples, Richardson undermines the continuity and consistency of the pica roman line by breaking a different eighteenth-century printing convention. For instance, Clarissa's Mad Paper X, by forcing readers to turn the book and realign the page, and to contemplate the meaning of skewed lines, violates the printer's tenet that a properly set page should simplify the reading

16. Philip Gaskell, *A New Introduction to Bibliography* (New York: Oxford University Press, 1972), 23.
17. 5:308.
18. 7:386; 7:387.

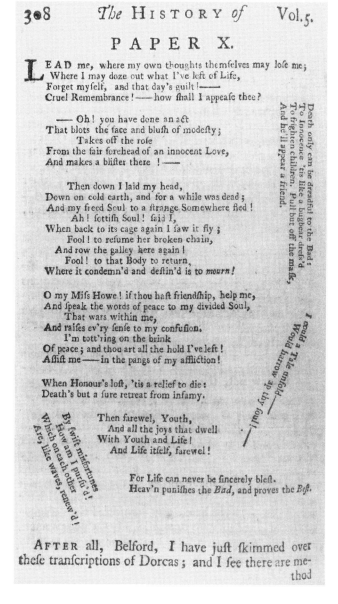

FIGURE 45.
Clarissa; or, The History of a Young Lady, third edition (1751), volume 5, page 308, "Paper X."

process. Joseph Moxon, for instance, in his *Mechanick Exercises on the Whole Art of Printing* (1683–84), specifies that a printed work should "shew graceful to the Eye, and [be] pleasant in Reading."[19] In the letters of Belford, Lovelace, and Brand, Richardson interrupts the pica roman lines with typographical anomalies,

19. Joseph Moxon, *Mechanick Exercises on the Whole Art of Printing* (London, 1683–84), ed. Herbert Davis and Harry Carter (London: Oxford University Press, 1958), 211.

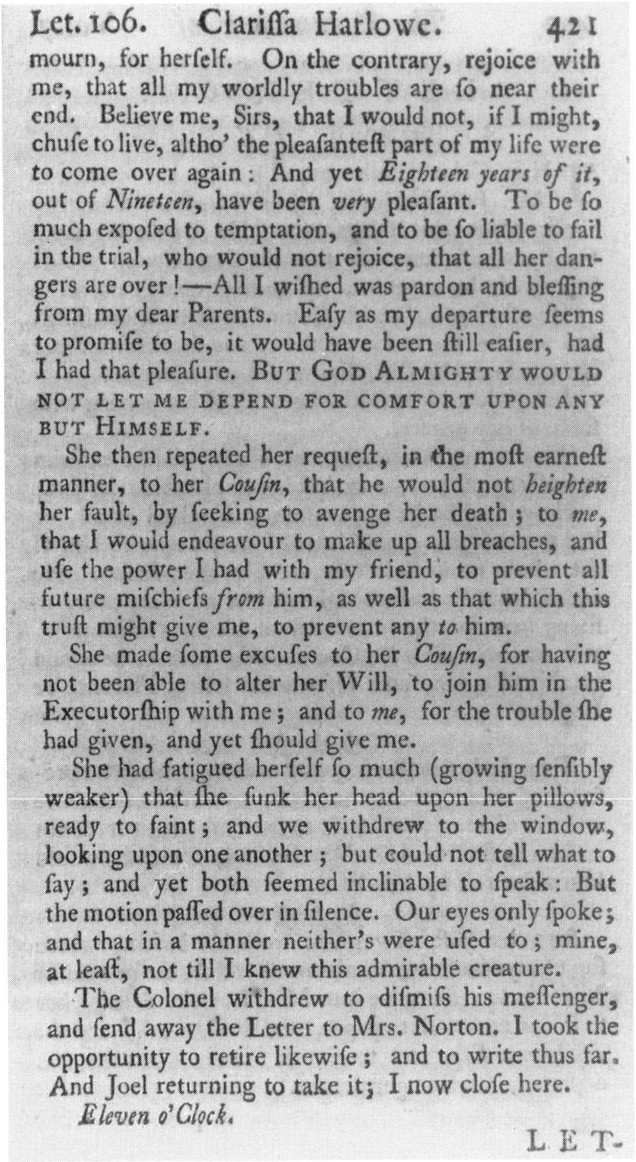

> Lct. 106.   Clariſſa Harlowe.   421
>
> mourn, for herſelf. On the contrary, rejoice with
> me, that all my worldly troubles are ſo near their
> end. Believe me, Sirs, that I would not, if I might,
> chuſe to live, altho' the pleaſanteſt part of my life were
> to come over again : And yet *Eighteen years of it,*
> out of *Nineteen,* have been *very* pleaſant. To be ſo
> much expoſed to temptation, and to be ſo liable to fail
> in the trial, who would not rejoice, that all her dan-
> gers are over !——All I wiſhed was pardon and bleſſing
> from my dear Parents. Eaſy as my departure ſeems
> to promiſe to be, it would have been ſtill eaſier, had
> I had that pleaſure. BUT GOD ALMIGHTY WOULD
> NOT LET ME DEPEND FOR COMFORT UPON ANY
> BUT HIMSELF.
>
>   She then repeated her requeſt, in the moſt earneſt
> manner, to her *Couſin,* that he would not *heighten*
> her fault, by ſeeking to avenge her death ; to *me,*
> that I would endeavour to make up all breaches, and
> uſe the power I had with my friend, to prevent all
> future miſchiefs *from* him, as well as that which this
> truſt might give me, to prevent any *to* him.
>
>   She made ſome excuſes to her *Couſin,* for having
> not been able to alter her Will, to join him in the
> Executorſhip with me ; and to *me,* for the trouble ſhe
> had given, and yet ſhould give me.
>
>   She had fatigued herſelf ſo much (growing ſenſibly
> weaker) that ſhe ſunk her head upon her pillows,
> ready to faint ; and we withdrew to the window,
> looking upon one another ; but could not tell what to
> ſay ; and yet both ſeemed inclinable to ſpeak : But
> the motion paſſed over in ſilence. Our eyes only ſpoke ;
> and that in a manner neither's were uſed to ; mine,
> at leaſt, not till I knew this admirable creature.
>
>   The Colonel withdrew to diſmiſs his meſſenger,
> and ſend away the Letter to Mrs. Norton. I took the
> opportunity to retire likewiſe ; and to write thus far.
> And Joel returning to take it ; I now cloſe here.
>   *Eleven o' Clock.*
>   L E T-

FIGURE 46. *Clarissa; or, The History of a Young Lady,* third edition (1751), volume 7, page 421. Note Richardson's use of small roman capitals at the end of the first paragraph.

often using them to excess. For instance, Moxon categorizes Belford's small capitals as one of the "seldomist used" type fonts from the compositor's upper box—
in the same auxiliary category as "Astronomical Signs"; by 1755, Smith finds the
small capitals more common but nevertheless discourages their use, calling them
"perplexing to the reader."[20] Lovelace's extensive use of the em dash, despite the

20. Ibid., 204; Smith, *Printer's Grammar,* 53.

FIGURE 47.
*Clarissa; or, The
History of a Young
Lady,* third
edition (1751),
volume 5, page
324. Note
Richardson's use
of em dashes.

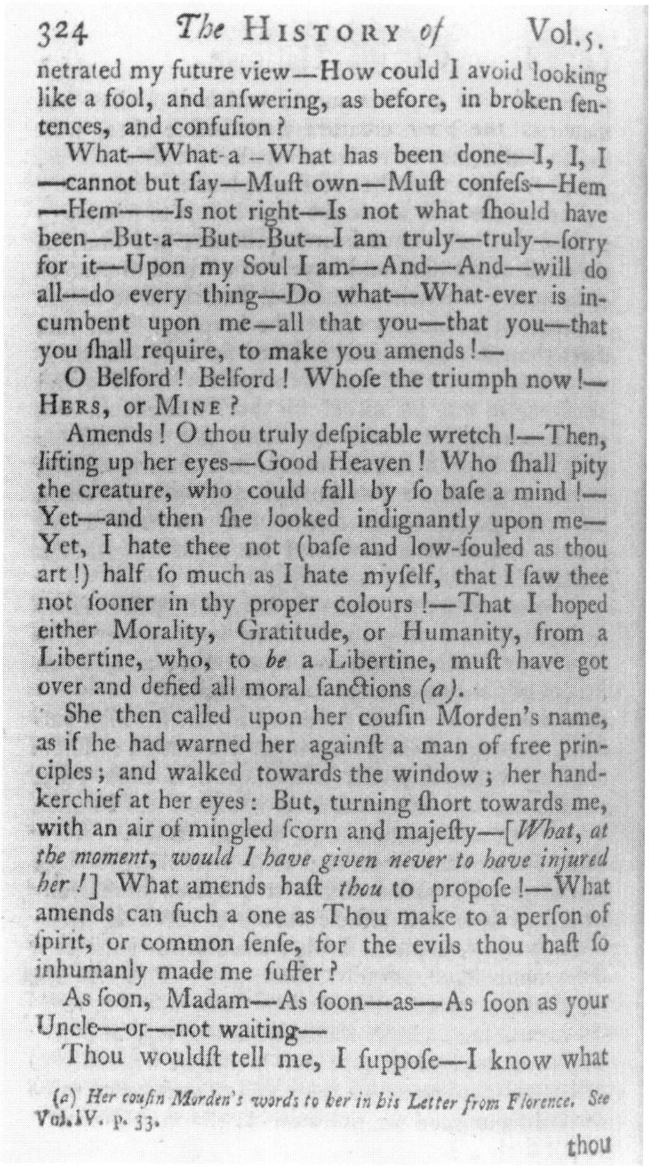

324   *The* HISTORY *of*   Vol. 5.

netrated my future view—How could I avoid looking
like a fool, and anfwering, as before, in broken fen-
tences, and confufion?

What—What-a—What has been done—I, I, I
—cannot but fay—Muft own—Muft confefs—Hem
—Hem——Is not right—Is not what fhould have
been—But-a—But—But—I am truly—truly—forry
for it—Upon my Soul I am—And—And—will do
all—do every thing—Do what—What-ever is in-
cumbent upon me—all that you—that you—that
you fhall require, to make you amends!—

O Belford! Belford! Whofe the triumph now!—
HERS, or MINE?

Amends! O thou truly defpicable wretch!—Then,
lifting up her eyes—Good Heaven! Who fhall pity
the creature, who could fall by fo bafe a mind!—
Yet—and then fhe looked indignantly upon me—
Yet, I hate thee not (bafe and low-fouled as thou
art!) half fo much as I hate myfelf, that I faw thee
not fooner in thy proper colours!—That I hoped
either Morality, Gratitude, or Humanity, from a
Libertine, who, to *be* a Libertine, muft have got
over and defied all moral fanctions *(a)*.

She then called upon her coufin Morden's name,
as if he had warned her againft a man of free principles; and walked towards the window; her hand-
kerchief at her eyes: But, turning fhort towards me,
with an air of mingled fcorn and majefty—[*What, at
the moment, would I have given never to have injured
her!*] What amends haft *thou* to propofe!—What
amends can fuch a one as Thou make to a perfon of
fpirit, or common fenfe, for the evils thou haft fo
inhumanly made me fuffer?

As foon, Madam—As foon—as—As foon as your
Uncle—or—not waiting—

Thou wouldft tell me, I fuppofe—I know what

(a) Her coufin Morden's words to her in his Letter from Florence. See
Vol. IV. p. 33.

thou

sign's prominence in Laurence Sterne's *Tristam Shandy* (1760–67), also violated
standard usage. Neither Moxon nor Smith identifies the dash as a primary printer's mark intended for extended use; and popular eighteenth-century stylebooks,
such as John Hill's *Young Secretary's Guide* (London, 1698), William Bradford's
Secretary's Guide (Philadelphia, 1737), and Hugh Blair's *Lectures on Rhetoric and
Belles Lettres* (London, 1783), do not mention the dash as an acceptable pointing

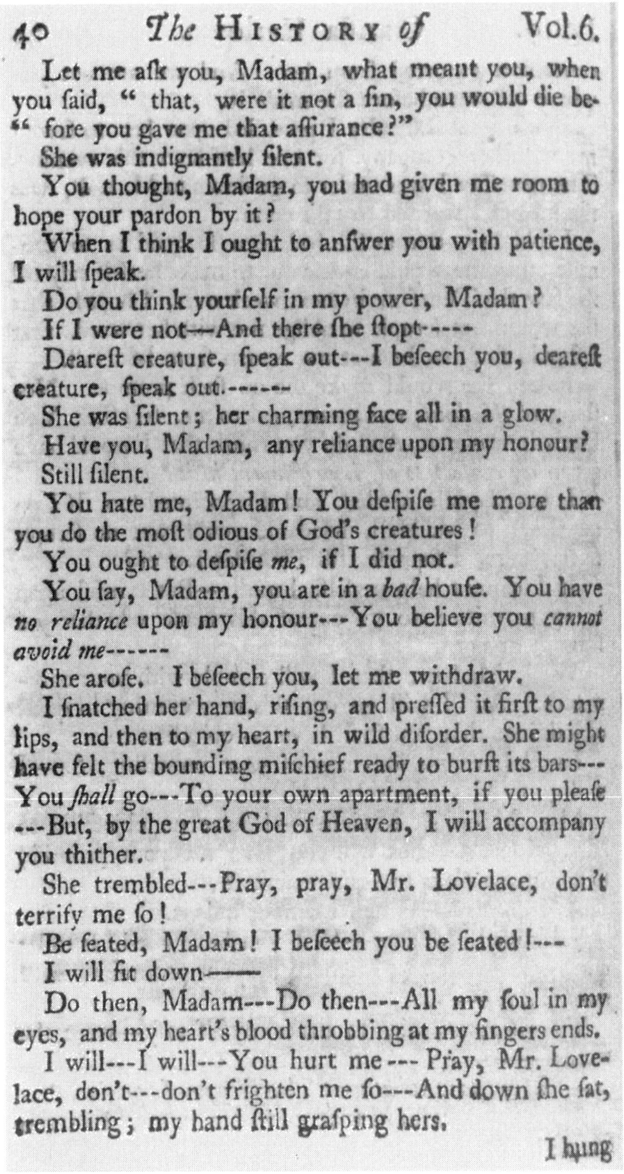

40   *The* HISTORY *of*   Vol.6.

Let me aſk you, Madam, what meant you, when you ſaid, " that, were it not a ſin, you would die be- " fore you gave me that aſſurance?"

She was indignantly ſilent.

You thought, Madam, you had given me room to hope your pardon by it?

When I think I ought to anſwer you with patience, I will ſpeak.

Do you think yourſelf in my power, Madam?

If I were not—And there ſhe ſtopt----

Deareſt creature, ſpeak out---I beſeech you, deareſt creature, ſpeak out.------

She was ſilent; her charming face all in a glow.

Have you, Madam, any reliance upon my honour?

Still ſilent.

You hate me, Madam! You deſpiſe me more than you do the moſt odious of God's creatures!

You ought to deſpiſe *me*, if I did not.

You ſay, Madam, you are in a *bad* houſe. You have *no reliance* upon my honour---You believe you *cannot avoid me*------

She aroſe. I beſeech you, let me withdraw.

I ſnatched her hand, riſing, and preſſed it firſt to my lips, and then to my heart, in wild diſorder. She might have felt the bounding miſchief ready to burſt its bars--- You *ſhall* go---To your own apartment, if you pleaſe ---But, by the great God of Heaven, I will accompany you thither.

She trembled---Pray, pray, Mr. Lovelace, don't terrify me ſo!

Be ſeated, Madam! I beſeech you be ſeated!---

I will ſit down——

Do then, Madam---Do then---All my ſoul in my eyes, and my heart's blood throbbing at my fingers ends.

I will---I will---You hurt me --- Pray, Mr. Love-lace, don't---don't frighten me ſo---And down ſhe ſat, trembling; my hand ſtill graſping hers.

I hung

FIGURE 48. *Clarissa; or, The History of a Young Lady*, third edition (1751), volume 6, page 40, illustrating Richardson's use of em dashes.

symbol for use in letter writing. Finally, Brand's random italic flourishes contrast the mid-eighteenth-century trend toward a more controlled, regularized use of the italic letter. According to Smith, printers used the italic letter "more sparingly" at the time of *Clarissa's* publication.[21]

By juxtaposing unusual and unconventional settings with the standard pica

21. Smith, *Printer's Grammar,* 13.

FIGURE 49.
Clarissa; or, The History of a Young Lady, third edition (1751), volume 7, page 384, illustrating Richardson's use of italic.

384   *The* HISTORY *of*   Vol. 7.
· *the Lady* (whom, being a *lover of learning* and *learn-*
· *ed men,* I fhall have great *opportunities* of *obliging—*
· For, when fhe departed from her Father's houfe, I
· had but juft the honour of her *notice,* and fhe feemed
· *highly pleafed* with my *converfation*); and, *next,* to
· be *thanked* and *refpected* by her *parents,* and *all her*
· *family;* as I am (I blefs God for it) by my *dear*
· *friend* Mr. John Harlowe: Who indeed is a man
· that profeffeth a *great efteem* for *men of erudition;* and
· who (with *fingular delight,* I know) will run over
· with me the *Authorities* I have *quoted,* and *wonder*
· at my *memory,* and the *happy knack* I have of re-
· commending *mine own fenfe of things* in the words
· of the *greateft fages of antiquity.*
· · Excufe me, my good friend, for this *feeming va-*
· *nity.* The great Cicero (you muft have heard, I
· fuppofe) had a *much greater* fpice of it, and wrote
· a *long Letter begging* and *praying* to be *flattered:* But
· if I fay *lefs of myfelf,* than other people (who know
· me) *fay of me,* I think I keep a *medium* between
· *vanity* and *falfe modefty;* the latter of which often-
· times gives itfelf the *lye,* when it is *declaring off* the
· *compliments,* that *every-body* gives it as its due: An
· hypocrify, as well as folly, that (I hope) I fhall for
· ever fcorn to be guilty of.
· · I have *another reafon* (as I may tell to you, my
· *old fchoolfellow*) to make me wifh for this *fine Lady's*
· *recovery* and *health;* and that is (by fome diftant in-
· timations) I have heard from Mr. John Harlowe,
· that it is *very likely* (becaufe of the *Slur* fhe hath re-
· ceived) that fhe will chufe to *live privately* and *pe-*
· *nitently*—and will probably (when fhe cometh into
· her *Eftate*) keep a *Chaplain* to direct her in her
· *devotions* and *penitence*—If fhe doth, who can ftand
· a *better chance* than *myfelf?*—And as I find (by *your*
· account, as well as by *every-body's*) that fhe is in-
· nocent as to *intention,* and is refolved never to think
· of Mr. *Lovelace more,* Who knoweth *what* (in time)
· *may*

roman type font, Richardson presents the print equivalent of an autograph manuscript page. Rather than producing what Joel A. Roth describes as "page after un-
relieved page of blocks of type,"[22] Richardson creates distinct pages marked with
idiosyncrasies that define each letter writer, much as readers would find in the

22. Joel A. Roth, "Excerpt: Typography That Makes the Reader Work," *Journal of Typographic Research* 3 (1969): 193.

handwriting of "Original Manuscripts." Brand's letters in particular demonstrate how typographical manipulation can replicate a manuscript reading experience. The italics in Brand's 2 September letter to Walton (figure 49) create a cluttered, aesthetically obnoxious page, and their overabundant thin strokes strain the readers' eyes. Rarely do four or five words pass without the italic letter appearing, and often, unexpected groups of words are emphasized, resulting in a clumsy cadence and an awkward reading experience. Brand emphasizes words on a whim, and with no distinguishable pattern to his italics, readers confront a visual muddle that must be deciphered in the same way that they would negotiate poor handwriting.

When Richardson modifies conventional pica roman lines, he creates metaphoric substitutions for the manuscript letters referred to on the third edition title page.[23] Richardson is not masquerading his typeset pages as the "Original Manuscripts" themselves. Rather, he creates metaphoric representations based on the perception of similarity between his printed page and autograph handwriting—similarities such as the variety and irregularity common in both.[24] These metaphoric representations allow Richardson to develop his characterization typographically. Readers might not consciously know the printing conventions specified in Moxon or Smith; but, as with handwriting, a visual critique identifies the pages as atypical and cues readers into the character's emotional or physical state. Thus, as if reading a handwritten manuscript, readers literally see Clarissa's rape-induced incoherence, Belford's reformed confidence, Lovelace's fallen loss of control, and Brand's absurd lack of introspection and self-restraint. It is important that metaphoric substitutions are only temporary replacements, allowing readers to return to the conventional pica roman line without negating the effects of the isolated autograph-in-print passages. Consequently, Richardson's metaphoric substitutions validate the manuscript motif, build characterization, and lend credibility to the novel's didactic message.

Richardson's second strategy for exploiting the manuscript motif alters conventional typography more drastically. Rather than modifying the standard pica roman type font, he occasionally abandons its use altogether in favor of an alternative type font, consequently elevating the manuscript verisimilitude beyond the metaphorical level. For instance, in the first edition of the novel, Richardson sets Clarissa's signatures to her final letter to Anna and to her will with a Grover's cursorial, a late seventeenth-century typeface modeled after Italian handwriting.[25]

23. For additional discussion of metaphoric and metonymic constructions, see Kaja Silverman, *The Subject of Semiotics* (New York: Oxford University Press, 1983), chap. 3, "Similarity and Contiguity."

24. Although a regularized hand was still taught in the eighteenth century, individual variations nevertheless occurred, as suggested by Lovelace's description of Anna Howe's handwriting: "Miss Howe's hand is no bad one; but is not so equal and regular [as Clarissa's]. That little devil's natural impatience hurrying on her fingers, gave, I suppose, from the beginning, her hand-writing, as well as the rest of her, its fits and starts, and those peculiarities, which, like strong muscular lines in a face, neither the pen, nor the pencil, can miss" (5:154).

25. Geoffrey Dowding, *An Introduction to the History of Printing Types* (London: Wace, 1961), 129. Angus Ross reproduces the first edition signatures in his one-volume reprint, Samuel Richardson, *Clarissa or The History of a Young Lady* (Harmondsworth: Penguin, 1985), 1349, 1420.

Signatures in every other letter appear in roman small capitals. Presumably, Richardson hopes to foreground the two thematically significant letters and accentuate the message of Christian patience that Clarissa extols above each signature.

However, Richardson resets the atypical signatures in the third edition with the more consistent roman small capitals.[26] I believe that he does so not because of a more conservative approach to type fonts, as has been argued,[27] but because he realizes that in one instance the typographically embellished signature contradicts the letter's narrative context. In Clarissa's final letter, readers actually encounter Belford's *transcription* of Clarissa's signature, a signature she herself wrote only with the assistance of her friend Mrs. Lovick because of her grave illness. Belford witnesses Clarissa's belabored attempt to conclude the final letter, and he offers the following emotional description for Lovelace: "She dictated the Farewel part, without hesitation; and when she came to the blessing and subscription, she took the pen, and dropping on her knees, supported by Mrs. Lovick, wrote the Conclusion; but Mrs. Lovick was forced to guide her hand."[28] Belford then explains that he "endeavoured to imitate the subscriptive part" in his transcription, or the version presented to readers. Visually, then, the decorative ligatures and precise, narrow width of the Grover faces in the first edition fail to reflect Clarissa's incapacitated, weakened state.

A second example, found in both the first and third editions of *Clarissa,* demonstrates how Richardson more effectively exploits the manuscript motif, and embellishes characterization, by replacing the pica roman type font. In her 24 March letter to Anna, Clarissa laments her impending, arranged marriage to the contemptible Roger Solmes. To cope with her "angry passions,"[29] she tells Anna how she reexamines the poem "ODE TO WISDOM. By a LADY," which has been circulating the neighborhood. Clarissa describes the poem as "not unsuitable to my unhappy situation,"[30] an accurate assessment given the poem's plea for support to Pallas Athena in stanza nine:

> By Thee protected, I defy
> The Coxcomb's Sneer the stupid Lye
> Of Ignorance and Spite:
> Alike contemn the leaden Fool,
> And all the pointed Ridicule
> Of undiscerning *Wit*.[31]

In her letter to Anna, Clarissa encloses the text of the sixteen-stanza ode as well as the harpsichord accompaniment for the last three stanzas which she herself has

---

26. 7:408 and 8:113.
27. Tom Keymer, "Jane Collier, Reader of Richardson, and the Fire Scene in *Clarissa,*" in *New Essays on Samuel Richardson,* ed. Albert J. Rivero (New York: St. Martin's Press, 1996), 155.
28. 7:407.
29. 2:50.
30. 2:50.
31. 2:53.

FIGURE 50. *Clarissa; or, The History of a Young Lady,* third edition (1751), engraved foldout leaf appearing in volume 2, page 54.

composed. Like Anna, readers of *Clarissa* have access to the poem and its music, the latter presented on an engraved foldout leaf measuring twice the size of a standard duodecimo page (figure 50).

The textual history of the "Ode to Wisdom" is worth briefly mentioning here, because it illustrates Richardson's willingness to alter the material as well as linguistic features of his novel. In actuality, Elizabeth Carter, a member of the Bluestocking Society (a mid-eighteenth-century circle of female intellectuals) and a close friend of Samuel Johnson, wrote the poem, and Richardson inserted the verses into *Clarissa*'s first edition (December 1747) without her knowledge.[32] Not only did he questionably appropriate the ode, but he also altered its linguistic text. Carter voiced her disapproval to Edward Cave, also a friend of Johnson's, who printed a second version of the poem, retitled "To Wisdom. A nocturnal Ode," in the December 1747 number of the *Gentleman's Magazine.* As a preface to the poem, Cave included an editorial disclaimer stating that the text previously "appeared in *Clarissa* with several faults."[33] Richardson initially planned to in-

32. For additional information on the Richardson-Carter controversy, see T. C. Duncan Eaves and Ben D. Kimpel, *Samuel Richardson: A Biography* (Oxford: Clarendon Press, 1971), 214–18; Ross, ed., *Clarissa*, 1514, n. "L54."

33. *Gentleman's Magazine* 17 (December 1747): 585. Cave politely minimizes the scope and significance of Richardson's emendations by referring to them as "several faults." In just the final three stanzas of the first edition text, presented on the engraved foldout leaf, Richardson makes thirty-four alterations to the

clude the entire sixteen-stanza ode in *Clarissa's* second edition (1749). Given Carter's displeasure, however, he canceled the leaf on which the ode began but retained the final three stanzas and the musical plate,[34] offering the following appeal to Carter: "it is hoped, that the Lady will not be displeased with the continuing of those, for the sake of the Music, which we will venture to say is set in so masterly a manner as to do credit to her performance."[35] Richardson eventually apologized to Carter, and in the third edition he restores the canceled stanzas with her consent. He makes further emendations to the third edition ode, though, and in the process creates the linguistic text that would become the basis for the final two editions published in his lifetime. Two significant substantive alterations are made to the engraved plate: in line one, Richardson changes "the" to "Thee" (similar to the *Gentleman's Magazine* version, though without the exclamation point) and in line two, he capitalizes "Thee" (a deviation from the *Gentleman's Magazine*), both of which more overtly accentuate the ode's concluding didactic praise of Wisdom. In the 1751 octavo fourth edition, Richardson removes the engraved foldout leaf and replaces it with a standard octavo leaf; additionally, he replaces the engraved script font of the third edition musical plate with standard pica roman type.[36] In the fifth edition of 1759 (also referred to as the duodecimo fourth edition), Richardson reintroduces the engraved foldout leaf and the script font, retaining the formatting and text of the third edition. The third edition version, then, is significant in that it shows Richardson the printer actively experimenting with the visual page by manipulating the pica roman type font.

First, Richardson disrupts the standard pica roman line, not with atypical type font settings, as in the letters of Belford, Lovelace, and Brand, but with extravagant formatting of the lines (figure 51). Readers of the third edition find the first thirteen stanzas of the "Ode to Wisdom" set in the standard pica roman type font. However, in contrast to the typical third edition page, Richardson expands the vertical distance between each line of the "Ode to Wisdom" with leading. As a result, the twenty-line measurement grows from an average of 82 millimeters

---

ode's accidentals and substantives. Concerning accidentals, Richardson generally emends Carter's enjambed lines to end-stopped lines, creating a more disciplined and rigid poetic verse. Concerning substantives, Richardson tends to capitalize important words, thereby more overtly emphasizing his own didactic message. He also amends words, with Carter's personified "THEE!" changed to "the" and her verb "Is" changed to "Are." My collation uses the text of the *Gentleman's Magazine* and a first edition of *Clarissa* from the University of Colorado–Boulder (PR 3664 C4 1748).

34. Sale's speculation regarding the nonextant cancellandum is convincing. See Sale, *Bibliographic Record,* 52. Richardson makes one emendation to the second edition musical plate, adding a superscript "e!" to "the" of line one to form "Thee!," which awkwardly fits between the preexisting words "To" and "Supreme."

35. *Clarissa* (2d ed., 1749), 2:48. Quoted in Eaves and Kimpel, *Samuel Richardson,* 216.

36. Richardson simultaneously published the octavo fourth and the duodecimo third editions in 1751, with the more expensive fourth edition apparently printed as a gift for friends. See Sale, *Bibliographical Record,* 58, and Stuber, "On Original and Final Intentions," 236. My textual comments are based on examination of a 1751 octavo fourth edition of *Clarissa* from the Noel Collection, Louisiana State University at Shreveport.

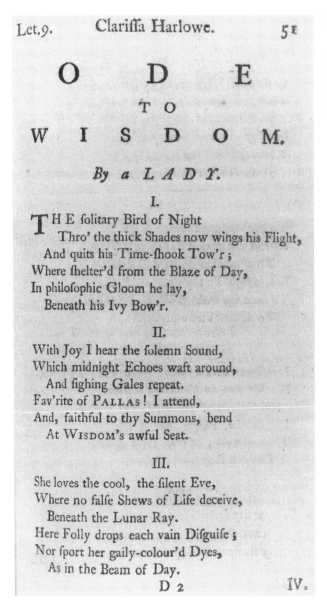

FIGURE 51.
Clarissa; or, The History of a Young Lady, third edition (1751), volume 2, page 51: "Ode to Wisdom" title page.

on the standard page to an average of 100 millimeters for the "Ode to Wisdom," adding approximately an extra page of type. In addition, the relatively short iambic trimeter and iambic tetrameter lines, formatted with left margin justification, create exceptionally large white space on the right margins. The increased vertical spread of the lines and the large amount of unused paper cause the thirteen stanzas to run to a generous and uncluttered four duodecimo pages. Richardson further accentuates the poem by setting the last three stanzas on the engraved fold-out leaf, tipped in as a recto page facing stanzas eleven through thirteen. The poem's commissioned music, engraving, extra paper, and oversized foldout leaf (left blank on the opposite side) no doubt came at significant cost to Richardson's print shop.[37] Despite the added expense, Richardson distinguishes the heavily didactic linguistic text of the "Ode to Wisdom" by disrupting the conventional pica roman page.

Richardson's second method of type font manipulation in the "Ode to Wisdom" is to abandon the use of the pica roman face altogether, as seen in the engraved musical plate. Aside from the musical notes themselves, which Janine Barchus convincingly describes as "augment[ing] [the] noble characterization of the heroine,"[38] the engraved script font is the most distinct feature of the fold-out leaf. Script fonts rarely appeared in England during the mid-eighteenth century, and neither Caslon's nor Baskerville's specimen sheets contained a script face.[39] Richardson's display, then, would have captured his readers' attention. Although the engraved script font in the musical plate appears as regular as a conventional typeset page, the type font nonetheless suggests actual handwriting. Richardson's engraver constructs the script font with realistic traits of an eighteenth-century hand, including parallels with quilled letters. For instance, the heavily inked serifs on the descenders of the capital letters A, H, I, M, N, R, S, and T give the appearance of excess ink common at the beginning of a pen stroke. Also, the heavy contrast between fat and lean strokes, as seen in the lower case e, o, and g, as well as in the vertical rule separating stanzas fifteen and sixteen, is consistent with quilled letters. Comparison of the engraved script font with eighteenth-century autograph manuscripts shows other similarities. For instance, the smooth continuity of the engraved letters parallels the repetitive vertical strokes seen in the poet Thomas Gray's (1716–71) handwriting. Additionally, the heavily inked descender serifs and the formation of a various letters, including

37. The exact cost for the musical plate is unknown. Ross, however, believes that the plate was produced at "considerable cost" (Ross, ed., *Clarissa,* 1514, n. "L54"). In a 18 December 1747 letter to Elizabeth Carter, Richardson refers to the "trouble" and "expense" of producing the musical plate. Quoted in Janine Barchus, "The Engraved Score in *Clarissa:* An Intersection of Music, Narrative, and Graphic Design," *Eighteenth-Century Life* 20 (1996): 5, and Eaves and Kimpel, *Samuel Richardson: A Biography,* 215. The musical plate continues to raise production costs in modern editions. Jim Springer Borck, project director and text coordinator for the *Clarissa* Project, reports that AMS Press incurred "considerable additional cost" when printing the musical plate for its 1990 facsimile reprint of the third edition. Because the plate requires separate printing and must be glued by hand onto a bound stub, the machine-press book requires effort similar to that which Richardson employed in the hand-press era. Interview with Jim Springer Borck, 25 November 1997.

38. Barchus, "The Engraved Score," 10. Barchus argues that the formatting of the engraved plate imitates popular musical lesson books. My central argument differs, in that I see the engraved script font evoking images not of other printed texts but of manuscript handwriting.

39. For a facsimile of Caslon's 1734 specimen sheet, see *Two Centuries of Typefounding: Annals of the Letter Foundry established by William Caslon in Chiswell Street, London, in the Year 1720* (London: Printed by George W. Jones at The Sign of the Dolphin in Gough Square, Fleet Street, 1920); for Baskerville's 1762 broadside specimen (reduced), see Daniel Berkeley Updike, *Printing Types: Their History, Forms, and Use* (Cambridge: The Belknap Press of Harvard University Press, 1966), fig. 270.

the capitals A, T, and F, occur in John Gay's (1685–1732) handwriting, described by P. J. Croft as "thoroughly of its period."[40]

By recognizing important features of handwriting, Richardson increases the verisimilitude lacking in the conventional appearance of the pica roman type font. Consequently, through the engraved script font, he offers readers a visual model of Clarissa's exemplary handwriting, described in the novel before her rape as "delicate" and "charming."[41] For eighteenth-century readers, the quality of a person's handwriting was a material indicator of the person's inner character and emotional state. After Clarissa's death, for instance, Anna equates handwriting with character when portraying her friend to Belford: "The hand she wrote, for the neat and free cut of her letters (like her mind, solid, and above all *flourish*) for its fairness, evenness, and swiftness, distinguished her as much as the correctness of her orthography, and even punctuation, from the generality of her own Sex."[42] Readers hear of Clarissa's "solid" and unassuming character throughout the novel, but the musical plate's script font allows them momentarily to *see* her through an image of her handwriting. As a result, the text of the printer temporarily displaces the text and characterization of the author. Because the musical plate occurs early in the second of eight volumes, its script font provides readers with a concrete example upon which to base their conceptual images of Clarissa's handwriting and character later in the novel.

Like the examples from Clarissa, Belford, Lovelace, and Brand, Richardson's musical plate, as an autograph manuscript in print, symbolically represents a handwritten manuscript page. However, in contrast to the metaphorical substitutions that occur when he disrupts the standard pica roman type font (substitutions based on the perception of similarity between the printed page and a handwritten manuscript page), Richardson creates in the musical plate a metonymic substitution for Clarissa's fictional handwriting. The metonymical substitution is a more powerful characterization device for Richardson because of its direct association with Clarissa. Richardson exploits the interpretive value of the engraved script font and uses its elegant though unassuming lines as a visual indicator of his heroine's upstanding yet humble character. Other nonlinguistic components of the musical plate heighten the direct association with Clarissa and encourage readers to acquiesce to the metonymic substitution. For instance, the plate promotes not only cognitive and visual readings but also, should the musical text actually be translated onto the strings of a harpsichord, tactile and audio readings. Clarissa undergoes a metonymic expansion as she can be seen, heard, and in a sense felt (the sensation of harpsichord keys upon the fingers). As in the metaphoric substitutions, the metonymic handwriting of the engraved script font

40. P. J. Croft, *Autograph Poetry in the English Language: Facsimiles of Original Manuscripts from the Fourteenth to the Twentieth Century,* 2 vols. (London: Cassell, 1973), 1:64. For a facsimile of Gray's hand, see Croft, 1:80; for a facsimile of Gay's hand, see Croft, 1:64.

41. 5:154; 6:206. Following the rape, Clarissa's handwriting is described as "trembling" (7:334) and "unstead[y]" (7:337).

42. 8:201.

only temporarily displaces the novel's conventional typography, thereby allowing readers' perceptions to slide back to the standard pica roman type font without prejudice and without negating the autograph manuscript verisimilitude. With its realistic features, Richardson's engraved script font accentuates the potential reality of Clarissa's hand. Like Lovelace, Anna, or Belford, readers encounter Clarissa's subjectivity through the material display of her handwriting. A plausible manuscript page temporarily emerges from the typography, and Clarissa's fictional thoughts acquire credibility as they temporarily could be the real thoughts of a real person.

Although Richardson's manipulation of type fonts occurs throughout the eight volumes of *Clarissa,* literary critics rarely note the significance of the novel's material features. Unfortunately, italic fonts and em dashes are dismissed as meaningless compositor's marks, and the musical plate is overlooked as a quaint appendage to a long work. The novel, however, exemplifies the influences of both an author and a master printer. Examination of Richardson's use of types fonts shows him struggling against print technology as well as exploiting its usefulness for presenting didactic fiction to a large audience. Richardson's creation of the autograph manuscript in print is an effective compromise, in that it allows the author to write epistolary fiction which retains the credibility typically reserved for "Original Manuscripts." Visual images as well as words carry meaning in *Clarissa.* Therefore, overlooking the importance of type fonts in Richardson's epistolary novel risks neglecting essential meaning.

Bridge Five

In the division of labor characteristic of modern literary professionalism, the compositor is central, standing between an author and his or her readers, mediating manuscript and transforming it into a printed and commodified object for purchase and consumption. In the preceding essay, Steven Price offers a case study focusing on Samuel Richardson as both author and printer. Combining two tasks typically assigned to separate individuals, Richardson was able to make and oversee crucial typographic decisions determining the visual appearance of his printed texts, especially the third edition of *Clarissa*. Price shows, for example, how Richardson used a variety of typefaces to signify the various hands of his characters. Like Benjamin Franklin in the 1740s, William Blake in the 1790s, and Walt Whitman in the 1850s, Richardson worked within an artisanal culture that eschewed divisions of labor, instead embracing the progressive mastery of the various stages of a mode of production. This craft-based training allowed him to bridge the gap between textual and technological modes of production.

As Leon Jackson argues in the following essay, by the time Edgar Allan Poe began to write in the 1830s, this artisanal culture was being eroded. Technological innovations and increasing specialization of labor in the printing trades leading to the eventual disappearance of master printers (like Richardson and Franklin) meant that few writers were able to supervise the production of their texts as Richardson had done in the eighteenth century. While he was well versed in the techniques and technologies of typesetting, Poe did not take a direct role in the production of texts, although he worried endlessly about the consequences. Aware of the semiotic significance of various typefaces, Poe fantasized about absolute control over the semiotics of print in his fictions while experimenting in his spare time with technologies that would sidestep the use of movable type altogether. In both lithography and anastatic printing, Poe believed that he had found techniques that merged the uniqueness of the written word with the infinite reproducibility of printed text. While Poe's own experiments in printing technology were ultimately unsuccessful, they both shaped his critical and creative practice and, Jackson notes, suggest that he was, in essence, fighting a rearguard action against the encroaching forces of industrialization. Ameri-

can printers would continue to enter the literary sphere—
Mark Twain, Joel Chandler Harris, and William Dean Howells
are only the most famous—but rarely again would writers take
as direct a hand in the printing of their texts as they had in the
eighteenth and early nineteenth centuries.

Chapter Six

"The Italics are Mine": Edgar Allan Poe and the Semiotics of Print

LEON JACKSON

In May 1849, just six months before his death in Baltimore, Edgar Allan Poe sent Edward H. N. Patterson a design for the cover of a magazine they planned to publish together. In a gentle arc, painstakingly hand-lettered by Poe to look like print, ran the title: "The Stylus: A Monthly Journal of Literature Proper, the Fine Arts, and the Drama." A sketch below depicted a hand holding a pen that was spelling out the word "Aletheia," the Greek for truth. Following a motto—"Aureus aliquando STYLUS, ferreus aliquando"—and mirroring the arc of the title, ran the equally neat legend "Edited by Edgar A. Poe" (figure 52).[1] Poe's scrupulously drawn title page both reflected and thematized a lifelong obsession with the skills of penmanship and stated with certainty his conviction that truth emerged from the handwritten word. Raised to a striking degree of explicitness on the cover of *The Stylus,* the motif of the manuscript hand as medium of truth more generally permeated Poe's work. Early tales such as "MS Found in a Bottle" and *The Narrative of Arthur Gordon Pym* suggested the power of the handwritten word to report the unspeakable; his essays on autography provided quirky yet authoritative analyses of celebrity signatures, while his popular series of bon mots were presented in the guise of a reader's casually penned marginalia. Poe's fascination with the handwritten word suggests an appreciation for what Walter Benjamin has called art's "aura," that essential and originary authenticity that both defines and guarantees authority through reference to the unique subjectivity of its creator.[2] "I am more than half serious," summarized Poe in 1844, "in all that I have ever said about manuscript, as affording indication of character. The general

I would like to thank Paul Gutjahr, Megan Benton, Meredith McGill, John Kneebone, and Stephen Rachman for their advice and encouragement.

1. Poe to Patterson, 23 May 1849, *The Letters of Edgar Allan Poe,* ed. John Ward Ostrom, 2 vols. (New York: Gordian Press, 1966), 2:443–444. This text is hereafter abbreviated *Letters.* Poe's design for the *Stylus* is discussed at length by Burton R. Pollin, "Poe's Iron Pen," in his *Discoveries in Poe* (Notre Dame, Ind.: University of Notre Dame Press, 1970), 206–29.

2. Walter Benjamin, "The Work of Art in the Age of Mechanical Reproduction," in *Illuminations,* ed. Hannah Arendt, trans. Harry Zohn (New York: Schocken, 1969), esp. 220–25.

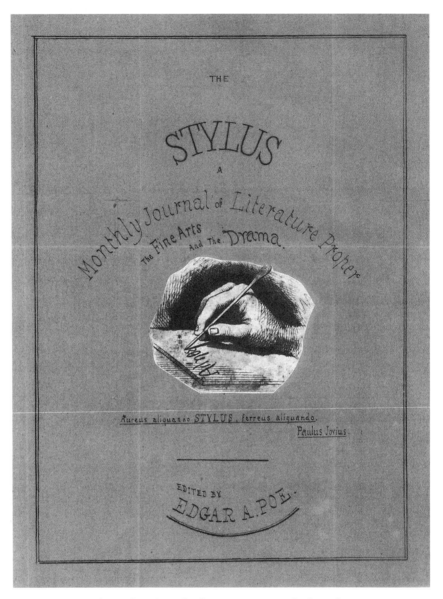

FIGURE 52. Poe's design for *The Stylus,* from *Some Letters of Edgar Allan Poe to E. H. N. Patterson of Oquawka, Illinois, with Comments by Eugene Field* (Chicago: The Caxton Club, 1898). By permission of the Houghton Library, Harvard University.

proposition is unquestionable—the mental qualities will have a *tendency* to impress the MS."[3]

Yet while Poe celebrated the unique and revelatory power of handwriting in so many of his writings, his celebrations were, themselves, ironically presented in printed form: uniform, impersonal, mediated, and infinitely reproducible. Poe's penmanship was forever refracted through the medium of the press, rendering his productions altogether more, yet frustratingly less, than he intended them to be. "I have written no books," he noted sourly in 1844.[4] Poe's attempts to write books were, indeed, inexorably doomed to failure, for as Roger Stoddard has pointedly explained, "authors do *not* write books. Books are not written at all. They are manufactured by scribes and other artisans, by mechanics and other engineers, and by printing presses and other machines."[5] The "truth" of the printed word, Poe came to believe, was not always the truth of the author's pen. Books were not only manufactured objects but also mediated, and many technologies stood between an author's manuscript and the publisher's text.

A good deal has been written about Poe's interest in handwriting and manuscripts, but almost nothing has been said about his very real fascination with what happened to the handwritten when it was committed to print.[6] Authors in antebellum America were far less distanced from the production side of publication than their modern counterparts, and Poe's interactions with editors, printers, and publishers led him to ponder deeply and comment frequently on the cultural meanings of typography and the typefaces that regularized the hand. In this essay, I consider Poe's heretofore overlooked obsession with printedness, especially as it manifested itself in his comments on typography and typographical errors. Poe, I argue, courted the social status and the convenient reproducibility of the printed word, while at the same time deploring its capacity to warp and distort authorial meaning. For much of his life, Poe attempted to close the gap between manuscript and print, first of all by making his handwriting imitate the uniformity

3. *Essays and Reviews,* ed. G. R. Thompson (New York: Library of America, 1984), 1322–23. This text is hereafter abbreviated *ER.*

4. Poe to Charles Anthon, [October] 1844, *Letters,* 1:270. In fact, Poe had published several "books" by 1844; what he meant by this disclaimer was that he had not produced a full-length, hardbound, thematically unified work that he believed deserved the title. The point I want to make here, however, is that Poe figures what is essentially a mechanical process in inappropriate, yet revealingly scribal, terms. For a pioneering exploration of Poe's theory of the book as form, see William Charvat, "Poe: Journalism and the Theory of Poetry," in *The Profession of Authorship in America, 1800–1870: The Papers of William Charvat,* ed. Matthew J. Bruccoli (Columbus: Ohio State University Press, 1968), 86–94.

5. Roger E. Stoddard, "Morphology and the Book from an American Perspective," *Printing History* 9 (1987): 4. Fittingly enough, the italics here are *not* mine.

6. In a recent survey of Poe scholarship, Kent P. Ljungquist predicted that work on the history of the book would lead critics to reconsider Poe's knowledge of, and interest in, the antebellum publishing world. See "Prospects for the Study of Edgar Allan Poe," *Resources for American Literary Study* 21 (1995): 180–81. While Ljungquist's prediction has indeed been borne out, most of what has been published along these lines focuses on Poe's responses to the professionalization of authorship. Considerations of Poe's interest in the intersections of the written and the printed, all excellent, are generally incidental to larger thematic studies. For a brief survey, see George Egon Hatvary, "Poe and the World of Books," in *A Companion to Poe Studies,* ed. Eric W. Carlson (Westport, Conn.: Greenwood Press, 1996), 541–44.

and regularity of print and later on by advocating printing technology that would allow one to print handwriting from etched zinc plates. Neither strategy fully succeeded, but both came to function as idealized preconditions for his literary and critical praxis.

"Words—printed ones especially—are murderous things."
Poe (*ER*, 1370)

When he was only ten, Poe composed a manuscript volume of love poems, addressed to various young girls in Richmond, which he begged his guardian, John Allan, to have published. Allan consulted with Poe's teacher, Joseph H. Clark, but Clark advised against the move, commenting that because Poe was so prideful, it would be "injurious" to him to be "flattered and talked about as the author of a printed book at his age."[7] Poe would have to wait another seven years until his first volume, *Tamerlane and Other Poems,* saw print. From his earliest experience, however, he idealized the experience of being printed as an elevation of status. Indeed, he sought to emulate the quality of printedness even in his handwriting. Commenting on Poe's manuscript submissions for an essay competition in the Baltimore *Saturday Visiter* in 1833, John Latrobe recalled that they were written in "Roman characters—an imitation of printing," almost as if Poe were using chirography to fantasize his way into print, while as late as 1847, Mary Bronson was struck by the fact that Poe's writing was "beautifully distinct and regular, almost like engraving."[8]

Distinction and regularity were two of the key traits of fine printing, and Poe dreamed about them in his work as a periodical editor. In campaigning on behalf of *Graham's Lady's and Gentleman's Magazine,* Poe wrote to contributors, noting that the type would be "new (always new) clear and bold, with distinct face."[9] Describing his projected magazine *The Penn* the same year, he envisaged "a good outward appearance—clear type, fine paper &c—double columns, I think, & brevier, with poetry running across the page in a single column." And while the prospectus for his *Stylus* was briefer, it was no less enthusiastic, promising that "in its typography, paper, and binding—it will far surpass all American journals of its kind."[10]

While Poe never got to edit the magazine he dreamed about, he continued to appreciate fine printing and commented upon it often in his book reviews. The poetry of Elizabeth Oakes Smith, for example, he believed made a "very pretty

---

7. Dwight Thomas and David K. Jackson, *The Poe Log: A Documentary Life of Edgar Allan Poe, 1809–1849* (Boston: G. K. Hall, 1987), 47; hereafter cited as *Poe Log.*
8. "Reminiscences of Poe by John H. Latrobe," in *Edgar Allan Poe: A Memorial Volume,* ed. Sara Sigourney Rice (Baltimore: Turnbull Brothers, 1877), 58; *Poe Log,* 707.
9. Poe to Washington Irving, 21 June 1841, *Letters,* 1:162. For almost identical phrasing, see Poe to John P. Kennedy, [21] June 1841, *Letters,* 1:164; Poe to Henry Wadsworth Longfellow, 22 June 1841, *Letters,* 1:167; and Poe to Fitz-Greene Halleck, *Letters,* 1:169.
10. Poe to Joseph Evans Snodgrass, 17 January 1841, *Letters,* 1:152; *ER,* 1033.

little volume, neatly printed." The poems of Henry B. Hirst were "beautifully printed"; those of Frances Osgood were "most beautifully printed"; while Appleton's Dante was "exquisitely printed."[11] Similarly, the typography of Seba Smith's *Powhatan* was deemed "clear beyond comparison," while the very highest praise was reserved for works like Harper and Brothers' 1836 edition of *Robinson Crusoe,* whose design, he believed, was "superlative." "In regard to the paper, typography, and binding" of *Crusoe,* Poe commented, "that taste must be fastidious indeed which can find any fault with either."[12]

Poe's fulsome praise of fine printing was sufficiently characteristic for some to accuse him of caring more for the form than for the content of the books he reviewed. In 1845, for example, the New York *Town* ran a parody of a typical Poe review in which the critic attacked an imaginary work as "a mass of insufferable trash, without one redeeming quality," while at the same time praising it for being "printed in a beautiful arabesque style by Wiley & Putnam."[13]

Yet while Poe was obsessed with typography, he was anything but a dilettante. In part, his concern for typographic quality reflected an appreciation for the idea that crisp letters facilitated easy reading and allowed browsers to process information more efficiently and effortlessly. In an age in which both spectacles and lighting were expensive, sloppy printing led to weak eyes and persistent headaches. "Novels are printed upon very poor paper and in small type," wrote J. Henry Clark in 1856, and the "power of vision" is thus "bartered away, for a very small price, to very little purpose."[14] Poe, that is, understood the importance of clarity in printed texts. Before taking up his first editorial position, at the *Southern Literary Messenger,* he had written to the proprietor, T. W. White, suggesting that he use a "lighter-faced type" for the headings of his articles as a way to "improve" their appearance. White followed Poe's advice and purchased a "beautiful fount of type" which was first used in the December 1835 issue of the *Messenger.*[15] A comparison of the *Messenger*'s old and new typefaces indicates that while the old font (figure 53) used heavy stems, the new type (figure 54) used thinner stems and finer serifs that took up less ink, giving a lighter and less compressed feel to the titles. The response to these and other seemingly small changes was remarkable. The new format, according to one reviewer, was "unquestionably one of the

11. *ER,* 90, 594, 1189; Edgar Allan Poe, *Writings in the Broadway Journal: Nonfictional Prose. Part I: The Text,* ed. Burton R. Pollin (New York: Gordian Press, 1986), 290.

12. *ER,* 918, 203.

13. *Poe Log,* 534–535.

14. J. Henry Clark, *Sight and Hearing* (New York: Charles Scribner, 1856), 70, quoted in Ronald J. Zboray, *A Fictive People: Antebellum Economic Development and the American Reading Public* (New York: Oxford University Press, 1993), 14–15. The earliest scientific experiments on the legibility of typefaces under varying conditions were conducted in France in the late 1790s and in England in 1825 and 1827. See Richard H. Wiggins, "Effects of Three Typographical Variables on Speed of Reading," *Journal of Typographic Research* 1 (1967): 5. Poe had written about the perils of near-sightedness, although not with reference to reading, in his 1844 tale, "The Spectacles."

15. Poe to Thomas W. White, 22 June 1835, *Letters,* 1:64. On White's purchase of new type for the *Messenger,* see White to Lucian Minor, 8 September 1835, quoted in David K. Jackson, *Poe and the Southern Literary Messenger* (New York: Haskell House, 1970), 99.

SOUTHERN LITERARY MESSENGER. 735

For the Southern Literary Messenger.

LOSS OF BREATH.

A TALE A LA BLACKWOOD. BY EDGAR A. POE.

O breathe not, &c.—*Moore's Melodies.*

The most notorious ill-fortune must, in the end, yield to the untiring courage of philosophy—as the most stubborn city to the ceaseless vigilance of an enemy. Salmanezer, as we have it in the holy writings, lay three years before Samaria: yet it fell. Sardanapalus—see Diodorus—maintained himself seven in Nineveh: but to no purpose. Troy expired at the close of the second lustrum: and Azoth, as Aristæus declares upon his honor as a gentleman, opened at last her gates to Psammitticus, after having barred them for the fifth part of a century.

* * * * * *

"Thou wretch!—thou vixen!—thou shrew!"—said I to my wife on the morning after our wedding—"thou witch!—thou hag!—thou whippersnapper!—thou sink of iniquity!—thou fiery-faced quintessence of all that is abominable!—thou—thou—" Here standing upon tiptoe, seizing her by the throat, and placing my mouth close to her ear, I was preparing to launch forth a new and more decided epithet of opprobrium which should not fail, if ejaculated, to convince her of her insignificance, when, to my extreme horror and astonishment, I discovered that *I had lost my breath.*

The phrases "I am out of breath," "I have lost my breath," &c. are often enough repeated in common conversation, but it had never occurred to me that the terrible accident of which I speak could *bonâ fide* and actually happen! Imagine—that is if you have a fanciful turn—imagine I say, my wonder—my consternation—my despair!

There is a good genius, however, which has never, at any time, entirely deserted me. In my most ungovernable moods I still retain a sense of propriety, *et le chemin des passions me conduit*—as Rousseau says it did him—*à la philosophie veritable.*

Although I could not at first precisely ascertain to what degree the occurrence had affected me, I unhesitatingly determined to conceal at all events the matter from my wife until farther experience should discover to me the extent of this my unheard of calamity. Altering my countenance, therefore, in a moment, from its bepuffed and distorted appearance, to an expression of arch and coquettish benignity, I gave my lady a pat on the one cheek, and a kiss on the other, and without saying one syllable, (Furies! I could not,) left her astonished at my drollery, as I pirouetted out of the room in a *Pas de Zephyr.*

Behold me then safely ensconced in my private *boudoir*, a fearful instance of the ill consequences attending upon irascibility—alive with the qualifications of the dead—dead with the propensities of the living—an anomaly on the face of the earth—being very calm, yet breathless.

Yes! breathless. I am serious in asserting that my breath was entirely gone. I could not have stirred with it a feather if my life had been at issue, or sullied even the delicacy of a mirror. Hard fate!—yet there was some alleviation to the first overwhelming paroxysm of my sorrow. I found upon trial that the powers of utterance which, upon my inability to proceed in the conversation with my wife, I then concluded to be totally destroyed, were in fact only partially impeded, and I discovered that had I, at that interesting crisis, dropped my voice to a singularly deep guttural, I might still have continued to her the communication of my sentiments; this pitch of voice (the guttural) depending, I find, not upon the current of the breath, but upon a certain spasmodic action of the muscles of the throat.

Throwing myself upon a chair, I remained for some time absorbed in meditation. My reflections, be sure, were of no consolatory kind. A thousand vague and lachrymatory fancies took possession of my soul—and even the phantom Suicide flitted across my brain; but it is a trait in the perversity of human nature to reject the obvious and the ready, for the far-distant and equivocal. Thus I shudderd at self-murder as the most decided of atrocities, while the tabby cat purred strenuously upon the rug, and the very water-dog wheezed assiduously under the table, each taking to itself much merit for the strength of its lungs, and all obviously done in derision of my own pulmonary incapacity.

Oppressed with a tumult of vague hopes and fears, I at length heard the footstep of my wife descending the staircase. Being now assured of her absence, I returned with a palpitating heart to the scene of my disaster.

Carefully locking the door on the inside, I commenced a vigorous search. It was possible, I thought, that concealed in some obscure corner, or lurking in some closet or drawer, might be found the lost object of my inquiry. It might have a vapory—it might even have a tangible form. Most philosophers, upon many points of philosophy, are still very unphilosophical. William Godwin, however, says in his "Mandeville," that "invisible things are the only realities." This, all will allow, is a case in point. I would have the judicious reader pause before accusing such asseverations of an undue quantum of absurdity. Anaxagoras—it will be remembered—maintained that snow is black. This I have since found to be the case.

Long and earnestly did I continue the investigation: but the contemptible reward of my industry and perseverance proved to be only a set of false teeth, two pair of hips, an eye, and a bundle of *billets-doux* from Mr. Windenough to my wife. I might as well here observe that this confirmation of my lady's partiality for Mr. W. occasioned me little uneasiness. That Mrs. Lackobreath should admire any thing so dissimilar to myself was a natural and necessary evil. I am, it is well known, of a robust and corpulent appearance, and, at the same time somewhat diminutive in stature. What wonder then that the lath-like tenuity of my acquaintance, and his altitude which has grown into a proverb, should have met with all due estimation in the eyes of Mrs. Lacko'breath? It is by logic similar to this that true philosophy is enabled to set misfortune at defiance. But to return.

My exertions, as I have before said, proved fruitless. Closet after closet—drawer after drawer—corner after corner—were scrutinized to no purpose. At one time, however, I thought myself sure of my prize, having, in rummaging a dressing-case, accidentally demolished a bottle (I had a remarkably sweet breath) of Hewitt's "Seraphic and Highly-Scented Extract of Heaven or Oil of Archangels"—which, as an agreeable perfume, I here take the liberty of recommending.

FIGURE 53. T. W. White's original font, as seen in the *Southern Literary Messenger* (September 1835). Courtesy of the American Antiquarian Society.

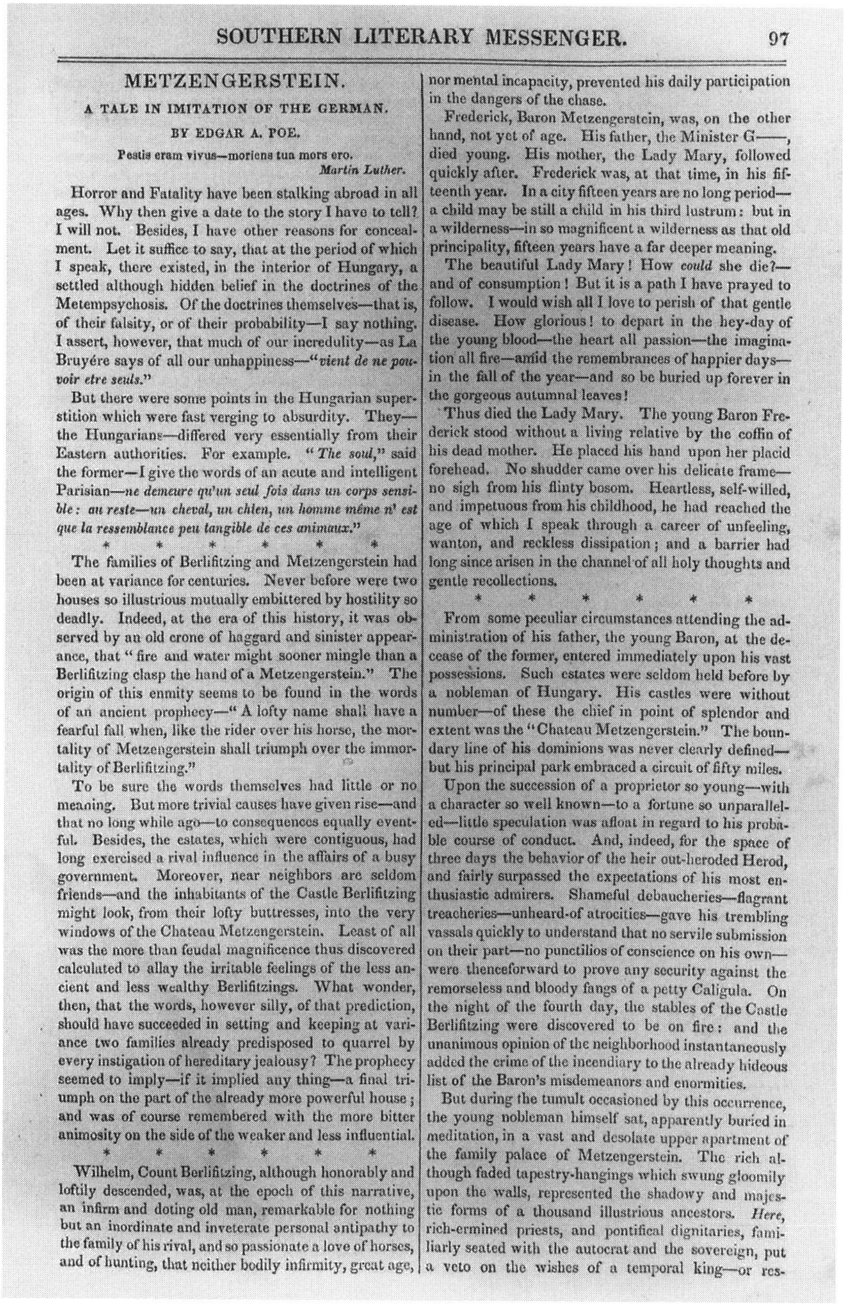

SOUTHERN LITERARY MESSENGER.   97

METZENGERSTEIN.

A TALE IN IMITATION OF THE GERMAN.

BY EDGAR A. POE.

Pestis eram vivus—moriens tua mors ero.
Martin Luther.

Horror and Fatality have been stalking abroad in all ages. Why then give a date to the story I have to tell? I will not. Besides, I have other reasons for concealment. Let it suffice to say, that at the period of which I speak, there existed, in the interior of Hungary, a settled although hidden belief in the doctrines of the Metempsychosis. Of the doctrines themselves—that is, of their falsity, or of their probability—I say nothing. I assert, however, that much of our incredulity—as La Bruyére says of all our unhappiness—"*vient de ne pouvoir etre seuls.*"

But there were some points in the Hungarian superstition which were fast verging to absurdity. They—the Hungarians—differed very essentially from their Eastern authorities. For example. "*The soul,*" said the former—I give the words of an acute and intelligent Parisian—*ne demeure qu'un seul fois dans un corps sensible: au reste—un cheval, un chien, un homme même n' est que la ressemblance peu tangible de ces animaux.*"

*   *   *   *   *   *

The families of Berlifitzing and Metzengerstein had been at variance for centuries. Never before were two houses so illustrious mutually embittered by hostility so deadly. Indeed, at the era of this history, it was observed by an old crone of haggard and sinister appearance, that "fire and water might sooner mingle than a Berlifitzing clasp the hand of a Metzengerstein." The origin of this enmity seems to be found in the words of an ancient prophecy—"A lofty name shall have a fearful fall when, like the rider over his horse, the mortality of Metzengerstein shall triumph over the immortality of Berlifitzing."

To be sure the words themselves had little or no meaning. But more trivial causes have given rise—and that no long while ago—to consequences equally eventful. Besides, the estates, which were contiguous, had long exercised a rival influence in the affairs of a busy government. Moreover, near neighbors are seldom friends—and the inhabitants of the Castle Berlifitzing might look, from their lofty buttresses, into the very windows of the Chateau Metzengerstein. Least of all was the more than feudal magnificence thus discovered calculated to allay the irritable feelings of the less ancient and less wealthy Berlifitzings. What wonder, then, that the words, however silly, of that prediction, should have succeeded in setting and keeping at variance two families already predisposed to quarrel by every instigation of hereditary jealousy? The prophecy seemed to imply—if it implied any thing—a final triumph on the part of the already more powerful house ; and was of course remembered with the more bitter animosity on the side of the weaker and less influential.

*   *   *   *   *

Wilhelm, Count Berlifitzing, although honorably and loftily descended, was, at the epoch of this narrative, an infirm and doting old man, remarkable for nothing but an inordinate and inveterate personal antipathy to the family of his rival, and so passionate a love of horses, and of hunting, that neither bodily infirmity, great age, nor mental incapacity, prevented his daily participation in the dangers of the chase.

Frederick, Baron Metzengerstein, was, on the other hand, not yet of age. His father, the Minister G——, died young. His mother, the Lady Mary, followed quickly after. Frederick was, at that time, in his fifteenth year. In a city fifteen years are no long period—a child may be still a child in his third lustrum : but in a wilderness—in so magnificent a wilderness as that old principality, fifteen years have a far deeper meaning.

The beautiful Lady Mary! How *could* she die?—and of consumption! But it is a path I have prayed to follow. I would wish all I love to perish of that gentle disease. How glorious! to depart in the hey-day of the young blood—the heart all passion—the imagination all fire—amid the remembrances of happier days—in the fall of the year—and so be buried up forever in the gorgeous autumnal leaves!

Thus died the Lady Mary. The young Baron Frederick stood without a living relative by the coffin of his dead mother. He placed his hand upon her placid forehead. No shudder came over his delicate frame—no sigh from his flinty bosom. Heartless, self-willed, and impetuous from his childhood, he had reached the age of which I speak through a career of unfeeling, wanton, and reckless dissipation ; and a barrier had long since arisen in the channel of all holy thoughts and gentle recollections.

*   *   *   *   *

From some peculiar circumstances attending the administration of his father, the young Baron, at the decease of the former, entered immediately upon his vast possessions. Such estates were seldom held before by a nobleman of Hungary. His castles were without number—of these the chief in point of splendor and extent was the "Chateau Metzengerstein." The boundary line of his dominions was never clearly defined—but his principal park embraced a circuit of fifty miles.

Upon the succession of a proprietor so young—with a character so well known—to a fortune so unparalleled—little speculation was afloat in regard to his probable course of conduct. And, indeed, for the space of three days the behavior of the heir out-heroded Herod, and fairly surpassed the expectations of his most enthusiastic admirers. Shameful debaucheries—flagrant treacheries—unheard-of atrocities—gave his trembling vassals quickly to understand that no servile submission on their part—no punctilios of conscience on his own—were thenceforward to prove any security against the remorseless and bloody fangs of a petty Caligula. On the night of the fourth day, the stables of the Castle Berlifitzing were discovered to be on fire : and the unanimous opinion of the neighborhood instantaneously added the crime of the incendiary to the already hideous list of the Baron's misdemeanors and enormities.

But during the tumult occasioned by this occurrence, the young nobleman himself sat, apparently buried in meditation, in a vast and desolate upper apartment of the family palace of Metzengerstein. The rich although faded tapestry-hangings which swung gloomily upon the walls, represented the shadowy and majestic forms of a thousand illustrious ancestors. *Here*, rich-ermined priests, and pontifical dignitaries, familiarly seated with the autocrat and the sovereign, put a veto on the wishes of a temporal king—or res-

FIGURE 54. T. W. White's new font, as seen in the *Southern Literary Messenger* (January 1836). Courtesy of the American Antiquarian Society.

most beautiful specimens of the art of printing we have ever witnessed." "In point of typographical execution it is unequalled by any similar work in the United States," said another. According to a third, its "typographical appearance" was "neat and beautiful," while in the words of a fourth, "No magazine in this country or elsewhere now excels it in the beauty of its *typography*—it is printed in the neatest manner, with the handsomest type, on the best paper."[16] The praise this typographic format garnered in the press vindicated Poe's intuition and helped land him the editorial position. Ten years later, long after Poe had left Richmond, he wrote the new editor, Benjamin Blake Minor, to see if he would print "The Raven" in the "beautiful typography of the *Messenger*."[17]

The reviewer for the *Petersburg Intelligencer* was one of the many who praised the *Messenger's* typography, but although he was content to admire the fine lettering, he did not dwell on it as others had done, for he believed that type was the "mere medium, or vehicle, by which mind is made to commune with mind."[18] Poe disagreed. While the clarity of the new typeface gave the impression of transparency, allowing the reader to see through the inked-up medium to the abstract message, it was his conviction that the medium *was* a message, if not *the* message intended by an author; for that reason, he said, it behooved the critic to read the printedness of a text as closely as one read what was printed. In his reviews, Poe typically examined typographic signification before contrasting it to, and playing it off against, the linguistic significance of the text. Praise of printing in a Poe review often signaled the onset of a bathetic onslaught. Thus, while he praised Hirst's poems as "beautifully printed," he also noted that "there is nothing in the book which is fairly entitled to be called original, either in its conception, execution, or manner as a whole" (*ER,* 594). And, while the typography of Smith's *Powhatan* was "clear beyond comparison," the poem itself, according to Poe, was an "absurdly *flat* affair" with a "grotesque . . . air of bombast and assumption" to it (*ER,* 918).

While Poe appreciated fine printing, then, he did not allow typography to distract his literary judgment. Indeed, he sought to expose just such complacency in others, arguing that in certain circumstances fine typography was used deliberately and strategically to suggest a quality that was substantially lacking in the literary caliber of the text. Most notoriously, in the course of an 1845 review of Longfellow, he suggested that the poet's publishers manipulated the typography of his works in order to elevate their prestige. With some bitterness, he wondered aloud "how much their success may be attributed to the luxurious manner in which, as merely physical books, they have been presented to the public" (*ER,*

16. "Supplement to the Southern Literary Messenger," *Southern Literary Messenger* 2 (January, 1836): 134, 136, 137, 135. The examples could be multiplied. See also "Supplement," *Southern Literary Messenger* 2 (April, 1836): 344, 348.

17. *Poe Log,* 497.

18. Quoted in "Supplement to the Southern Literary Messenger," *Southern Literary Messenger* 2 (January, 1836): 134.

761).[19] Poe also speculated that the reputation of the unjustifiably acclaimed Rufus Dawes was cemented permanently when his poems were published as "the *initial* volume of a series, the avowed object of which was the setting forth, in the best array of paper, type, and pictorial embellishment, the *élite* of the American poets" (*ER*, 491).

That it was possible to gull readers into regarding the works of Longfellow and Dawes as great literature by virtue of their fine binding, typography, and paper simply underscored for Poe, as it should do for us, the idea that the materiality of the text signifies in ways independent of, and sometimes divergent from, the semantic level of textual meaning. In antebellum America, fine printing and elaborate binding suggested not only an eminently readable book, but also the taste and discrimination of the book owner, who was only sometimes also a book reader.[20] "If you hear one praising a new publication, now-a-days," complained an anonymous critic in 1806, "and ask him in what its merit consists, he will describe them thus: 'Sir, it is printed on Whatman's best wire-wove paper, (soft as a glove,) the type is beautiful, bound in morocco, and, in a word, as elegant and *tasty a thing* as ever was seen."[21] The substitution of the book's "tastiness" for the reader's "taste" here suggests the emergence of an ethos in which books have become just one more luxury commodity, to be consumed by the wealthy. The gourmandization of literature was a phenomenon Poe well understood, and as Alexander Hammond points out, gastronomic figures permeated both his critical and creative writings. Poe's story "Bon Bon," in particular, details the life of an author-chef known equally for "his *essais* and his *omlettes*."[22] In serving up elegantly printed texts, Poe believed, publishers encouraged the public to consider them, generically and unthinkingly, as literarily superior regardless of their contents.

There was, moreover, a decidedly class-oriented dimension to Poe's critique of typographic showmanship, since he was painfully aware that only the wealthiest publishers and their favored clients could avail themselves of the best types and the newest presses. Deprived, for the most part, of such grandiose resources himself, Poe felt justified in lashing out at the "evident toadyism" of a reading public

19. The background of Poe's campaign against Longfellow is detailed by Sidney P. Moss, *Poe's Literary Battles: The Critic in the Context of His Literary Milieu* (Carbondale: Southern Illinois University Press, 1963), 132–89.

20. For an nuanced account of how books functioned as "multivalent objects" in nineteenth-century America, see Ronald J. Zboray and Mary Saracino Zboray, "Books, Reading, and the World of Goods in Antebellum New England," *American Quarterly* 48 (1996): 587–622. Equally suggestive, although focused quite specifically on bindings, is Jeffrey D. Groves, "Judging Literary Books by Their Covers: House Styles, Ticknor and Fields, and Literary Promotion," in *Reading Books: Essays on the Material Text and Literature in America*, ed. Michele Moylan and Lane Stiles (Amherst: University of Massachusetts Press, 1996), 75–100.

21. "Customers of a Circulating Library," *The Emerald* 1 (1806): 68. Again, the italics here are not mine.

22. See Alexander Hammond, "Consumption, Exchange, and the Literary Marketplace: From the Folio Club Tales to *Pym*," in *Poe's "Pym": Critical Explorations,* ed. Richard Kopley (Durham, N.C.: Duke University Press, 1992), 153–66; Poe, *Poetry and Tales,* ed. Patrick F. Quinn (New York: Library of America, 1984), 166. This text is hereafter abbreviated *PT*.

that would give to Longfellow's "fine paper and large type, to his morocco binding and gilt edges . . . and to the illustrations of his poems by Huntington, that
amount of indiscriminate approbation which neither could nor would have been
given to the poems themselves" (*ER,* 1172).[23] At their best, then, elegant fonts
could enhance and amplify an author's status; at worst, they could be used by
publishers to distract a reader's attention from works of poor literary quality.

The signifying qualities of letterforms were more socially stable. Ideally, Poe
believed, a particular font or case could convey a subtle message or enhance the
semantic level of signification. Thus, in the midst of an 1845 controversy with
the pseudonymous 'Outis' over Longfellow's alleged plagiarism, Poe paused to
question why Outis had referred to the title of one of Dana's poems in capitals,
as "THE DYING RAVEN." There was, Poe believed, an "argument embodied in the
capital letters." The argument, quite specifically, was that Poe had plagiarized his
own best known poem, "The Raven," from Dana's less well known piece. The
title was "so printed," he concluded, "for the purpose of safely insinuating a
charge which not even an Outis had the impudence openly to utter" (*ER,* 726).[24]

The idea that specific fonts carried particular tones or meanings was not a new
one. Blackletter or gothic type was typically used in legal texts, while the master
typefounder James Rolandson noted in 1816 that his Long Primer No. 2 and
Small Pica No. 2 were "suited only for works of fancy."[25] Poe's sometime friend
Nathaniel P. Willis also commented suggestively on the semiotics of type, praising
the visual effect of the *Boston Transcript,* with the observation that "The *type* is
captivating—a kind of insinuating, piquant, well-bred *brevier,* that catches the
eye like a coquette in a ball-room."[26] Others theorized the connection between
type and tone more thoroughly. In 1787, for example, Francis Hopkinson, a Philadelphia man of letters, published an essay in which he called for a more reasoned
selection of letter face "so as to make it expressive not only of an author's narrative, opinions, or arguments, but also of the peculiarities of his temper, and the

23. Poe was not the only author to level a class-based critique against typographic showmanship. Reviewing the poetry of Rufus Dawes, William Joseph Snelling wrote: "Say what we please, there is nothing
like fair paper and well cut type to set off a graceful poem or enliven a plainly told story. A bad poem in
beautiful dress, however, entirely destroys our philosophy, and we throw it out of the window with the
greater gusto from that very circumstance; on the same principle that we kick an impudent valet down the
stairs with more pleasure, when he is dressed like a gentleman." *The Amateur* 1 (15 June 1830): 10.

24. In a discriminating analysis of the Poe-Outis exchange, Meredith McGill notes correctly that Poe
equivocates in his reading of the offending capitals, since reiterating them seems to grant them fresh authority. The very danger they suggest, however, simply underscores the symbolic freight of the typography.
Poe's reading is more resonant still if one accepts, with Burton R. Pollin, that the Outis letter was written
by Poe himself, although the jury is still out on the question of his authorship. See McGill, "Poe, Literary
Nationalism, and Authorial Identity," in *The American Face of Edgar Allan Poe,* ed. Shawn Rosenheim and
Stephen Rachman (Baltimore: Johns Hopkins University Press, 1995), 296; Pollin, "Poe as Author of the
'Outis' Letter and 'The Bird of the Dream,' " *Poe Studies* 20 (1987): 10–15; and Kent Ljungquist and
Burford Jones, "The Identity of 'Outis': A Further Chapter in the Poe-Longfellow War," *American Litera-
ture* 60 (1988): 402–15.

25. Quoted in Rollo G. Silver, *Typefounding in America, 1787–1825* (Charlottesville: University Press
of Virginia, 1965), 26.

26. Nathaniel P. Willis, "Ephemera," *Compete Works* (New York: J. S. Redfield, 1846), 702.

vivacity of his feelings." By way of example, Hopkinson described an imaginary controversy in which contending authors resorted to increasingly large fonts to express their "degree of vociferation."[27] This was a scenario Poe well understood, and something much like it occurs in his satiric tale of 1844, "The Literary Life of Thingum Bob, Esq." Poe's squib recounts the course of a furious controversy following the submission of plagiarized poems to four neighboring literary magazines. The plagiarizer, Thingum Bob, looks on as the magazines attack first him and then one another, and in recording the fray, he provides a running commentary on the rhetoric of controversiality. While Bob is keenly and humorously alive to the drubbings dealt him by each periodical, he is especially aware of the resonances carried by particular letterforms. Attacked by a wag in the local press as being "entirely devoid of imagination," which is "not only the soul of POESY, but also its very heart," Bob concedes the judgment to be "very severe," but believes the "unkindest cut" was to print the word poesy in "small caps." "In those five preeminent letters," he writes, "what a world of bitterness is there not involved!" (*PT,* 769). The word *periodical*—"in Italics, too"—strikes Bob as the height of sarcasm. Likewise, an editorial using a lower case "them" and an upper case "WE" creates for Bob the image of a critic "looking down" on his competitors "in gigantic capitals!" The effect to Bob is overpowering. "It was too *bitter!*" he exclaims, "it was wormwood—it was gall" (*PT,* 769, 771). While Bob was manifestly an object of, as well as a vehicle for, Poe's literary satire, Poe himself held that specific fonts could be manipulated to inflect conventionally signified meanings and to insinuate additional meanings to the conventionally signified.

On occasion, Poe manipulated font size to accentuate his message, most notably in his review of George Jones's *History of Ancient America* (1843). A bizarre work that claimed Christianity had been brought to pre-Columbian America by the Apostle Thomas, the *History of America* was both arrogant in tone and luxurious in execution, utilizing dozens of customized fonts and featuring no less than five separate title pages (figure 55). In part, Poe poked fun at the specifically historical claims of the author; he devoted more energy, however, to mocking the materiality of the book, which he judged, not entirely without truth to be, "one of the most magnificent things ever put forth from a press" (*ER,* 644). Just as he had read nastiness into the upper case text of Outis, Poe read smugness in Jones's elaborate typography. He derided the title pages, excoriated the engravings, and

27. Quoted in Rollo G. Silver, *The American Printer, 1787–1825* (Charlottesville: University Press of Virginia, 1967), 145. In 1787 as in 1827, when Poe's first volume was published, the idea that type expressed voice stood in contrast to the popular idea that printedness engendered impersonality. As Michael Warner and others have pointed out, print culture came to be associated with the emergence of a bourgeois public sphere characterized by the evacuation of personality; revealingly, Poe rejected the practice of anonymous reviewing and sought to read the identity of an author even when it wasn't public knowledge. On conflicting understandings of printedness and presence in early America, see Michael Warner, *Letters of the Republic: Publication and the Public Sphere in Eighteenth-Century America* (Cambridge: Harvard University Press, 1990), and Leon Jackson, "Jedidiah Morse and the Transformation of Print Culture in New England, 1784–1826," *Early American Literature* 34 (1999): 2–31.

AN

ORIGINAL HISTORY

OF

ANCIENT AMERICA.

Founded upon the

RUINS OF ANTIQUITY:

THE

Identity of the Aborigines

with the People of

TYRUS AND ISRAEL:

and the Introduction of Christianity by

THE APOSTLE S^T THOMAS.

BY

GEORGE JONES, R.S.I.: M.F.S.V.; &c

DEDICATED TO HIS GRACE

THE ARCHBISHOP OF CANTERBURY.

Published by Longman, Brown, Green & Longmans, London.

Harper & Brothers, New-York.

Alexander Duncker, Berlin.

& Frederick Klienchsieck, Paris.

1843.

COPYRIGHT SECURED IN ENGLAND AND AMERICA.

FIGURE 55. One of George Jones's five title pages for *The History of Ancient America* (1843). Widener Library, Harvard University.

150

mocked Jones's obsequious capitalization of King and Monarch (Jones had dedicated the work to Frederick William of Prussia) by suggesting that he could, perhaps, "render the compliment more pointed" by in future using "only a small *g*"
when referring to "his GOD." As his coup de grâce, Poe offered an analysis of
a single Jonesian exclamation point, "by which he means," said Poe, " 'See that!
listen to GEORGE JONES!' " Pursuing the idea that letter face shaped meaning to
absurd lengths, Poe wondered that Jones "did not instruct his printer to put two
[exclamation points] in the place of one, or have a Brobdignagian one founded
on purpose" (*ER*, 644).[28] Lacking his own Brobdignagian fonts, Poe limited himself to satirizing Jones's egotism by using his whole name often and always in
small caps, mocking his self-inflation by imitating on a Lilliputian scale his typographic bluster.

"The italics are mine." Poe (*ER*, 1427)

Although Poe's comments on letterforms and typefaces are scattered, when put
together they offer the outlines of what is, essentially, a semiotic theory of typography, according to which culturally sanctioned meanings are manifest within the
specific dimensions of printing types. In typography as in cryptography, Poe as-
pired to be the "king of secret readers," able to determine the hidden grammars
of signifying systems and willing to lay them bare for an appreciative public. But
as Shawn Rosenheim has brilliantly demonstrated in his study of semiology and
cryptography, exploration of coded languages led Poe disturbingly close to the
idea that the meanings of signs were merely arbitrary and capable of any, or no,
meaning at all.[29] Ironically, while Poe published and solved the cryptograms sent
to him by the reading public, he found his faith in the stable meanings of letterforms challenged in the process. Reproducing the cryptograms demanded the
"wildest typography" of the printing office, dislocated the conventional contexts
of alphabetic signification, and rendered conventionally resonant letterforms
meaningless (*ER*, 1281).[30]

As an author and editor, too, Poe struggled to fix meaning through fixed typographic convention. The passage of a text from pen to print was so characterized
by a division of labor that careless errors could leave an author's text as meaningless as a cryptogram. Typesetting was a physically and mentally demanding task,
and because compositors were paid by units of type set, they tended to work at

28. Throughout the review, Poe refers to exclamation points by the archaic name "admiration note,"
thereby offering another commentary on Jones's tone of self-congratulation. See *Oxford English Dictionary*,
s.v. "admiration." On Poe's abiding interest in the power of punctuation to inflect meaning, see *ER*,
1424–26.
29. Shawn Rosenheim, "The King of 'Secret Readers': Edgar Poe, Cryptography, and the Origins of the
Detective Story," *ELH* 56 (1989): 375–400.
30. Many of the cryptograms Poe solved have been conveniently reproduced by Clarence S. Brigham,
Edgar Allan Poe's Contributions to "Alexander's Weekly Messenger" (Worcester, Mass.: American Antiquarian
Society, 1943).

speed.[31] Errors almost inevitably crept into texts and were often left—undetected and uncorrected—since proofreading was not enforced with any great rigor. In the smallest printing shops, responsibility for proofreading began and ended with the compositors themselves, who would check proofs and, if necessary, "correct in metal." Larger establishments did, on occasion, hire proofreaders, especially when important texts were in press, but almost none could afford to employ them full time.[32] Moreover, at even the best-supervised printing shops, compositors still had to contend with authors' nearly illegible manuscripts. Hours could be spent "in deciphering their words," recalled a former compositor, Uriel Crocker. "Frequently, if we could not succeed in making out the words, we would put in words of about the same length that made nonsense, or would leave a vacant space or turn the type upside down."[33] Failing to "decipher" the hand of the author, the compositors would thus create unsolvable cryptograms of their own.

Poe's anxiety over loss of authorial control of his medium (and thus his message) is dramatized humorously in "X-ing a Paragrab," a tale that recalls the creative antics of Crocker and his colleagues. Here, the theft of all the letter *o*s from a printer's case compels a compositor to substitute the letter *x* throughout a newspaper editorial he is setting up, a move that quite literally renders it cryptographic to the bemused reading public. Stumped by the editorial, which begins "Sx hx, Jxhn! hxw nxw? Txld yxu sx, yxu knxw," readers declare the text "in-X-plicable" (*PT*, 922, 923). The irony, of course, is that it is not. In Poe's semiological universe, x always equals o or some other equally determinate unit of meaning. The last laugh is on the reading public.[34] More dramatically, but no less conveniently, Poe corrects a typographical error in "A Tale of the Ragged Mountains," to solve the mystery of Augustus Bedloe, who has, perhaps, through metempsychosis re-experienced the life of a fifty-seven-years-dead colonial agent named Oldeb. When Bedloe dies in circumstances that parallel Oldeb's murder the previous century and the local newspaper "misprints" his name as Bedlo, the narrator infers a palindromic connection, "for Bedlo, without the *e*," he mutters, "what is it

31. The use of sliding pay scales encouraged compositors to work hastily; in the 1840s, one typesetter began to initiate speed and endurance competitions. See Walker Rumble, "A Time of Giants: Speed Composition in Nineteenth-Century America," *Printing History* 28 (1992): 14.

32. On the responsibility of the compositor to proofread his sheets, see Edward Grattan, *The Printer's Companion* (Philadelphia: Printed and Published by the Proprietor, 1846), 24–27, 49–56. On more developed practices, see Rollo G. Silver, "Mathew Carey's Proofreaders," *Studies in Bibliography* 17 (1969): 123–33, and Silver, *American Printer*, 93–94.

33. *Memorial of Uriel Crocker* (Boston: n. p., 1891), 33.

34. This story is dismissed by almost all critics as a slight effort. Arthur Hobson Quinn calls it a "satiric trifle," while Kenneth Silverman considers it "scarcely more than a humorous bagatelle." See Quinn, *Edgar Allan Poe: A Critical Biography* (1941; Baltimore: Johns Hopkins University Press, 1998), 596–97, and Silverman, *Edgar A. Poe: Mournful and Never-ending Remembrance* (New York: Harper, 1992), 406. The only extended treatment is that by Leroy Perkins and Joseph A. Dupras, "Mystery and Meaning in Poe's 'X-ing a Paragrab,'" *Studies in Short Fiction* 27 (1990): 489–94. My own reading, however, is at odds with their claim that "in the 'aporia' or gap of comprehensibility which the X'd paragraph presents, Poe typographically demarcates a zone of interpretive freedom, a break from the tyranny of authorial intention" (492). While Poe is obsessed by indeterminacy, I believe, he always holds out the promise of determinate knowledge.

but Oldeb conversed?" Convinced that his acquaintance has, indeed, transmigrated souls, the narrator all too quickly dismisses the suggestion of the editor that this is "a mere typographical error," instead finding in the variant spelling suggestions of a "truth" that is "stranger than any fiction" (*PT*, 665). "X-ing a Paragrab" and "A Tale of the Ragged Mountains" suggest Poe's anxieties regarding the capacity of poorly placed type to warp or totally obliterate meaning, while at the same time allowing him to suppress his fear by decoding such errors to reveal the truth.[35]

Poe's fictional depictions of typesetting error are, however, just that: fictions. As carefully crafted fantasies, they allowed him to regain control of an essentially mediated process that took meaning out of an author's hands and placed it into those of compositors, pressmen, and editors. In reality, he was less calm. When he was reading copy for his own journal, recalled a colleague, "even a typographical error threw him into an ecstasy of passion."[36] Poe's anger reflected a longstanding frustration with the way in which his own manuscripts had been treated.

The appearance of Poe's first volume, *Tamerlane*, in 1827, offers a case study in the pitfalls of rendering a manuscript in print. Produced by a Boston job printer, Calvin Thomas, *Tamerlane* was a wretched piece of workmanship, and forty pages of cheap paper, shoddy composition, and smudgy ink marred Poe's maiden effort. Barely older than his client, Thomas was a careless compositor and repeatedly misread Poe's manuscript: "list" became "lisp," "fever" became "ferver," "steep" became "sleep," and, somehow, the line "In climes of my imagining" became "Inclines of my imaginary."[37] Poe's second and third volumes were scarcely better. The printers of *Al Aaraaf, Tamerlane, and Minor Poems,* Matchett & Woods, possessed a far wider selection of types, but their use of a fat-faced font on the title page suggested they were more at home in the world of job printing than in producing literary works (figure 56).[38] However, it was Poe's third volume—*Poems by Edgar A. Poe*—that marked the author's typographic nadir. Paid for with subscriptions from his West Point colleagues, *Poems* was, one recalled, "a puny volume, of about fifty pages, bound in boards and badly printed on course

35. G. R. Thompson argues that Poe uses the narrator's reading of the typographic error as proof of metempsychosis to suggest his naiveté. We need, however, to distinguish the narrator's position of gullibility from Poe's own position, which promises both typographic and metaphysical proofs. See Thompson, "Is Poe's 'A Tale of the Ragged Mountains' a Hoax?" *Studies in Short Fiction* 6 (1969): 454–60.

36. Charles F. Briggs, quoted in Kenneth K. Cameron, "A Late Defense of Poe by N. P. Willis," *American Transcendental Quarterly* 36 (1977): 74. For an enumeration and discussion of typographic errors in the *Broadway Journal,* see Edgar Allan Poe, *Writings in the Broadway Journal: Nonfictional Prose. Part 2: The Annotations,* ed. Burton R. Pollin (New York: Gordian Press, 1986), xlv–xlvi.

37. The textual history and publication of *Tamerlane* are detailed by Thomas Ollive Mabbott, introduction to *Tamerlane and Other Poems,* by Edgar Allan Poe (1827; New York: Facsimile Text Society, 1941), esp. xx–xliv.

38. See *Al Aaraaf, Tamerlane, and Minor Poems* (1829; New York: Facsimile Text Society, 1933). On the development of Fat Faces and their association with commercial and job printing, see Geoffrey Dowding, *An Introduction to the History of Printing Types* (Clerkenwell, Eng.: Wace, 1961), 161–67. Poe had written to his guardian, John Allan, requesting one hundred dollars so that *Al Aaraaf* could be printed "in a style equal to any of our American publications." Allan, needless to say, refused. Poe to Allan, 29 May 1829, *Letters,* 1:20.

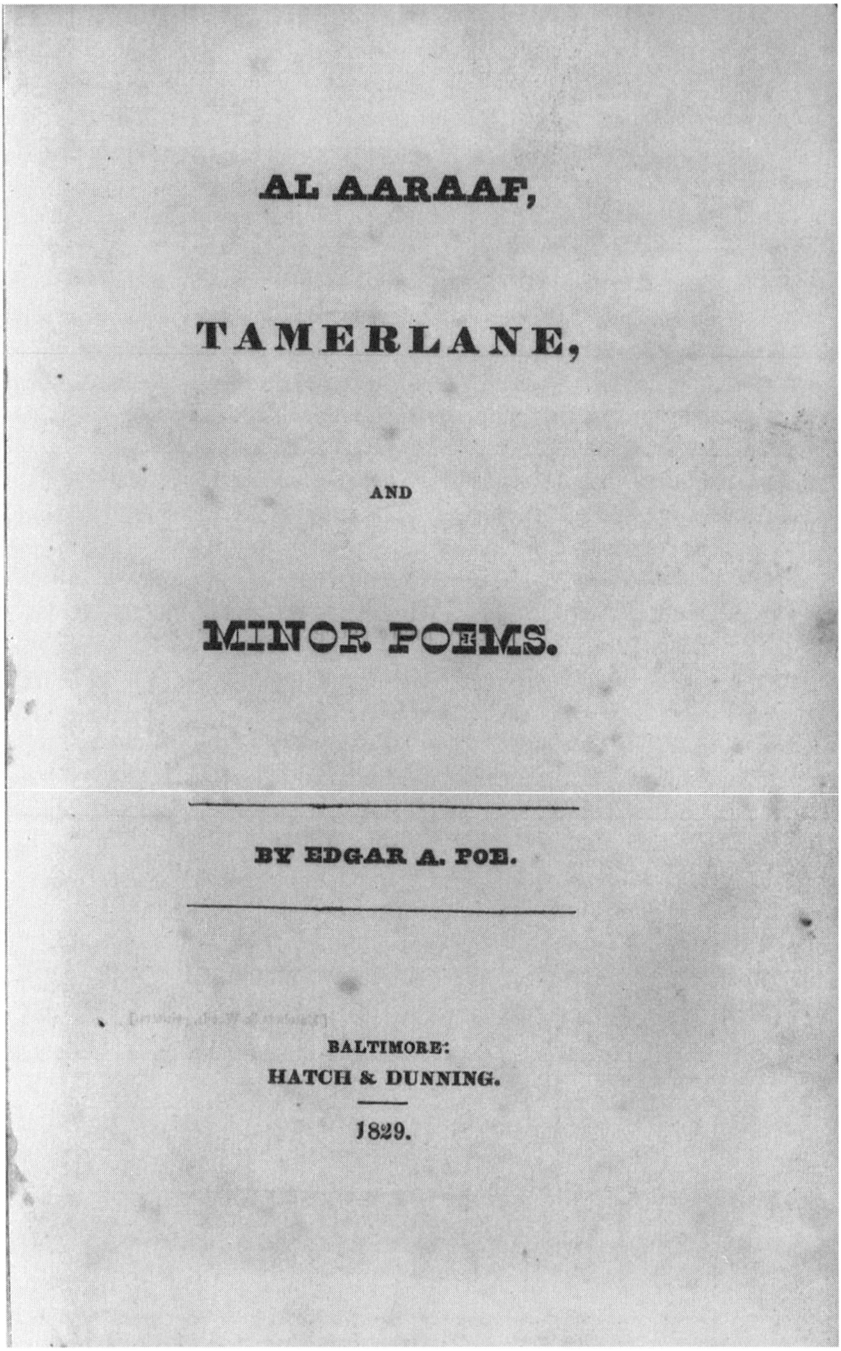

AL AARAAF,

TAMERLANE,

AND

MINOR POEMS.

BY EDGAR A. POE.

BALTIMORE:
HATCH & DUNNING.

1829.

FIGURE 56. The title page of Poe's *Al Aaraaf, Tamerlane, and Minor Poems* (1829). By permission of the Houghton Library, Harvard University.

[*sic*] paper." The text was greeted at the Point "with a general expression of disgust," one cadet scrawling in his copy "This book is a damn cheat."[39] Desperate for the approval if not the admiration of his peers, Poe was evidently mortified by his books' typographical errors; in a biographical account dictated to Henry Hirst in 1843, he simply wrote his first out of existence, while complaining that the others were victims of "slovenly printing."[40]

Temperamentally, then, Poe was not inclined to trust printers. Throughout his critical career, he whined ceaselessly about the liberties they took and the errors they made. He complained of the "distortion of his sentences by the printer's . . . general substitution of a semi-colon, or comma, for the dash of the MS" (*ER*, 1425). He raged about the "thousand outrageous typographical blunders" he discovered in an otherwise beautifully printed book he was reviewing (*ER*, 991). And he fretted about the "vexatious *errata*" that began to creep into his own magazine (*ER*, 1093). In submitting what was to be his final poem to *Sartain's Magazine* in February 1849, Poe provided detailed instructions on exactly how the poem was to be printed; predictably enough, his instructions were not followed.[41]

If Poe "invented" the detective story to fix the relation between signs and meanings, he also invented himself as a proofreader for the same reason and in much the same way. A veritable Dupin of the press room, Poe had a wholly deserved reputation for typographical sleuthing. "He was a minute detector of slips of the pen," recalled a fellow editor, "and, probably, was unequalled as a proof reader."[42] Indeed, in an 1844 article, he boasted of finding the only error—an inverted *o*—an an otherwise perfect imprint (*ER*, 1342). When, in the course of quoting and commenting on the text of another, Poe wrote "The italics are mine," this was, perhaps, as close as he could get to wresting typographic as well as semantic authority from the hands of his compositors (*ER*, 1427). Ultimately, however, it was not enough.

Poe was by no means the only writer who felt either distrust for, disgust with, or exclusion from the world of printedness. Most, however, contented themselves by immersion in a culture of manuscript production and scribal reproduction. It was a world Poe both knew and understood. At the University of Virginia and at West Point, students participated in a full-fledged scribal culture, generating and disseminating manuscript productions for the consumption of discrete coteries of readers. While at West Point, Poe himself had produced "vicious doggerel" on the officers he disliked which he had his roommate copy left-handed and

39. *Poe Log*, 118; Silverman, *Edgar A. Poe*, 69. In point of fact, Poe's 1831 *Poems* was 124 pages in length and not fifty. See *Bibliography of American Literature*, comp. Jacob Blanck, Virginia L. Smyers and Michael Winship (New Haven: Yale University Press, 1955–91), 7:115 (item 16125).

40. Quoted in Mabbott, introduction to *Tamerlane*, xxxix.

41. See Heidi M. Schultz, "Edgar Allan Poe Submits 'The Bells' to 'Sartain's Magazine,' " *Resources for American Literary Study* 22 (1996): 166–81. Schultz points out, however, that, after their own fashion, the compositors did make concessions to accommodate Poe's lineation.

42. Charles F. Briggs, *Holden's Dollar Magazine* 4 (December 1849): 766, quoted in *Edgar Allan Poe: The Critical Heritage*, ed. I. M. Walker (London: Routledge & Kegan Paul, 1986), 333.

"post . . . around the building." "Poems and squibs of local interest were daily issued" from his room, recalled another cadet.[43] In a more serious vein, Poe might also have belonged to West Point's Dialectic Society, a group that met weekly to read aloud members' manuscript essays and poems. Whether he attended their meetings or not, it was a clear anticipation of the Folio Club he would invent to frame his earliest short stories less than two years later.[44] Unlike the Dialecticians, however, the members of Poe's fictitious club are fiercely competitive, voting on who has the worst manuscript and leaving the unfortunate author to pay for the group's food and wine. As Poe described the Folio Club story, the newest member of the club, distraught at being voted the worst author, "seizes the seventeen M.SS. upon the table, and, rushing from the house, determines to appeal, by printing the whole, from the decision of the Club, to that of the public."[45] Like the luckless member of the Folio Club, Poe emerged from and was drawn back toward the world of manuscript production, yet rushed time and again into the world of print.

Unwilling to confine himself to the world of scribal production but unable to accept the contingencies of the typographic medium, Poe sought for ways to bring the authenticity of the one and the efficiency of the other into fruitful coordination. In part, as we have seen, he achieved at least a semblance of coordination by imitating printedness in his handwriting. His most interesting experiments, however, found him attempting to imitate and reproduce handwriting in print. His first attempt is seen in the "Autography" series published in the *Southern Literary Messenger* in 1836. Predicated on the idea that when analyzed carefully, handwriting revealed personality traits, "Autography" broke typographic ground in providing facsimiles of twenty-four celebrity autographs, to which Poe added satiric letters and semi-serious handwriting analyses (figure 57).[46] The entire series, as Meredith McGill has pointed out, was riven with irony: signatures, which are typically seen as a mark of authenticity, are here copies; the letters to which they are appended and which they guarantee are fake; and the series, while

43. *Poe Log,* 108. On the importance of scribal production in American colleges, see Dean Grodzins and Leon Jackson, "Books and Colleges, 1790–1840," in *An Extensive Republic: Print, Culture, and Society in a New Nation,* ed. Robert A. Gross and Mary Kelley, vol. 2 of *A History of the Book in America* (Cambridge: Cambridge University Press, forthcoming). On the place of manuscript in an essentially print-oriented civic culture, see, more generally, David S. Shields, "The Manuscript in the British American World of Print," *Proceedings of the American Antiquarian Society* 102 (1992): 403–16.
44. On the Dialectic Club and literary activity at West Point, see Karl E. Oelke, "Poe at West Point: A Revaluation," *Poe Studies* 6 (1973): 1–6.
45. Poe to Harrison Hall, 2 September 1836, *Letters,* 1:104. On the *Folio Club* project, see Alexander Hammond, "A Reconstruction of Poe's 1833 'Tales of the Folio Club': Preliminary Notes," *Poe Studies* 5 (1972): 25–32. Hammond suggests that Poe's model was, in all likelihood, the Delphian Club of Baltimore (25).
46. "Autography," as many reviewers at the time noted, was not an original idea but was derived, quite explicitly, from an 1833 essay in the popular British periodical *Fraser's Magazine,* in which autographs were reproduced in facsimile and analyzed. On the development of handwriting analysis as an index of unique character, I have found especially useful Tamara Plakins Thornton, *Handwriting in America: A Cultural History* (New Haven: Yale University Press, 1996), 77–107.

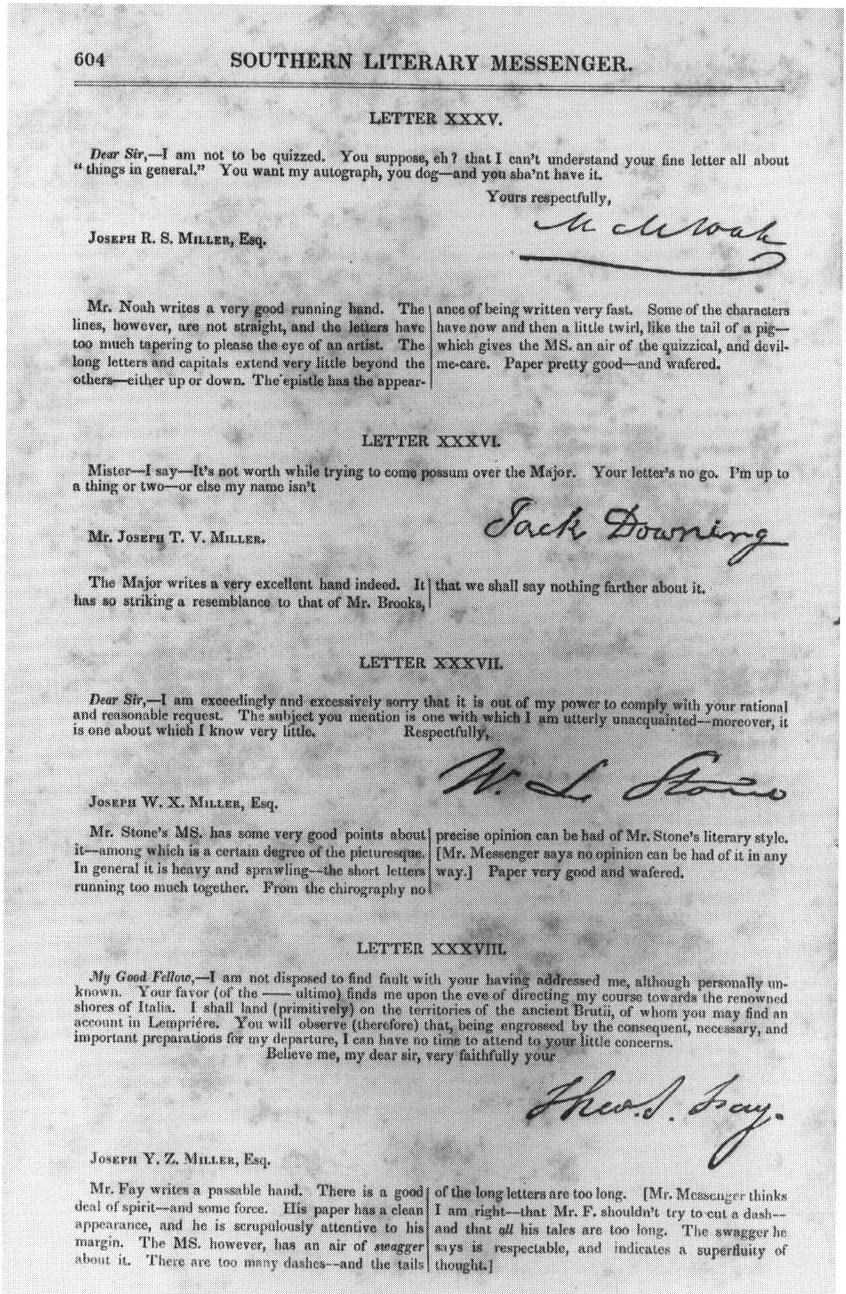

604   SOUTHERN LITERARY MESSENGER.

LETTER XXXV.

Dear Sir,—I am not to be quizzed. You suppose, eh? that I can't understand your fine letter all about "things in general." You want my autograph, you dog—and you sha'n't have it.

Yours respectfully,

JOSEPH R. S. MILLER, Esq.

Mr. Noah writes a very good running hand. The lines, however, are not straight, and the letters have too much tapering to please the eye of an artist. The long letters and capitals extend very little beyond the others—either up or down. The epistle has the appearance of being written very fast. Some of the characters have now and then a little twirl, like the tail of a pig—which gives the MS. an air of the quizzical, and devil-me-care. Paper pretty good—and wafered.

LETTER XXXVI.

Mister—I say—It's not worth while trying to come possum over the Major. Your letter's no go. I'm up to a thing or two—or else my name isn't

Mr. JOSEPH T. V. MILLER.

The Major writes a very excellent hand indeed. It has so striking a resemblance to that of Mr. Brooks, that we shall say nothing farther about it.

LETTER XXXVII.

Dear Sir,—I am exceedingly and excessively sorry that it is out of my power to comply with your rational and reasonable request. The subject you mention is one with which I am utterly unacquainted—moreover, it is one about which I know very little.   Respectfully,

JOSEPH W. X. MILLER, Esq.

Mr. Stone's MS. has some very good points about it—among which is a certain degree of the picturesque. In general it is heavy and sprawling—the short letters running too much together. From the chirography no precise opinion can be had of Mr. Stone's literary style. [Mr. Messenger says no opinion can be had of it in any way.] Paper very good and wafered.

LETTER XXXVIII.

My Good Fellow,—I am not disposed to find fault with your having addressed me, although personally unknown. Your favor (of the —— ultimo) finds me upon the eve of directing my course towards the renowned shores of Italia. I shall land (primitively) on the territories of the ancient Brutii, of whom you may find an account in Lempriére. You will observe (therefore) that, being engrossed by the consequent, necessary, and important preparations for my departure, I can have no time to attend to your little concerns.
Believe me, my dear sir, very faithfully your

JOSEPH Y. Z. MILLER, Esq.

Mr. Fay writes a passable hand. There is a good deal of spirit—and some force. His paper has a clean appearance, and he is scrupulously attentive to his margin. The MS. however, has an air of *swagger* about it. There are too many dashes—and the tails of the long letters are too long. [Mr. Messenger thinks I am right—that Mr. F. shouldn't try to cut a dash—and that *all* his tales are too long. The swagger he says is respectable, and indicates a superfluity of thought.]

FIGURE 57. Poe attempted to break down the barriers between print and handwriting in his "Autography" analyses, *Southern Literary Messenger* (August 1836). Courtesy of the American Antiquarian Society.

itself printed, is essentially irreproducible since the woodcuts from which the signatures were taken are the property of the *Messenger* and are too expensive for others to reproduce.[47] To Poe, however, the series was an immense success for more immediately personal reasons, since it enabled him to capture the elusive and unique "aura" of the handwritten while remaining in the context of the printed.

Of course, the technology utilized to reproduce the autographs was at least two centuries old by the time the *Messenger* came to employ it on Poe's behalf. The signatures were carefully traced onto blocks of hard wood which were then carved so that the lettering stood out in relief. So designed, the blocks could be locked into forms along with type, inked up, and printed from. The production of the blocks for "Autography" was probably a somewhat slow and expensive process, but for Poe it held out the promise of mechanical reproduction that retained the originality of an author's hand while obviating the pitfalls associated with typographic errors. Poe returned to "Autography" again in 1841–42, running a second and more extensive series of analyses in *Graham's Magazine.* By this time, however, he was looking at more advanced technologies of reproduction.

In particular, Poe took an interest in lithography, beginning an informal apprenticeship under Peter Duval in Philadelphia.[48] Developed by Alois Senefelder in the 1790s, lithographic printing utilized smooth limestone blocks onto which designs were drawn with a grease pencil and etched with acid. Ink took to the designs and was repelled by the dampened, etched portions of the stone, allowing the reproduction of remarkably clear images. Lithography marked an advance on wood engraving, for as Philip Gaskell explains, the stones were quickly prepared, extremely durable, and easily reused.[49] Of more interest to Poe, however, would have been the fact that lithography was less mediated than conventional printing, since it could reproduce something like an author's handwriting and did not involve thousands of misplaceable letter types. Poe's apprenticeship and any sustained involvement with lithographic printing were cut short when he found that the stooping posture demanded by the process was taking a toll on his health, although his enthusiasm might also have been dampened by a sneaking disrespect for Duval and a growing realization of how painfully inefficient lithographic

47. See Meredith L. McGill, "The Duplicity of the Pen," in *Language Machines: Technologies of Literary and Cultural Production,* ed. Jeffrey Masten, Peter Stallybrass, and Nancy Vickers (New York: Routledge, 1997), 62–63.

48. On Poe's study of lithography, see Lambert A. Wilmer, *Merlin, Baltimore, 1827: Together with "Recollections of Edgar A. Poe,"* ed. Thomas Ollive Mabbott (New York: Scholars' Facsimiles & Reprints, 1941), 33. On Duval, see Joseph J. Moldenhauer, "Beyond the Tamarind Tree: A New Poe Letter," *American Literature* 42 (1971): 474–75. Poe had, in all likelihood, been familiar with lithography since his student days, as professors at the University of Virginia had purchased a lithographic press in 1826 to reproduce lecture notes and class outlines. See Philip Alexander Bruce, *History of the University of Virginia, 1819–1919: The Lengthened Shadow of One Man,* 5 vols. (New York: Macmillan, 1920), 2:130–31.

49. Philip Gaskell, *A New Introduction to Bibliography* (Winchester: St. Paul's Bibliographies, 1995), 267–68.

printing was when compared to increasingly speedy letter presses.[50] By 1845, Poe could refer to lithography as a "comparatively frivolous invention."[51]

The ease with which Poe could dismiss lithography as a viable technology of reproduction was a clear indication of the extent to which, by 1845, he had reinvested his aspirations in the newer and more promising technique of anastatic printing. Developed in Germany and England in the early 1840s, anastatic printing was essentially a mode of textual reproduction rather than of production. Printed sheets were brushed with highly diluted nitric acid, blotted, and then pressed firmly onto copper plates. The acid ate into the copper plate but in so doing left a lightly etched impression of the printing from the original sheet. The plate, when treated and inked, could then be used, in much the same way as a stereotype plate, to produce as many or as few reproductions as the printer desired.[52]

In an essay on anastatic printing published in the *Broadway Journal* in January 1845, Poe announced and described the process before advancing the fantastic claim that it would, quite literally "revolutionize the world" (154). In the first instance, Poe believed, anastatic printing would render conventional printing processes more efficient and cost-effective by allowing durable plates to be made quickly and cheaply from any printed text. To this extent, anastatic printing promised the same advantages as printing from stereotype plates; rather than tying up precious founts in potentially unmarketable works, plates could be produced quickly and, from these, texts printed in exactly the quantities demanded by the market, whether this was "a hundred thousand impressions per hour" or "no more than a dozen" (156). Moreover, anastatic plates, as Poe pointed out, could be produced more quickly and efficiently than stereotype plates, since the etchings on them could be taken from any copy of the desired printed text rather than from expensive standing type. Such innovations, he believed would take the risk out of printing and so allow the affordable dissemination of important but recherché texts such as his own.

Poe's subsequent claims for the anastatic process, however, were far more visionary. Because anastatic plates could be made from handwritten as well as

50. On the physical discomfort experienced by Poe while studying lithography, see Wilmer, *Merlin,* 33. Poe expressed his low opinion of Duval's artistry in a letter to Thomas Wyatt, 1 April 1841, quoted in Moldenhauer, "Beyond the Tamarind Tree," 468–69. On the relatively slow speed of lithographic presses in this period, see M. Twyman, "The Lithographic Hand Press, 1796–1850," *Journal of the Printing Historical Society* 3 (1967): esp. 41–40.

51. "Anastatic Printing," in *The Complete Works of Edgar Allan Poe,* ed. James A. Harrison, 17 vols. (New York: Society of English and French Literature, 1902), 14:154. Subsequent references to this essay will be cited, parenthetically, in the text.

52. The process is described briefly by Poe in "Anastatic Printing," 154–55. For more detailed and technical descriptions, upon which I have drawn for my discussion, see Geoffrey Wakeman, "Anastatic Printing for Sir Thomas Phillips," *Journal of the Printing Historical Society* 5 (1969): 24–27, and Gaskell, *A New Introduction to Bibliography,* 269. The technique was patented in 1844 and popularized in England, by Michael Faraday, in 1845. Poe's information might have come by way of Duval; it is more likely, however, that he learned of it through reading *Art Union,* an English periodical to which he refers in his essay.

printed sheets of paper, Poe believed that, once they overcame their conventional veneration of print, authors would choose to reproduce their own manuscripts, "without the expensive interference of the type-setter" or the "ruinous intervention of the publisher" (157). In anastatic printing, then, Poe believed he saw a means of overcoming the seemingly unbridgeable gap between manuscript production and mechanical reproduction, between aura and efficiency; anastatic technology would eventually render Gutenberg's printing press obsolete. And while Poe had not yet "written" a book, he believed that with the help of anastatic printing he would be able to do so. Moreover, in "writing" an anastatic book, it would not be necessary for an author to state "the italics are mine," since everything in the book *would* be the work of the author and only the work of the author. The collapse of the Gutenberg Galaxy, Poe implied, would also herald the richly deserved and long overdue demise of Typographic Man.

Yet Poe's vision went further still. With the onset of the anastatic revolution, the world would see three further paradigmatic transformations. The first would be an autographic revolution as authors began to "pay some attention to legibility" in their manuscripts (157). For the benefit of those whose handwriting was not as beautiful as Poe's, the art of scrivening would also be revived, with the "female amanuensis" taking the role currently occupied by the "male type-setter" (158). Books would start, once again, to resemble the illuminated manuscripts from whose scripts, in any case, the first types had been derived.

Following the scribal revolution, the world would also witness an epistemological revolution, since clarity in handwriting engendered clarity in thought and, ultimately, in "philosophy at large" (158). No longer would shoddy thought be concealed under a show of dazzling yet pointless typography.

Anastatic printing, finally, would demand a revolution in copyright law. As Poe was writing, American copyright law understood printedness as an essentially public medium in which an author could enjoy only limited property rights; anastatic printing circumvented what Meredith McGill has called the "instantaneous and absolute" transformation the law recognized in the act of going into print.[53] The anastatic revolution, wrote Poe, in language that recalled his attack on Longfellow's textual coquetry, would depreciate "the value of the *physique* of a book," while at the same time inflating "the value of its *morale*" (159). Since this was all a copyright should ever protect, the transformation of printing technologies would make the development of international copyright laws "only the more urgent" (159).

To paraphrase in the language of Walter Benjamin, anastatic printing would facilitate the presence of the aura in the mechanically reproducible work of art; in the language of Poe, it would herald the displacement of typography by chirography. The italics would, finally, belong to Poe.

53. See Meredith L. McGill, "The Matter of the Text: Commerce, Print Culture, and the Authority of the State in American Copyright Law," *American Literary History* 9 (1997): 21–59 (quotation, 23), and McGill, "The Duplicity of the Pen," 41–42.

Poe, however, was to be sorely disappointed. In the first place, he soon discovered that the promises held out by the technology would not be realized in practice; while the production of anastatic plates was relatively simple, it was just not possible to print from them with any great efficiency. Indeed, by 1846 the technology's pioneer had himself decided to abandon the process as costly and unreliable.[54] More immediately, Poe's plans to employ anastatic technology were quickly derailed by the overwhelming debts he assumed upon becoming the sole proprietor of the *Broadway Journal*. Fittingly, and ironically, enough, his only use of anastatic printing was to reproduce a letter to subscribers begging for financial support. Less than a month later, his journal was dead.

Three years after the death of the *Broadway Journal*, Poe was found semiconscious in a Baltimore tavern by Joseph Walker, who relayed a desperate message to the author's nearby friend Joseph Snodgrass. Together, the two managed to get Poe to a hospital where, four days later, he died.[55] Poe's rescuers, it turns out, were a typesetter and an editor. Yet their kindness notwithstanding, Poe had little cause to love members of either group. For most of his professional career, he had clashed with both, struggling to get into print and when there struggling against the medium itself. Poe was, without a question, struck by the capacity of typefaces to enhance and extend the power of the written word, but the process of printing was too controlling, and yet, ultimately, too uncontrollable to fulfill either his aesthetic or emotional needs. "To be controlled," Poe wrote in 1848, "is to be ruined."[56] It is, perhaps, the greatest irony of all, then, that Poe should have left responsibility for his literary estate to a former printer, Rufus Griswold, who with his inaccurate editions, forged manuscripts, and malicious lies would scandalize the literary world by printing, controlling, and ruining the posthumous hand of Edgar Allan Poe.[57]

54. Wakeman, "Anastatic Printing for Sir Thomas Phillips," 27–28.

55. *Poe Log*, 844.

56. Poe to G. W. Evleth, 4 January 1848, *Letters*, 2:356.

57. On Griswold's deliberate distortions of Poe's manuscripts, see Killis Campbell, "The Poe-Griswold Controversy," in *The Mind of Poe and Other Studies* (New York: Russell & Russell, 1962), 63–98; on his executorship more generally, see Joy Bayless, *Rufus Wilmot Griswold: Poe's Literary Executor* (Nashville, Tenn.: Vanderbilt University Press, 1943).

Bridge Six

Edgar Allan Poe's ultimately frustrated attempts to circumvent traditional typography, as described by Leon Jackson in the preceding essay, were echoed in France at nearly the same time. In a similar quest to reproduce directly the authorial trace of handwriting, Rodolphe Töpffer—considered by some historians to be the first modern cartoonist—championed what he called "autographie" (akin to Poe's "anastatic printing," not Poe's "autography") in his 1845 "Essay on Physiognomy." Töpffer's printed cartoons contained both pictures and handwritten text, and their accurate reproduction was intrinsic to Töpffer's aesthetic—just as it is to cartoonists today.

In the following essay, Gene Kannenberg Jr. argues that the cartoonist's hand reveals a prime difference between traditional, text-based literature and the graphic, design-intensive realm of comics. For the cartoonist, as Poe wished it for himself, the accurate reproduction of authorial marks—be they images or text—is essential in the publication of these graphic texts. In comics, the text (often hand-lettered, hence the common term *lettering*) is never an incidental formal element, but rather an essential graphic component of the overall page design. The accurate reproduction of the text's original appearance is linked directly to the reproduction of the images with which the text shares space on the page.

In the field of comics study in America, there exists a movement to explicate the formal properties of comics. Yet when it comes to lettering, scholars most often treat that element as if it were "unmarked," a transparent vehicle of language: in short, as a nearly nongraphic component in the form's almost fundamental amalgamation of word and image. Kannenberg asserts that textual, typographic forms in comics themselves contribute to *graphic narrative*. He proposes a threefold heuristic model for examining the ways in which the appearance of the text in comics influences larger verbal/visual narrative patterns.

The narrative qualities of lettering, such as placement within and across compositions on the page, influence the acquisition of information by the reader in flexible, fluid ways. Metanarrative qualities comment to varying degrees on a given work in areas such as timing, characterization, and theme. And lettering's extranarrative qualities can identify a work's status as an example either *by* a particular creator or *of* a certain title or type, beyond the specific plot or other story content.

By focusing on a wide range of examples of comic art, Kannenberg's essay demonstrates how careful attention to the graphic nature of comics lettering can affect interpretation on multiple levels and across all types of comics texts. Some comic books feature the work of professional "letterers" instead of the work of a single cartoonist, while the advent of computer-aided lettering allows for innovations such as individually designed fonts that mimic a cartoonist's own hand: commercial font suppliers sometimes provide the entire publication design of a comic book series. Examining the varied nature of lettering in contemporary comics, Kannenberg offers a template for typographic inquiry into the narrative art form known as comics.

Chapter Seven

Graphic Text, Graphic Context: Interpreting Custom Fonts and Hands in Contemporary Comics

GENE KANNENBERG JR.

The text in comics, known as *lettering,* plays an important yet often overlooked role in that art form's visual storytelling.[1] Most critical definitions of the term *comics* note that the dynamic interplay of image and text is a significant, if not essential, element in the medium, although much debate exists as to qualifying particulars.[2] Yet these two components—image and text—generally have not been regarded equally by comics criticism. Scholars discuss drawings in terms of their aesthetic and narrative qualities, but they generally downplay the aesthetic contributions of text in favor of concentrating on its presumably transparent capacity as the vehicle for narration.[3] Given the typography scholar Johanna Drucker's assertion that "the most potent aspect of typography [is] its refusal to resolve into either a visual or verbal mode," however, it would seem that careful attention to the typographic qualities of lettering could provide useful insights into this hybrid, verbal/visual narrative form.[4]

1. The term *comics* began as a plural form, describing humorous newspaper strips; today it is used ambiguously as a label for the medium. The term's misleading association with humor has led some scholars to seek an alternative label, with uneven results. As this critical debate has not been settled, and *comics* is the still the term most immediately recognizable, I use it as a singular, collective form to refer to the medium.

2. Among the more significant and influential aesthetic analyses of comics, see Lawrence L. Abbott, "Comic Art: Characteristics and Potentialities of a Narrative Medium," *Journal of Popular Culture* 19, no. 4 (1986): 155–76; Lewis J. Davies Sr., "The Multidimensional Language of the Cartoon: A Study in Aesthetics, Popular Culture, and Symbolic Interaction," *Semiotica* 104, nos. 1/2 (1995): 165–211; Will Eisner, *Comics & Sequential Art* (Tamarac, Fla.: Poorhouse Press, 1985); Scott McCloud, *Understanding Comics: The Invisible Art* (Northampton, Mass.: Kitchen Sink Press, 1993); R. C. Harvey, *The Art of the Funnies: An Aesthetic History* (Jackson: University Press of Mississippi, 1994); David Kunzle, "Introduction," *The Early Comic Strip: Narrative and Picture Stories in the European Broadsheet from c. 1450 to 1825* (Berkeley: University of California Press, 1973), 1–8; Pascal Lefèvre and Charles Dierick, "Introduction," in *Forging A New Medium: The Comic Strip in the Nineteenth Century,* ed. Lefèvre and Dierick (Brussels: VUB University Press, 1998); and Art Spiegelman, "Commix: An Idiosyncratic Historical and Aesthetic Overview," *Print* 42, no. 6 (1988): 61–73, 195–96.

3. For example, Harvey, in his insightful *Art of the Funnies,* convincingly champions the blending of words and pictures in comics, but he focuses on both the content and the appearance only of pictures; for text, his remarks remain, with few exceptions, almost entirely devoted to narrative content.

4. Johanna Drucker, *The Visible Word: Experimental Typography and Modern Art, 1909–1923* (Chicago: University of Chicago Press, 1994), 4. Most lettering in comics is not, strictly speaking, typeset; however,

This essay seeks to develop a much-needed conceptual framework for comics study by identifying key relationships between the graphic qualities of comics lettering and the various narrative consequences of those qualities. These relationships fall into three categories: (1) *Narrative* qualities, including the ways the text's position within compositions influences the order in which discrete units combine into an aggregate narrative whole; (2) *Metanarrative* qualities, including the way the appearance of text can enhance the narrative in areas such as timing, characterization, or theme, as opposed to plot or structure; and (3) *Extranarrative* qualities, including how the way design can identify a work as an example either *by* a particular creator or *of* a certain title or type, regardless of specific story elements.

This essay presents this new interpretive framework in detail, discussing lettering history and practice where appropriate and analyzing two significant bodies of lettering work that showcase recent developments in lettering practice and technology. I hope that this strategy will not only contribute to the understanding of the possibilities for narrative sophistication in comics as a whole, but also allow for comparative studies with investigations of textual practices in other literary and artistic fields.[5]

The reasons for slighting the aesthetic dimensions of text in comics have been at least partially well founded. Early comics—books as well as strips—are sometimes critically lauded *despite* their ill-considered hand-lettering. Perhaps the ultimate example is the work of Winsor McCay, the early twentieth-century cartoonist who created *Dream of the Rarebit Fiend* and the classic *Little Nemo in Slumberland* (figure 58); note that, while the graceful title lettering suggests the shape of the waves in the images to follow, the speech-balloon text looks, to be charitable, ill considered.[6] Naturally, exceptions have always existed, including the highly expressive work of creators such as Walt Kelly, whose strip *Pogo* was known for its graphic innovation as well as its incisive political satire. Through the use of emblematic fonts for characters like the Barnum-esque P. T. Bridgeport (figure 59), Kelly attempted, as he wrote, "to indicate the tone of voice of the

---

I believe it is fruitful to follow Kimberly Elam's notion of *expressive typography,* which "expands the traditional definition of typography to include all means of creating written language" (*Expressive Typography: The Word as Image* [New York: Van Nostrand Reinhold, 1990], vii). A. Kibédi Varga notes that "*calligraphy* is the purest and most radical example of fusion of word and image because in it we cannot decide whether a letter becomes an image or an image a letter" ("Criteria for Describing Word-and-Image Relations," *Poetics Today* 10 [1989]: 37).

5. Of course, while most comics do include text, a strong tradition of wordless comics exists around the globe. See Thierry Groensteen, "Histoire de la BD muette (première partie)," *9e Art* 2 (1997): 60–75, and "Histoire de la BD muette (deuxième partie)," *9e Art* 3 (1998): 92–105.

6. McCay's "sloppy lettering" is especially troubling to modern critics. Bill Watterson, creator of the comic strip *Calvin and Hobbes,* comments: "You know something is wrong when a man of McCay's obvious composition and drafting skills draws such pathetic-looking dialogue balloons. The balloons themselves often impede the visual flow of the panel, and McCay rarely allowed enough space for the words. Were the words a complete afterthought?" See Winsor McCay, *The Best of Little Nemo,* ed. Richard Marschall (New York: Stewart, Tabori and Chang, 1997), 195. Harvey concurs: "You'd think a man of [McCay's] graphic genius would improve upon the prevailing conventions [of lettering] when they so clearly disfigure his otherwise flawless artwork": *The Art of the Funnies,* 28.

FIGURE 58. Winsor McCay, *Little Nemo in Slumberland,* 21 April 1907, panels 1–3. Note the elegant title lettering as well as the decidedly inelegant word-balloon text. From *The Complete Little Nemo in Slumberland, Volume II,* published by Fantagraphics Books, Seattle.

FIGURE 59. P. T. Bridgeport's expressive speech patterning, suggesting tone of voice and characterization. Walt Kelly, *Pogo,* 9 July 1951. © 1997 O.G.P.I.

FIGURE 60. Beauregard and Albert's speech balloons reflect the material context of their words. Walt Kelly, *Pogo,* 23 March 1954. © 1997 O.G.P.I.

character."[7] In this example, the use of multiple display fonts attempts to render graphically the sound of blustery hucksterism. Other Kelly experiments collapsed spoken and written text in innovative fashions, as in a sequence featuring Beauregard the detective (figure 60); note the dialogue that uses *faux*-type to reflect preprinted paperwork and script for handwriting, emphasizing the materiality of the text as well as its content. Yet for the majority of comics creators, lettering remained distinctly a secondary consideration.

Critical disregard of lettering's visual characteristics also stems from a desire among some contemporary critics to assert the form's literary leanings, thereby establishing a link to "proper" academic study. Thus the text is treated, as in most literary studies of prose, as if it were *unmarked* (wherein literary content is key, regardless of its form) as opposed to *marked* (wherein formal distinctions hold value, more than does content), to use Johanna Drucker's terminology.[8] By treating comics text as if it were unmarked, one can focus, misleadingly, on its supposed "literary" quality. To do so, however, neglects the visuality of the medium as a whole, to say nothing of the actual text.

Thus, historically, the text itself in comics has been considered successful if it simply maintains a graceful legibility. Increasing self-promotion by comics creators and the growing sophistication of comics readers, however, have led to a reevaluation of the contribution of lettering and letterers to the art form.[9] Comics creators—encouraged, perhaps, by the cartoonist Will Eisner's observation, in his influential practitioner treatise *Comics & Sequential Art,* that "text reads as an image"[10]—have increased their attention to the impact of lettering, both intrinsically and as part of the graphic surface of the page. This attention has resulted in a multifaceted relationship between text and image, serving to enhance the form's already complex narrative possibilities.

7. Walt Kelly, *Ten Ever-Lovin' Blue-Eyed Years with Pogo* (New York: Simon and Schuster, 1959), 43.

8. Drucker traces these categories to Gutenberg, who printed Bibles as unmarked texts, "uninterrupted blocks of text in which the words on the page 'appear to speak for themselves' without the visible intervention of the author or printer," and Indulgences that "displayed the embryonic features of a marked typography" (*The Visible Word,* 95). This split led to the use of unmarked text for literary prose and marked text for, especially, rhetoric-heavy advertising. Although the dichotomy blurred briefly with the experimental work of Dada, Cubist, and Futurist poets in the early twentieth century, according to Drucker, this general distinction still holds. The use of highly "marked" (in several senses) text in comics helps to make concrete the popular assertion that the form itself, by the very nature of its graphic-intensive appearance, cannot have a literary purpose.

9. This recognition began most prominently during the early 1960s, when full credits, earlier included haphazardly at best in most comic book stories, began to appear regularly at Marvel Comics under Stan Lee's editorial hand. Soon other companies followed suit, allowing readers to better recognize, follow, and study the work of individual creators, not just titles or characters. For an extended discussion of the rise of comic book fandom in conjunction with a growing recognition of creators and their work, see Bill Schelly, *The Golden Age of Comic Fandom* (Seattle: Hamster Press, 1995).

10. Eisner, *Comics & Sequential Art,* 10. Compare Elam's observation that "it is possible to combine successfully typography and image, by returning to and acknowledging the recent roots of graphic design in the late nineteenth and early twentieth centuries. . . . This collaborative development of the image and typography enables the word to become the image and the image to become the word" (*Expressive Typography,* vii).

If comics critics are to explore these possibilities fully, however, they need to address the visual appearance of lettering in a systematic and illuminating fashion. Important to this practice is the recognition of *design* as a significant element in comics structure and the realization that the appearance of the lettering itself (from typeface to placement) is a significant portion of that design. In a way, the comics page may be viewed as, in David Scott's sense, a spatial text.

> "Spatial" texts are those which, in foregrounding the materiality of the word as a (visual) signifier, depend for their full impact on visual—as well as aural— attention. . . . [Spatial texts,] in most cases, emerge from a literary tradition saturated with the visual arts, one in which composition is conceived as being partly dependent on the organization of constituent elements within a visible framework. In this way, the interrelationship of the various parts of the text tends to be seized simultaneously or through multiple—and multidirec- tional—strategies of reading, of which the traditional linear, horizontal model is only one of a variety of options open to the reader.[11]

While here Scott refers to nineteenth-century prose poetry, this quotation never- theless prepares the way for a discussion of comics text. The design of the comics page organizes constituent elements within its own visual framework, as does each panel on that page. The physical proximity of the images to the text, wherein each may in fact contain the other, necessitates multiple strategies of reading. In this essay I introduce terminology aimed to identify the various types of spatial textual properties and effects in comics, with particular emphasis on the graphic appearance of the text itself.[12]

The comics form allows for an almost limitless range of narrative types, from deeply felt memoirs like Art Spiegelman's Pulitzer Prize–winning *Maus* to educa- tional photo-novellas to vintage issues of *Superman's Girlfriend, Lois Lane.* As op- posed to the single-creator paradigm, which holds for many comics strips and alternative comic books, the most familiar comic books in America (*Superman, Archie, X-Men,* etc.) are produced in an assembly-line fashion, with different indi- viduals responsible for writing, drawing, lettering, coloring, and editing the pub- lications.[13] This structure allows publishers to produce many books on schedule and encourages creative staff to choose and master a particular area of expertise.

11. David Scott, *Pictorialist Poetics: Poetry and the Visual Arts in Nineteenth-Century France* (Cambridge: Cambridge University Press, 1988), 116, 123.

12. This essay's emphasis on the appearance of text adds a new dimension to the analysis already done on text/image relationships; works such as Kibédi Varga's "Criteria for Describing Word-and-Image Rela- tions" note the perceptual shift between reading (text) and (viewing) images, but they do not attempt to address how the viewing of the text's visual form contributes to this perceptual situation.

13. Letterers in comic strips work in a similar fashion. Many strips are produced by one cartoonist, although some employ assistants, usually uncredited. For simplicity's sake, this discussion will focus on the somewhat larger role of the comic *book* letterer, although it should be understood that the strip letterer's job is nearly identical.

Cartoonists who publish in smaller comics presses, or (occasionally) through mainstream book publishers, have less editorial demand for "product" and often strive to produce "literary" works in the comics form. Similarly, comics study is itself wide-ranging, an inter- and multidisciplinary field; its scholars have backgrounds in such areas as art history, literature, communications, philosophy, or social sciences. The terminology used in this essay is thus intended to aid all scholars in analyzing and discussing the content of any type of comic, regardless of its means of publication, intended audience, or literary aspirations.

Definition of Terms

Narrative. Text can affect the narrative dimension of a comic—that is, the structural formation and comprehension of that comic's intended message—by its placement within the overall composition of the panel or page. Text can serve many different purposes in comics: titles, narration, dialogue, sound effect, labels, part of the mise-en-scène, and more; when we refer to several different types of comics text, it may be useful to think of them as *lexias,* or textual divisions.[14]

Although a gridlike structure featuring regular tiers of panels is most common on the comics page, compositions can vary widely in the number, shape, and arrangement of panels: large panels for dramatic effect, layouts that frame action both horizontally and vertically, and other design elements can set a scene or tell the story not just sequentially but in toto. It is through composition that storytellers direct the order in which panels—and the elements within each panel—are to be read.[15] The placement of lexias within compositions can contribute to this narrative element by guiding the eye from panel to panel, particularly in non-traditional (i.e., nongridlike) compositions, as well as guiding the eye between textual elements within each panel.

As they ultimately control the text's placement, letterers are responsible for a

14. See Amy Spaulding, *The Page as a Stage Set: Storyboard Picture Books* (Metuchen, N.J.: Scarecrow Press, 1995). Spaulding acknowledges that her use of the term *lexia* differs from that of Roland Barthes in *S/Z* (New York: Hill and Wang, 1974). Barthes defines *lexia* as a "unit of reading of varying length, from a few words to several sentences, divided as a matter of convenience" (*S/Z,* 13, quoted in Spaulding, 27). Spaulding's use of the term to mean "strings of words that are read together, whether long or short" (26), is very useful in discussing comics text types.

15. In reading English-language comics, the eye moves in a left-right, top-down pattern, as in traditional "straight text" reading. In some other cultures' comics, such as Japanese *manga,* that reading pattern is mirrored (i.e., panels are read from right to left). This pattern affects both the arrangement of text and the composition of the page. Thus, in the United States, published translations of *manga* take one of three forms: (1) Each page is "flipped" vertically, to put the panels in left-right order, reproducing panels as mirror images of their exemplars; (2) The page is flipped, but the individual panels are then re-flipped; such a scheme is problematic when panels are of an irregular size or shape, and is thus used sparingly; (3) The book is published in its original state, and readers are told to start at the back and read right-left, which can cause momentary cognitive dissonance but restores the integrity of the original version. For more information on *manga* history, conventions, and publishing, see Frederik L. Schodt, *Manga! Manga! The World of Japanese Comics* (New York: Kodansha America, 1986) and *Dreamland Japan: Writings on Modern Manga* (Berkeley, Calif.: Stone Bridge Press, 1996).

portion of a comics story's narrative content. Letterers enter the creative process after the artwork has been drawn in pencil and the script has been finalized,[16] adding the text to the pencil artwork, drawing the balloons and caption boxes, and finally delineating the panel borders. Artists who provide their own lettering fulfill the same role as do letterers per se, thus allowing for even greater nuance in storytelling. Will Eisner in particular makes sophisticated use of text as compositional element and narrative marker. As such his work provides an excellent example of the narrative dimension of comics lettering. Figure 61, the opening page for the short story "Sanctum" from Eisner's collection *Invisible People,* offers a wealth of information conveyed purely through the appearance and placement of the text.

The page consists of a title and four visual elements (borderless panels) anchored as a single unit by a gray-and-black background. The image of young Pincus under his bed appears directly to the left of the image of his father in the doorway. These two images would normally follow from left to right (Pincus first, Father second), given their relative positions. By placing the father's speech balloon directly to the right of the title, Eisner indicates that this picture is to be "read" first on the page. Further, the snaking placement of lexias on the page serves gradually to focus the reader's gaze toward the bottom of the composition, where we find a mass of humanity, the entity upon which—figuratively and, in this image, quite literally—Pincus's fear focuses.

Eisner addresses the importance of guiding the reader's gaze, even while skimming, in the section of his *Comics & Sequential Art* addressed to aspiring cartoonists. He writes: "Remember that the reader's first action is to scan the page, then the panel. If the pictorial value of the images is very exciting or filled with great detail—there will be a tendency to 'skim' the balloon text. So a wise defensive stratagem is to try to deploy the bold face not only in service of sound but to 'telegraph' the message. The reader should be able to get the thrust or sense of the dialogue out of the bold-face letters alone."[17] Of course, Eisner's practice is not entirely typical, and his advice not universal. His description holds some sway for cartoonists like himself who use spare, nuggetlike dialogue; Eisner suggests that no more than thirty words should ever occupy a single panel. Cartoonists who offer more densely packed pages, however, cannot assume that their "message" will be clear from skimming alone. Indeed, many comics (including Eisner's)

---

16. There are two general approaches to creating collaborative comic books. In the first method, the writer drafts a complete script, indicating the number of panels per page and the accompanying text; the artist then interprets these directions. The second is known as the "Marvel Method" owing to its extensive use by writer Stan Lee (and subsequent writers) at Marvel Comics during the 1960s. The writer (with, sometimes, the artist) creates a brief plot; the artist then draws a full story based on this outline, providing the bulk of the story's narrative structure. After the pages are drawn, the writer then creates a full script based on the story breakdown provided by the artist. In this case "scripter" is more appropriate than "writer," as it is the artist who gives specific shape to the story's plot.

17. Eisner, *Comics & Sequential Art,* 152.

FIGURE 61. Characteristically for Eisner's work, balloon placement aids both in narrative acquisition and in metanarrative illumination, while the title typography serves a metanarrative function. Will Eisner, *Invisible People,* 10. Copyright Will Eisner.

demand and reward slow, careful reading. Still, even on a panel-to-panel basis, the effect of visual textual emphasis and placement is to guide the reader's comprehension of the narrative.[18]

Metanarrative. Besides influencing the structural qualities of a comics narrative, the appearance of text—and the borders that surround it, such as balloons or caption boxes—can provide information *about* the narrative, beyond the information in the grammatical content of the words and the order in which the objects on the page should be read. Through formal presentation and manipulation, text can convey metanarrative information such as sound/tone of voice, characterization, pacing, and thematic resonance.

Because of the cumulative nature of the comics form, this metanarrative relationship may be noticed both within individual panels or compositions and throughout the full comics story. Roland Barthes has termed this type of relationship *relay:* "Here text (most often a snatch of dialogue) and image stand in a complementary relationship; the words, in the same way as the images, are fragments of a more general syntagm and the unity of the message is realized at a higher level, that of the story, the anecdote, the diegesis (which is ample confirmation that the diegesis must be treated as an autonomous system)."[19] Thus, by the relay process, the appearance of lettering can at some times enhance our understanding of a specific element within a single panel, and at other times influence theme or characterization over the course of an entire story.

Text in comics has traditionally been presented in simple block capital, sans serif letters, which reproduce clearly when the artwork is reduced in size (usually by about one-third) for final printing.[20] The use of simple capitals dates at least from the earliest widely disseminated comics in America, the comic strips in the late nineteenth and early twentieth centuries, which depended upon clarity (and cleverness) to attract a large and varied newspaper readership.[21] However, intentional

18. In his discussion of Roy Lichtenstein's *Eddie Diptych* in "Comic Art," Lawrence L. Abbott examines the nonlinear eye movements that typify the reading of comics (159–61). Similarly, A. Kibédi Varga notes that, at the object level, text and image in comics are viewed (at least initially) simultaneously ("Criteria for Describing Word-and-Image Relations," 33); however, once readers perceive a page or even a panel as a whole, they must then make their way through the layout, and here the placement of text serves as one guidepost.

19. Roland Barthes, "Rhetoric of the Image," in *Semiotics: An Introductory Anthology,* ed. Robert E. Innis (Bloomington: Indiana University Press, 1985), 198.

20. The use of capital letterforms in comics may be a contributing factor to the continued misperception of comics as a medium suitable only for children. Spaulding notes that "Watts [Lynne Watts and John Nisbett, *Legibility and Children's Books: A Review of Research* (New Windsor, Berkshire, Eng.: NFER, 1974), 21] discusses the fact that the general rule about all capitals being less-easily read than lowercase does not hold for children. Studies have shown that children who have recently learned to read find all capitals easier to read" (*The Page as a Stage Set,* 176–77).

21. Many early strips relied also upon ethnic humor and stereotypes. Especially in ethnically diverse New York City—where many of the comic strips were created—accents were part of everyday life, and this fact was reflected in the dialect-laden speech balloons of comic strips. For three slightly different discussions of the developing popularity of comic strips, see Harvey, *The Art of the Funnies;* Ron Goulart, *The Funnies: 100 Years of American Comic Strips* (Holbrook, Mass.: Adams, 1995); and Bill Blackbeard and Dale Crain, eds., *The Comic Strip Century: Celebrating 100 Years of an American Art Form* (Northampton, Mass.: Kitchen Sink Press, 1995).

stylistic variation in fonts, once less pervasive, is rapidly gaining precedence. The examples from Walt Kelly's work discussed earlier showed some ways in which enhancing the font can add metanarrative characterization information.

The text's appearance, combined with that of the balloon or box that contains it, will determine how words are understood by the reader—as various forms of speech, thought, broadcast messages, narration, sound effects, and so on. The specific distinguishing characteristics may be dictated by the scriptwriter, the letterer, or both. Often the letterer is responsible for the placement of the word balloons on the page or in the panel. Balloons generally consist of an oval, scalloped, or rectangular "cloud" around the text, with a small tail pointing toward the speaker's mouth. Of course, some comics avoid the use of balloons entirely, having their dialogue "float" above characters' heads while often including a line, analogous to the balloon's tail, to identify the speaker. Even then, the text is still set off compositionally within its own discrete display space.

The shape of balloons can enhance the message of the text. Scott McCloud reproduces a small variety of balloon examples in *Understanding Comics,* although he relies on his readers' prior experience to understand the shapes' various connotations. To note but a few examples: For *thought,* the balloon's edge is scalloped and the tail is replaced by a series of small circles or bubbles.[22] *Whispering* is indicated either by forming the balloon with a dashed line or by using smaller-than-normal text. To convey *shouting,* a balloon's edge is spiked, or the text is made relatively larger than that used for normal speech, or both. Similarly, *electronic speech* can be simulated by a jagged-edge or geometrically shaped balloon. *Sarcasm* has even been awarded its own iconic representation, the "dripping" word balloon. Innovative creators continue to develop new effects as the need or opportunity arises.

Visual emphasis of certain words within balloons, usually through boldface text, is used not only to guide skimming (as described in the Eisner quotation above), but also to represent spoken cadence or other metanarrative effects. In figure 59, Kelly exaggerates cadence in P. T. Bridgeport's circus-poster hyperbole. Eisner states, "The 'control' of the *reader's ear* is vital if the meaning and intent of the dialogue is to remain as the writer intended it."[23] McCloud concurs, noting—and illustrating, but without further comment—that "even the variations of lettering *styles,* both in and out of balloons, speak of an *ongoing struggle* to capture the very *essence* of sound"[24] (figure 62). The sound of characters' voices in radio, film, or television contributes greatly to audience interpretation; comics, developing in this century along with these other media, uses visual emphasis as a metanarrative device in order to replicate this additional characterization tool in its own, mute medium.

22. Early attempts to indicate thought included placing the dialogue in parentheses, often in a spoken-dialogue balloon, but the puffy "thought balloon" has become a standard signifier.
23. Eisner, *Comics & Sequential Art,* 125.
24. McCloud, *Understanding Comics,* 134.

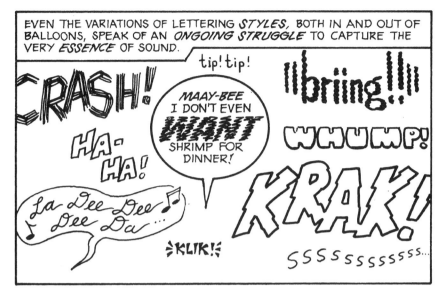

FIGURE 62. McCloud suggests, via representative examples, a wide range of sound effect types commonly seen in comics lettering. Scott McCloud, *Understanding Comics* 134.5. © 1999 Scott McCloud.

The placement of lexias can also affect the pace of a story. As Eisner observes, "The arrangement of balloons which surround speech—their position in relation to each other, or to the action, or their position with respect to the speaker, contribute to the measurement of time."[25] Densely packed or overlapping panels create the impression of compressed or quickly passing time, while open panel compositions with a few, widely scattered balloons connote longer, slower time frames.[26] Additionally, the placement of balloons relative to the position of speakers can embellish relationships between speakers.[27]

The letterer is also responsible for the final appearance of sound effects. Like emphasized text, sound effects represent an attempt to render the audible visible. Usually onomatopoeic, sound effects also function as design elements, balancing compositions and serving to guide the reader's eye. While dialogue and narration have usually been produced in simple hands or fonts, sound effects have long been elaborately designed and presented, an acceptable place for letterers to flaunt their calligraphic finesse without fear of compromising the integrity of the narration.

Eisner's "Sanctum" page (figure 61) displays some of these sophisticated meta-

25. Eisner, *Comics & Sequential Art,* 26.
26. See McCloud, *Understanding Comics,* chap. 4, "Time Frames."
27. For an example of narrative analysis in which balloon placement is considered as an integral storytelling element, see Richard Reynolds's discussion of selected pages from Marvel Comics' *X-Men* no. 122 in that author's *Super Heroes: A Modern Mythology* (London: B. T. Batsford, 1992; Jackson: University Press of Mississippi, 1994), 86–90.

narrative techniques. Besides carefully situating his lexias, Eisner makes his lettering, especially in titles, exceptionally expressive. The title's wedgelike serifs and the slight decorations on the *S* suggest stone carving, such as one might find on a temple or other religious building. More significantly, by making the *C* and the *U* smaller than the other letters and placing them beneath the crossbar of the *T*, suggesting arms hugging children, Eisner uses the text in the title itself to suggest the act of sanctuary.

The placement of the text on this page also imparts metanarrative information. To elaborate upon the earlier discussion of the page's first two panels: The co-equal position of these panels introduces simultaneously both Pincus's tendency to hide and one reason for this behavior. Further, Eisner creates a slight graphic tension here, using the text placement to make the apparent "second" panel of the page the first one to be read. This structure also works on a thematic level, mimicking the tension that exists between the characters. Finally, by placing the introductory narration on the side of the bed under which Pincus hides, and emphasizing the word *sanctum* within, Eisner draws attention to the protective qualities of the bed itself. Thus, the appearance of the text, regardless of its narrative content, can operate on thematic levels to embellish the narrative.

Extranarrative. The appearance of text can further impart information not simply about the particular story in which it appears; it can also reinforce the materiality of the narrative by drawing attention to its status either as a particular type of work (the product of a particular company, a title in a certain genre) or as an example of an effort by a particular cartoonist. Neither of these distinctions pertains to individual narratives; rather, they are elements of the bibliological codes that serve to identify texts to readers.

Such codes are readily apparent in mainstream comics publishing concerns, such as Marvel (*X-Men*) and DC (*Superman*). As primarily dealers in commodities, large companies need to ensure brand recognition, and thus brand loyalty. Package design plays an important role in this process, and lettering—particularly with the typographic sophistication afforded by computer technology—is an integral part of design.[28] The subsequent discussion of computer lettering explores the issue of industrial or "brand-name" recognition in greater detail.

A second form of brand-name recognition holds sway in comics produced by a single cartoonist. In these instances, the harmonious blending of text and art styles labels a work as the product of that cartoonist. This harmony is another example of extranarrative content. In Kimberly Elam's words, "When [handwritten typography] is used to communicate messages, it is chosen because it offers so

---

28. For an exhaustive overview of package design for the text-based book see Gérard Genette, *Paratexts: Thresholds of Interpretation*, trans. Jane E. Lewin (Cambridge: Cambridge University Press, 1997). Genette defines *paratext* as "what enables a text to become a book and to be offered as such to its readers and, more generally, to the public" (1). For Genette, the realm of the paratext lies not with the author, who creates the base text, but rather with the publisher, who gives the text final shape. As we have seen in comics, however, the designer of the text, often down to the indicia, is the letterer or the cartoonist; as such, the metanarrative paratext is not divorced from authorship but rather is integral to the process of presentation.

FIGURE 63. Speech text, narration, drawn text, and artwork all share the same rough-hewn line, an extranarrative cue that *Maus* is an intensely personal work. Art Spiegelman, *Maus: A Survivor's Tale. I: My Father Bleeds History* 112.1. Copyright 1973, 1980, 1981, 1982, 1983, 1984, 1985, 1986 by Art Spiegelman. Reprinted by permission of Pantheon Books, a division of Random House, Inc.

much more than specific information, as handwritten messages become dynamic statements of individual style, personal communication, and spontaneous creation and placement."[29] Although books created by a single cartoonist are rare in the world of mainstream comics publishing, they are much more common in what is termed the "alternative" or "small press" marketplace; such books are generally intended for an audience of adults, rather than one of children.[30]

The types of lettering produced by these artists serve to mark such comics as unique, personal creations produced by a single hand—from the delicate fantasy line work and equally delicate letters of Charles Vess (*The Book of Ballads and Sagas*) to the angst-ridden, gestural, and expressive pictures and words of Roberta Gregory (*Naughty Bits, Artistic Licentiousness*). Many other alternative cartoonists are highly regarded for their innovative use of lettering conventions (e.g., Dave Sim in his long-running, self-published *Cerebus*) or have integrated their art and calligraphy styles to such an extent that the forms of their balloon/panel compositions are unlike any others (e.g., Dame Darcy's elaborate and ornate *Meat Cake*).

For his *Maus: A Survivor's Tale*,[31] Art Spiegelman paid close attention to this extranarrative surface of his work (figure 63): "It's really clear [in *Maus*] that the writing and drawing are made by the same hand. And that quality of line is something that seemed important to me in *Maus* as well; I found myself drawing and

29. Elam, *Expressive Typography*, 25.

30. For one discussion of the development of the adult-oriented alternative marketplace out of the underground "comix" movement of the 1960s and 1970s, see Roger Sabin, *Adult Comics: An Introduction* (London: Routledge, 1993). Will Eisner was one of the first American cartoonists to produce long-form comics narratives for adults, beginning with *A Contract with God and Other Tenement Stories* (New York: Baronet, 1978).

31. Art Spiegelman, *Maus: A Survivor's Tale. I: My Father Bleeds History* (New York: Pantheon, 1986), *Maus: A Survivor's Tale. II: And Here My Troubles Began* (New York: Pantheon, 1991).

writing with the same tools. The lettering was done with the same tool that I drew with, which was a fountain pen. . . . I wanted to keep it close to writing so that what I was making was a manuscript, something made by hand. It's one of the reasons that *Maus* is drawn in a one-to-one ratio, that the book is printed the same size that it's drawn, so that it's really as close to getting a clear copy of somebody's diary or journal as one could have."[32] The specifics of Spiegelman's example run to extremes compared to most comics practice, particularly of popular, mainstream titles. It is rare, for instance, for comics to be printed at the same size as they are drawn, and specialized pens exist for both lettering and drawing. Spiegelman's reasoning, however, indicates his deep understanding of the extranarrative qualities which cartoonists' own lettering can bring to their work. Self-aware creators facilitate the dynamic interplay of image and text through extra-narrative identification far more thoroughly than can the piecemeal workers in mainstream comics, who (unless they have the ability to mimic an artist's own lettering)[33] instead rely on different types of graphic interplay.

Focus on a Distinctive Style: Todd Klein

Some professional letterers, through close consultation with their writer and artist colleagues, have attained a skillful, artistic balance between their calligraphic style and the graphic and narrative style and content of the books on which they work. The lettering of many professionals is not simply clear and competent, but, rather, artistic and expressive in its own right. It lies beyond the scope of this essay to attempt to cover all or even most of these artisans, many of whose names became synonymous with either titles (Tom Orzechowski with Marvel's *Uncanny X-Men*) or artistic collaborators (John Workman with many of the comics of the writer/artist Walt Simonson). The work of one letterer, however, deserves examination in some detail: Todd Klein, whose lettering on a wide variety of comics, for publishers large and small, contributes to both extranarrative "book identity" and metanarrative characterization to a degree that few other professional letterers have achieved.

Like the work of most letterers, Klein's traditional hand consists of clear, relatively undistinguished block capitals; what makes his style particularly noteworthy, however, is his knack for using—and often creating—different calligraphic hands to add both graphic identity and storytelling content to the comics he letters, especially in relation to individual characters. His lettering often speaks more to character than to page design or to stylistically complementing the artwork, primarily because of the mainstream, multi-artist nature of many of the

32. Art Spiegelman, *The Complete Maus* (CD-ROM; Voyager, 1994).

33. Calligraphic mimicry is rare in mainstream comics, given the traditional assembly-line system. Mimicry is somewhat more common in the realm of comics published in translation. Coedited by Art Spiegelman and Françoise Mouly, the anthology *Raw* (1980–91) published English translations of much international comics work, taking great pains to ensure that the text in the English versions matched the style of each cartoonist's hand as closely as possible.

books in which he has had a role. Klein may perhaps be best known for his work on the popular, high-concept fantasy comics series *Sandman,* written by Neil Gaiman and drawn by a wide variety of artists, published from January 1989 through March 1996 by DC Comics and its Vertigo imprint.

Klein's work on *Sandman* offers particularly rich examples that illuminate both his talent and the expanded meta- and extranarrative storytelling roles of a good professional letterer. The *Sandman* series, running for seventy-five individual issues and collected into ten bookshelf volumes, chronicles the life of Morpheus (Dream) and his interactions with characters both human and otherwise.[34] Klein, letterer over the series' entire run, was, along with the cover illustrator Dave McKean, one of the few graphic constants in the books; while Gaiman wrote every issue, individual artists were chosen for specific stories as the content or theme of a story dictated (e.g., the "cartoony" artist Mike Allred for the light-hearted tale of "Prez, the Teenage President," the fantasy artist Charles Vess for versions of *A Midsummer Night's Dream* and *The Tempest*). Klein's lettering, then, provided a sense of extranarrative graphic continuity over a large and visually dissimilar body of texts. Between the styles of McKean's photomontage covers and Klein's letters, readers could tell that a particular issue was a *Sandman* issue even without seeing the title or Gaiman's name.

Klein's customized lettering styles in *Sandman* accompany most of the fantasy series' nonhuman characters; each race, sometimes each individual being, is assigned a "signature font" which reflects aspects of the character itself. Morpheus, the series' eponymous Sandman, is given immediately recognizable speech: written in mixed case, it is printed in white-upon-black within almost amoeba-like balloons, their many pseudopod tendrils only slightly shorter than the main tail for the balloon (figure 64, panel 1). The inverted color scheme of the text adds a degree of sober seriousness to the brooding Morpheus above and beyond the rhetorical content of the sentences themselves. Near the end of the series, Morpheus dies and is replaced by a new incarnation, this one as bright and innocent as the former was dark and foreboding. To metanarratively reflect the change in the character's outlook as well as continuity with his previous incarnation, Klein's lettering and balloon style remain the same, save for rendering the letters in traditional black text upon a white background. Combined with pictures by various artists which also present the "new" Morpheus as a fair-haired and-clothed entity, the text serves as a key element for readers in recognizing and understanding this "new/old" character.

Each of Morpheus's siblings is differentiated by a characterizing font. Destiny,

34. This fantasy series grew out of the superhero tradition. Earlier versions of the "Sandman" included a gas-mask-wearing dandy, like Batman or the Shadow, in the early 1940s; a costumed superhero version of that character in the later 1940s by Joe Simon and Jack Kirby, creators of Captain America as well as entire comics genres such as "kid gang" and romance comics; and a revised superhero version, again by Simon and Kirby, in 1974. Gaiman's plots occasionally borrowed (often ironically) from the earlier versions, but his Morpheus was an original character whose tales generally avoided the superhero genre trappings of his previous namesakes.

FIGURE 64. Todd Klein's lettering helps metanarratively to identify both speakers and their characterizations. Characters in order of appearance: Death, Dream (Morpheus), Despair, Delirium, Desire, Destiny. Neil Gaiman (writer), Mike Dringenberg (penciller), Malcom Jones III (inker), Todd Klein (letterer). *The Sandman* 21 © 1990 DC Comics. All rights reserved. Used with permission.

the eldest of the Endless, speaks in italics, enhancing the narrative aspect of his character: He speaks what will come to pass (figure 64, panel 6).[35] Despair's letters are typical Klein block capitals, but the edges of her word balloons themselves appear rough and misshapen, as if to suggest that the words themselves cause pain in their uttering (figure 64, panels 1 and 3). Delirium (who was once Delight), as her name implies, finds herself continuously situated in a whirlwind world of ideas, sensations, and actions. The size and shape of her text fluctuates from word

35. The character Destiny had been used in previous DC mystery anthologies as a "host" who introduced stories. Italics were used to differentiate Destiny's narration from story content. In this case, both the character and his font were to some extent predetermined, although in the context of the *Sandman* series both take on additional (meta)narrative significance.

to word, even from letter to letter, and the lines of text themselves rise and fall with only the slightest sense of order or decorum; the shapes of the balloons are similarly malleable, and they contain an ever-shifting rainbow of color to match Delirium's continuously altering perceptions (figure 64, panels 2, 4, 5, and 6).

Desire, whose appearance often resembles, intentionally, the androgynous paintings of Patrick Nagel, is given standard speech balloons but stylized, sharply formed text, implying the daggerlike danger inherent in his/her sphere of influence (figure 64, panels 3–5). Conversely, Destruction has standard text enclosed by balloons with thick, heavy, black borders, suggesting how the weight of his role affects his speech, and why he eventually chooses to abandon that role. Finally, Death's speech is represented, curiously, as absolutely standard, with the same appearance of text and balloons as any normal human in the series has (figure 64, panel 1). This apparently odd aesthetic association makes sense given Gaiman's characterization of Death as the most likable, most "human" of the Endless. For Gaiman, death (and Death) is not something to be feared but, rather, accepted as a natural aspect of life. The character's speech marks her as at one with human beings, whereas the rest of the Endless' actions—and visual speech—place them apart from humanity.

Many other fantastic characters—gods, goddesses, forces of nature, faery folk—receive similar textual treatment. The appearance of their speech balloons, for all their variety, follows the same pattern of reflecting, and providing, metanarrative characterization. Klein is also skilled in placing lexias to direct the reader's eye. While Gaiman is the acknowledged author and primary creative force behind the *Sandman* series, Klein's contributions to both the books' extranarrative appearance and their metanarrative content are substantial.

Klein's numerous industry awards are indicative of the high regard in which his work is held by both readers and other creators, including the cartoonist Linda Medley. The first volume of her fairy-tale-inspired book *Castle Waiting*, subtitled *The Curse of Brambly Hedge*, was printed using a typeset but graphically inelegant font in hopes of gaining acceptance and sales in the bookstore (as opposed to comic book store) marketplace (figure 65).[36] For the subsequent comic book series, as well as for a reprinting of the first volume, Medley has used Klein's letters to provide a more integrated extranarrative surface for the story. Klein's lettering in this series—in a dual-case, slightly more ornate style than normal—does not display as many character-based variations as seen in *Sandman,* although it does suggest an appropriately ethereal, fairy-tale quality. Klein varies the shape and weight of word balloons for some characters and renders sound effects and other inherently expressive text with distinctive appeal (figure 66). Even without

36. "The first edition of *Brambly Hedge* used normal typeface in an effort to make the book more appealing to bookstores and people who were not regular readers of comics. However, this seemed to make no difference in sales outside comic stores at all, and the typeface was in fact the only thing about the book that readers did not seem to like. So, for the new edition, the very talented Todd Klein, who is the letterer for the regular *Castle Waiting* series, relettered all the pages": John Kelly, Olio editorial assistant, personal communication, 10 June 1999.

FIGURE 65. The first version of *Castle Waiting: The Curse of Brambly Hedge,* aesthetically hampered by a mechanical serif font. *Castle Waiting: The Curse of Brambly Hedge* (Olio, 1996), n.p. "Castle Waiting" story and art by Linda Medley.

FIGURE 66. The revised version, in which the art is complemented by Todd Klein's graceful letterforms. *Castle Waiting: The Curse of Brambly Hedge* (Olio, 1999), 14. "Castle Waiting" story and art by Linda Medley, lettering by Todd Klein.

an excess of formal variation, his more ornate style blends more harmoniously with Medley's artwork than did the earlier typeset font, fostering—if not the illusion that text and image were created by the same hand—at least the impression that the words and pictures belong to the same aesthetic family. By working closely with his fellow creators and focusing on both meta- and extranarrative embellishments, Klein contributes to and enhances both verbal and visual storytelling.

The Impact of Computers

Many comics letterers, including Klein, have begun to make the transition from pen to keyboard in their work. Ready-made computer fonts (from those specially created for use by comics professionals and available commercially to even the "Comic Sans MS" font included with Microsoft software products) have drastically altered the appearance of many comic books in the American marketplace, from the slickest superhero magazine to the smallest independent, copy-machine-produced mini-comic. Numerous cartoonists have turned to computers to enhance the visual appeal of their creations by offering clearly formed, legible computer lettering.

Of course, mechanical type was used in comics before the advent of the computer. Occasionally publishers have courted respectability by using pre-printed or stenciled character fonts instead of lettering by hand. As Eisner notes, "Typesetting does have a kind of inherent authority but it also has a 'mechanical' effect that intrudes on the personality of free-hand art. Its use must be carefully considered because of its effect on the 'message' as well."[37] For example, Gilberton Publishing's popular *Classics Illustrated* series combined often stiff artwork with bland, expressionless type.[38] EC Comics, publishers in the 1950s of *Tales from the Crypt, Shock SuspenStories,* and many other comics, often used Leroy stenciling for its letters, causing the text to read as cold and detached—well suited to the tone of some stories but highly inappropriate for many others.[39] Regularized mechanical type lacks the human element which the comics form demands for the harmonious visual and thematic blending of text and image. For that reason, today's computerized fonts attempt to mimic handwriting, combining the convenience of set type with the expressive benefits of hand-lettering.

Like traditional hand-lettering, computer fonts can contribute to the narrative, metanarrative, and extranarrative dimensions of comics storytelling. The computer's ability to manipulate the appearance of fonts with relative ease and less

37. Eisner, *Comics & Sequential Art,* 27.
38. For an extended discussion of one *Classics Illustrated* adaptation and its relation to both its source material and to another, more sophisticated comics version, see "Comic Books as History: The First Shot at Fort Sumter," chap. 1 of Joseph Witek's *Comic Books as History: The Narrative Art of Jack Jackson, Art Spiegelman, and Harvey Pekar* (Jackson: University Press of Mississippi, 1989).
39. EC comics edited by Harvey Kurtzman, however, often featured bold and expressive hand-lettering, which contributed greatly to the aesthetic achievement of his stories.

effort than hand-lettering can affect the narrative in any number of ways, allowing especially for more pervasive extranarrative techniques.

Increasingly, many comics creators who utilize computers in their work are approaching fonts in the same way that they approach the rest of the visual surface of comics, as an integral part of the entire page's design; they strive for text which conveys ideas not only grammatically but graphically as well. The most successful computer comics letterer, Richard Starkings, has built an entire company, ComiCraft, upon the idea that lettering in comics can affect the tone of a series not simply by supplying text to a publisher, but rather by adding significant meta- and extranarrative visual elements into this profoundly visual art form.[40]

Starkings, whose company is hired primarily by large publishers such as Marvel (*Amazing Spider-Man, X-Men*) and Image Comics (*Kurt Busiek's Astro City*), began to use computer fonts as a way to increase the number of jobs he could take on per month. By scanning in his own writing, he found he could increase his productivity without sacrificing quality. His work became so popular that he began to hire assistants; ComiCraft now employs over thirty people engaged in various aspects of font application and design. The company also sells some of its fonts to other comics creators, both amateur and professional, in a variety of styles: *Balloon Fonts* for dialogue text; *Display Lettering* for titles and other large-scale text; *Caption Lettering* for captions, thought balloons, and so forth; and of course *Sound Effects.*

The ComiCraft approach to lettering seeks to utilize computer fonts efficiently in order to create graphically interesting lettering, well placed to ensure readability and in service to the story. Often for a high-profile book (e.g., *Kurt Busiek's Astro City,* a title created and owned by the popular writer Kurt Busiek), ComiCraft will create a new dialogue font, in addition to designing text pages (letter columns, editorials).[41] Specialized dialogue fonts are designed to subtly reflect the book's general mood and graphic style, though in practice the dialogue fonts vary only slightly from standard block capitals.

Where computer lettering of the ComiCraft variety makes its mark most visibly, however, is in other types of lexias: titles, captions, footnotes and symbols, page numbers, and the like. In these instances the computer letterer helps to create not a psychologically reflective, characterization-driven lettering style, but rather an extranarrative identity for the book as a whole, uniting cover copy and design, internal narration, editorial copy, and other design elements. Of course,

40. Information on ComiCraft's history and procedures comes from the company's website, <http://www.comicraft.com>, visited 30 July 1998.

41. As an indication that mainstream comic book readers have become increasingly creator-conscious, many mass-produced comics now display the names of their writers and artists on their covers. When Busiek, a highly regarded superhero comic book writer for Marvel Comics, created his own superhero comic for another company, it was titled *Kurt Busiek's Astro City,* using his own name-recognition to "brand" the book and boost sales. The covers to this comic list his name, the names of the artists, *and* the "Starkings/ComiCraft" label, connoting the respect with which at least one corner of comics publishing and readership regards Starkings's work.

it is not always possible to give each book a completely unique treatment; but especially on the more popular comics much attention is paid toward integrating the entire graphic package. This practice thus ensures the name-brand recognition crucial in commercial comics, where writers and artists often work for only brief periods of time on long-running series. Computer design brings with it regularized extranarrative identity, thus allowing products by various hands to blend more easily with one another.

For a flagship title such as Marvel Comics' *Amazing Spider-Man,* ComiCraft adds numerous decorative details that enhance the book's overall presentation through an emphasis on the character's "spider" theme. Some caption boxes, particularly introductions, are emblazoned with a spider motif, which also appears in page-number design. Footnotes (necessitated by the complex issue-to-issue story continuity of such comics) also are given an arachnid treatment, the traditional asterisk replaced with a similarly shaped spider icon; a different font distinguishes note-text from narration (figure 67). Note how the fourth narrative caption box in this figure appears to have been hand-lettered, most likely a result of a last-minute editorial decision once the book had been lettered by ComiCraft and returned to the editorial office (a not uncommon situation in mainstream comics). This hand-lettering, while serviceable in and of itself, nevertheless disturbs the extranarrative integrity of the page through its addition of a recognizably second narrative face. Another computer font is used for the creator credits at the bottom of the page, again distinguishing this text from the narrative.

Similarly, the long-running series *Fantastic Four* has benefited from Comi-Craft's design work. Introductory caption boxes contribute to the book's overall appearance by both the addition of a stylized "4" and the use of a stylized initial capital letter; the font for this letter is based upon the font used for the book's cover logo; the use of this literal "logo type" can also be found in other narration, such as the caption "Next:" in figure 68. The company also has added distinctive metanarrative touches to the dialogue of some characters. The fiery Human Torch speaks with flaming, red-tinted word balloons, while the rocklike, monstrous Thing uses a chiseled font. Even the denizens of the undersea kingdom of Atlantis have a unique word-balloon design, utilizing thought-balloon-like but intensified bubbles instead of a tail, denoting that their speech "bubbles" through the water which fills their helmets.

At times, the desire to match an appropriate font to a particular image works only on the microlevel of the panel. Some books boast a dizzying number of additional fonts simulating computer read-outs, radio speech, exclamations, and other lexias. In the larger context of the page—not to mention the entire book—the bombastic use of such effects by overzealous craftspeople can serve to overwhelm their aesthetic and storytelling impact. However, the computer merely makes such a possibility easier than it is with hand-lettering; the difference is one of degree, not kind.

The computer makes it easy to scale the size of lettering, allowing more text to

FIGURE 67. A wide range of computer-generated fonts, apart from one apparently hand-lettered caption box. Tom DeFalco (writer), Joe Bennett (penciller), Bud LaRosa (inker), RS & ComiCraft's Kiff Scholl (letterer). *Amazing Spider-Man* 1.430 (Marvel, January 1998), 1. TM & © 2000 Marvel Characters, Inc. Used with permission.

FIGURE 68. The font used for the caption "Next:" is based on the comic book's cover logo, while the Human Torch's fiery word balloons (above) and the Thing's rough-hewn text (below) reflect both their appearances and their characterizations. Chris Claremont (writer), Salvador Laraoca (penciller), Art Thibert (inker), RS/ComiCraft/DL (letterer). *Fantastic Four* 3.8 (Marvel, August 1998), n.p. TM & © 2000 Marvel Characters, Inc. Used with permission.

FIGURE 69. Alternating font sizes can produce intriguing, although perhaps unintended, narrative effects. Tom DeFalco (writer), Joe Bennett (penciller), Bud LaRosa (inker), RS & ComiCraft's Kiff Scholl (letterer). *Amazing Spider-Man* 1.430 (Marvel, January 1998), 12:3–5. TM & © 2000 Marvel Characters, Inc. Used with permission.

be forced into less space relatively easily. Hand-letterers tend to work at a regularly sized scale, using standard sets of ruled lines to guide their writing; if the need arises, they might choose to make the text a bit smaller to fit it all into the composition. This same option exists for computer letters as well, of course, but the ease with which the computer enables the letterer to adjust the size of text sometimes leads to narratively ambiguous situations.

For example, in a tier of panels from *Amazing Spider-Man* (figure 69), the changing size of the dialogue text has metanarrative implications, intended or otherwise. The first panel contains two large faces and very little open compositional space; to meet the need to fit in four word balloons, the computer letterer has made the text in balloons one and three smaller than that in the other balloons. This solution fits all of the text into the panel, but in so doing it creates the metanarrative impression, perhaps intentionally, that the smaller text balloons represents whispering, or at lease sotto voce comments. The second word balloon in the next panel also employs a reduced text size, yielding a similar interpretation. In the third panel, however, the textual shrinkage in balloons two and three is not so contextually appropriate; the third balloon in particular ("Make up your mind, Shantal! . . . ") appears, by nature of the exclamation point, to indicate shouting, usually metanarratively indicated by larger, not smaller, text.

One possible—and radical—interpretation of this panel would state that the text actually narratively directs our reading process as a camera and sound would in cinema.[42] The first balloon indicates a normal volume level as would befit a main subject speaker (not a background character), while the decreased size in balloons two and three indicate a camera pull-back to reveal the larger scene, including the passerby not present in the previous panels. The normal-sized text issuing from the radio indicates a shift in narrative focus within this single panel from the conversation to the radio message. Thus, the scene in the third panel would suggest not an instance of cinematic "deep focus" but rather a static representation of a camera pull-back, with the textual variations indicating a change in focus over the extended time frame contained in this single panel.[43]

The varying size of the text in this panel makes such an interpretation certainly possible, but it would reflect a decidedly nonstandard approach to comics storytelling. It is, in fact, just as likely that the size of the font was decreased in balloons two and three simply to make room for the large amount of text in this relatively small composition. The ease of textual alteration and experimentation offered by the computer makes this solution easier to employ than it would be with hand-

42. For a discussion of the comics form in relation to film terminology, see Charles Hatfield, "*Heartbreak Soup:* The Interdependence of Theme and Form," *inks: Cartoon and Comic Art Studies* 4.2 (May 1997): 2–17. This wide-ranging discussion does not, however, deal with point of view and sound in the way I am proposing here.

43. McCloud discusses how a comics panel may contain or represent not simply a frozen instant of time, but rather an extended sequence in which various elements of a single composition may portray differing instances of time; text, especially speech, is a key element in this effect (*Understanding Comics,* 95–97).

FIGURE 70. Jeff Smith mixes a computerized font for normal speech with hand-rendered display text for sound effects and irregularly formed speech. *Bone* 36 (May 1999), 17:1–2. *Bone*® is copyright 1999 by Jeff Smith.

lettering, whether by accident or design; but as this example demonstrates, alterations in the size of text do have narrative consequences.

Some independent comics creators have approached computer lettering as a substitute for their own letters in a different way, by utilizing computer fonts based on their own handwriting.[44] Jeff Smith, creator of the highly regarded fantasy series *Bone,* originally lettered his comic by hand. He eventually embraced the computer for some technical aspects of production, and soon Smith discovered he could use the computer to scan his own lettering and create a font which is a remarkable simulacrum of his own calligraphic style. Now, apart from exclamations, sound effects, or other nonstandard lexias, the text in *Bone* is produced on a computer, printed out, and placed onto Smith's penciled pages before they are inked (figure 70).[45] In this fashion Smith is able to take advantage of the computer's abilities without sacrificing the author-based extranarrative integrity of his page design.

Smith is certainly not alone in using a personalized computer font. Jill Thompson's *Scary Godmother* features lettering by Brenda Feikema "from a font created by Jill Thompson."[46] Dave McKean, creator of *Cages* as well as a sometime collaborator with Neil Gaiman, has co-created elaborate fonts for many of his comics, all of which combine graphics of many kinds (photos, paintings, line drawings)

44. This practice mimics the initial development of printing: "The first typefaces used in printing were designed to imitate as closely as possible the hand-drawn letterforms in calligraphic manuscripts" (Elam, *Expressive Typography,* 26).

45. For an overview of Smith's creative process from script to finished page, with examples of his computer font, see Craig Shutt, "Stripped to the *Bone,*" *Hogan's Alley* 4 (Summer 1997): 74–84.

46. Jill Thompson and Brenda Feikema (lettering). *Scary Godmother* (Dover: Sirius Entertainment, 1997), title page.

with text as equivalent graphic elements. The practice of custom computer lettering can be traced back at least as far as 1989, when Roxanne Starr, letterer for Bob Burden's quirky *Flaming Carrot,* used a deadpan block capital font scanned from her own printing into a Macintosh computer. These creator-specific fonts serve to reinforce the extranarrative identity of these cartoonists' work.[47]

The proliferation of computerization in the comics field has the potential to influence the production and appearance of the comics themselves, apart from lettering, in ways that are yet to be fully determined. Certainly the use of digital coloring methods, allowing artists to model or shape color gradations to provide the illusion of texture and volume, has become commonplace in mainstream comics. The nearly ubiquitous home computer, ever more powerful, has put technology into the hands of many comics artists who do not benefit from the support of a large publishing company. Computers have also helped put comics on the Internet, offering the potential for a multitude of effects unavailable to print. The widespread use of standardized computer comics fonts by cartoonists of all types (from seasoned professionals to the youngest neophytes) represents a first step in a process which—as it matures into more individualized applications—is poised to transform the comics art form into something distinctly *other* than its present paper incarnation.[48]

But that time is not yet here; and while some comics have begun a slow migration to electronic forms, most cartoonists are still content to remain bound to the realm of print. Many cartoonists do, however, show a tendency to embrace technology when it makes their job (or their art) easier and more successful. The popularity of do-it-yourself computerized fonts stems from their ease of use, their clarity, and their ability to mimic, to a certain extent, the human hand. Yet for all of the innovation they offer, they also present the possibility for various aesthetic and semiotic shortcomings which should be taken into account when one studies the comics page.

It takes a rare combination of hand-letterer and cartoonist to create a page as well integrated and harmonious as a single cartoonist can create. When artists hire others to do their lettering, either by hand or by computer, they delegate part of their storytelling duty. Such delegation may benefit their work if letterers are skilled in adapting or altering their style in order to facilitate the demands of a particular story, though such is not always the case. In so doing, creators run the risk of sacrificing the extranarrative aesthetic integrity of the page for expedi-

47. Bob Burden, *Flaming Carrot Comics* 23 (Dark Horse Comics: November, 1989), n.p. Computerized fonts were used earlier, for example, the Macintosh font used for the Peter B. Gillis (writer) and Michael Saenz (artist) comic book *Shatter,* cover-billed as "The First Computerized Comic!" (First Comics, 1985). *Shatter* used a ready-made font, however, which was not designed to mimic hand-created text. Since the entire comic was produced on a Macintosh, including computer-rendered artwork, the Macintosh font itself served as an extranarrative element marking the comic as a computer production.

48. The same, of course, may be said for all print technologies. For a range of views on possible new directions for print, see *The Future of the Book,* ed. Geoffrey Nunberg (Berkeley: University of California Press, 1996); Umberto Eco's Afterword seems to me eminently reasonable in its resistance to the simple binary of "digital text as utopia" and "print as dead."

ency, but they can gain a less specific although still recognizable extranarrative identity for the product as a gestalt. The former often characterizes independently produced comics with literary aims, while the latter generally reflects mass-market, genre material. The use of increasingly sophisticated computer fonts represents an attempt by cartoonists to overcome shortcomings of either talent or, more frequently, simple time. As the use of custom, "made by-and-for-the-cartoonist" fonts becomes more popular, more practical, and more personal, cartoonists can hope to benefit on aesthetic and narrative as well as practical levels.

Carefully considered and executed lettering can add additional information to the comics page apart from merely conveying grammatical narrative content, information which should be taken into consideration when comics are studied. By focusing on the narrative, metanarrative, and extranarrative qualities contributed by the graphic appearance of text, studies of comic books and strips can more fully address the graphic nature of the form's storytelling techniques.

The interpretive scheme presented in this essay marks, I hope, a starting point for typographic critique in comics; I do not view it as a "final word." Of necessity, this brief overview takes a generally ahistorical point of view in order to focus on common formal tropes; more thorough historical surveys will doubtless offer patterns of development and relationships with other media only hinted at here. I have also only tangentially addressed the wide variety of text/image combinations possible within individual panels; note that McCloud's seven (preliminary) categories of text/image combination barely acknowledge the appearance of the text.[49] Further, I do not wish to imply that formalist study alone is a sufficient or ultimate goal for comics criticism. I do believe, however, that a thorough understanding of comics' formal properties should lie behind any criticism which attempts to discuss the form's narrative aspects. To ignore the graphic presentation of the material in discussions of so-called story content is to misrepresent the visual dynamic through which those stories are told.

In addition, increased critical attention to interplay between the appearance of text and image on the comics page can shed light on other examples of graphic textual study in literature and art. Consider Scott's description of the work of Symbolist poets such as Arthur Rimbaud:

> Many of the semiotic processes operative in painting could be activated by poetry: the perception of the page itself as being the formal area of the poem's performance, the realization of the importance of the relationship between figure (text) and background (page), the visual hierarchization of linguistic elements (patterns of spacing and typography) within the format of the page. The foregrounding of the linguistic signifier (through spacing, syntactical, or stanzaic placing, the use of capitals, italics, etc.) could become in this way the poetic equivalent of the plastic qualities of paint. The literary text . . . was thus

49. McCloud, *Understanding Comics,* 153–55.

increasingly to consist of an artistic arrangement of signifiers, a visual diagram, as much as a linguistic structure of logically coordinated signifieds.[50]

The Symbolist "visual diagram" finds a not-so-distant cousin in the comics page, which adds the placement of discrete images along with text to create tales composed of highly charged, carefully designed units. By developing a better understanding of the nature of comics as "an artistic arrangement of signifiers"—"signifiers" in this case relating to both image *and* text as equivalently significant components—comics criticism is in a better position both to learn from and to contribute to broader academic discourse regarding typography and the various relationships between text and image which occur throughout other art forms. Leonardo da Vinci described the debate of poetry and painting, of word and image, as *pargone,* or a "war of signs." The comics page, where graphic text is included as an element of a larger graphic context, should be understood as a form in which text and image participate not in war but rather in mutually beneficial collaboration.[51]

50. Scott, *Pictorialist Poetics,* 37.
51. This essay itself is indebted to the collaborative process. A much shorter version was presented at "The Graphic Novel: A 20th Anniversary Conference," University of Massachusetts–Amherst, on 14 November 1998, where I benefited from the comments and questions of many audience members including Jan Baetens, Will Eisner, Scott McCloud, and Robin Varnum. Various drafts have received helpful comments from my editors, Paul Gutjahr and Megan Benton, as well as the anonymous reviewers for the University of Massachusetts Press. Finally, I am greatly indebted to Charles Hatfield, K. A. Laity, and Professor Tom Roberts at the University of Connecticut for their repeated and thoughtful feedback.

Notes on Contributors

Megan L. Benton is an associate professor of English at Pacific Lutheran University, where she directs an interdisciplinary program in publishing and printing arts. She is the author of *Beauty and the Book: Fine Editions and Cultural Distinction in America* and several articles on publishing, reading, and typographic history.

Paul C. Gutjahr is an assistant professor of English and American Studies at Indiana University. He is the author of *An American Bible: A History of the Good Book in the United States, 1777–1880*. He has published numerous articles and chapters on a wide range of subjects, including pedagogy, American literature, and religious publishing history.

Leon Jackson is an assistant professor of English at the University of South Carolina. He has published articles on eighteenth- and nineteenth-century literary and cultural history, and he is a contributor to volume 3 of *A History of the Book in America.* His current interests center on satire, shame, and print culture in antebellum America.

Gene Kannenberg Jr. is completing a dissertation titled "Form, Function, Fiction: Text, Image, and Design in the Comics of Winsor McCay, Art Spiegelman, and Chris Ware" in the English department at the University of Connecticut. He is a contributing writer for *The Comics Journal,* chair of the International Comic Arts Festival, and moderator of the Comics Scholars' Discussion List. He has published in *The International Journal of Comic Art,* where he also edits the "Critical Closure" scholarly resource section.

Sarah A. Kelen is an assistant professor of English at Nebraska Wesleyan University. She writes on medieval literature and early modern medievalism, and she is currently working on a book about the early modern reception and editing of Chaucer and Langland.

Beth McCoy is an assistant professor of English at SUNY Geneseo, where she teaches African American literature and coordinates the American Studies program. Specializing in the Harlem Renaissance, she has published essays on Jessie

Redmon Fauset, Carl Van Vechten, and Amiri Baraka. Her current project, titled "Defining the Definers," explores how novels by black women trace shifts in white masculinity.

Steven R. Price is an assistant professor of English at Mississippi College, where he teaches British literature and the eighteenth-century novel. He has served as assistant general editor of *The Eighteenth Century: A Current Bibliography*. His research interests include the redefinition of authorship in the eighteenth century and Samuel Richardson's roles as printer and editor as well as author.

Index